THE ASSOCIATION FOR SCOTTISH LITERARY STUDIES

NUMBER ELEVEN

THE PARTY-COLOURED MIND

Prose relating to the Conflict of Church and State
in Seventeenth Century Scotland

THE ASSOCIATION FOR SCOTTISH LITERARY STUDIES

ANNUAL VOLUMES PUBLISHED BY SCOTTISH ACADEMIC PRESS

1971 James Hogg. *The Three Perils of Man.* Ed. Douglas Gifford.

1972 *The Poems of John Davidson.* Vol. I. Ed. Andrew Turnbull.

1973 *The Poems of John Davidson.* Vol. II. Ed. Andrew Turnbull.

1974 Allan Ramsay and Robert Fergusson. *Poems.* Ed. Alexander M. Kinghorn and Alexander Law.

1975 John Galt. *The Member.* Ed. Ian A. Gordon.

1976 William Drummond of Hawthornden. *Poems and Prose.* Ed. Robert H. MacDonald.

1977 John G. Lockhart. *Peter's Letters to his Kinsfolk.* Ed. William Ruddick.

1978 John Galt. *Selected Short Stories.* Ed. Ian A. Gordon.

1979 Andrew Fletcher of Saltoun. *Selected Political Writings and Speeches.* Ed. David Daiches.

1980 *Scott on Himself.* Ed. David Hewitt

1981 *The Party-Coloured Mind.* Ed. David Reid.

THE ASSOCIATION FOR SCOTTISH LITERARY STUDIES

GENERAL EDITOR–DOUGLAS MACK

THE PARTY-COLOURED MIND

Prose relating to the Conflict of Church and State
in Seventeenth Century Scotland

EDITED BY

DAVID REID

SCOTTISH ACADEMIC PRESS
EDINBURGH
1982

Published by
Scottish Academic Press Ltd
33 Montgomery Street, Edinburgh EH7 5JX

First published 1982
SBN 7073 0304 4

Printed in Great Britain by
Clark Constable Ltd, Edinburgh

For my mother

ACKNOWLEDGEMENT

The Association for Scottish Literary Studies acknowledges the generous financial assistance of the Scottish Arts Council in the publication of this Volume.

CONTENTS

FOREWORD

Except with the selections from Leighton, Charteris, Peden and Pitcairne, where the earliest texts are eighteenth or nineteenth century editions, I have taken passages from seventeenth century first editions, or failing those from the best manuscripts available. I have retained original spellings, except that I have given "i" and "j", "u" and "v" according to modern usage, rendered initial double "f"'s as single ones and expanded contractions. With punctuation and capitals, I have modernized or at least simplified. I have supplied emendations in square brackets where they were necessary to make sense of passages. I have annotated only what I thought the general reader might find obscure or in need of explanation if the sense of a passage were to be clear or the significance of what it treated were to come out. In places I may have broken this rule of parsimony, but I have tried to avoid editorial officiousness. The index will supply some cross references.

I am conscious of many debts, of which the following are the most important. All the passages I have edited from manuscript have appeared in earlier editions. I am indebted to all of those, though some are rather inaccurate, for information and useful guesswork. In writing the historical and biographical notes, I have drawn especially on W. L. Mathieson, *Politics and Religion in Scotland, 1550–1695*, 2 vols. (Glasgow: Maclehouse, 1902), Gordon Donaldson, *Scotland, James V to James VII* (Edinburgh: Oliver & Boyd, 1971) and *The Dictionary of National Biography*. I am particularly grateful to Professor David Buchan, former general editor of this series, for much help and stimulation in planning this anthology – I was indeed lucky to be able to draw on his remarkable general knowledge of Scottish life and literature. I am also greatly indebted to my colleague, Dr. Neil Keeble, for his painstaking and helpful criticisms of an earlier draft, to the present editor of this series, Mr. Douglas Mack, for some useful suggestions and to Dr. Ronald Jack of the Department of English and Dr. Michael Lynch of the Department of Scottish History at the University of Edinburgh for corrections and comments that helped me to improve the book. And I must thank Mr. A. J. Aitken of *The Dictionary of the Older Scottish Tongue* for answering queries about vocabulary and Dr. I. B. Cowan of the Department of Scottish History at Glasgow University for help with a historical crux. The faults of this book are, of course, mine. Thanks are also due to the staff of the National Library of Scotland for their help with many inquiries, to Lord Binning for permission to print passages from Wariston's *Diary* and to Dr. W. D. Baston, archivist at Mellerstain, for making the MS of the *Diary* available, to the following for permission to print passages from their MSS: the Bodleian Library (Gilbert Burnet, *History of My Own Time*), the British Library (David Calderwood, *Historie of the Kirk of Scotland*; Gilbert Burnet, *Memoirs*), Edinburgh University Library (James Melville, *The True Narration of the Declyneing State of the Kirk of Scotland*), the Library of New College, Edinburgh (Robert Baillie, *Letters and Journals*), the National Library of Scotland (Archibald Napier, "Letter about the Soveraigne and Supreme Power"; James Kirkton, *The Secret and True History of the Church of Scotland*), The Society of Antiquaries of Scotland (William Drummond, *ΣΚΙΑΜΑΧΙΑ*). |Finally I wish to thank the secretaries of the Department of English Studies here, Miss Elspeth McLennan, Mrs. Katherine MacKenzie, Miss Olwen Peel, Miss Mamie Prentice, for typing a difficult MS.

University of Stirling
6th April 1981

INTRODUCTION

I won't quarrel with the view that the seventeenth century is the dullest in Scottish literature, since the fourteenth century anyway. The prose is in a better way than the poetry. Indeed we have a literature of genuine interest there, but distinctly a minor literature. We need only compare it with what English writers of the time achieved or what Scottish writers would achieve in the next century to have the meagreness, the backwardness, of the literary culture of the Scottish seventeenth century brought home to us.

The disappearance of Scots from literary currency is surely a sign of growing provinciality. Except with popular sermons, either printer or author came to look to England for a literary standard and anglified texts for publication. Memoirs come down to us with more Scots forms only because they were unpublished. In his preface to *The History of the Houses of Douglas and Angus* David Hume of Godscroft writes:

> For the language it is my mother-tongue, that is, Scottish: and why not, to Scottish-men? Why should I contemne it? I never thought the difference so great, as that by seeking to speak English, I would hazard the imputation of affectation. Every tongue hath [its] own vertue and grace. . . . For my own part, I like our own, and he that writes well in it writes well enough to me. Yet I have yeelded somewhat to the tyrannie of custome and the times, not seeking curiously for words, but taking them as they came to hand. I acknowledge also my fault (if it be a fault) that I ever accounted it a mean study and of no great commendation to learn to write or to speak English and have loved better to bestow my pains on forreigne languages, esteeming it but a dialect of our own, and that (perhaps) more corrupt. ([Edinburgh: Tyler, 1644], n.p.)

In spite of these professions it is hard to find any trace of Scots here or elsewhere in the *History*. Still it is a spirited defence and contrasts agreeably with the contempt for Scots at the end of the century in Pitcairne's *Assembly*, where Scots is put into the mouths of

Presbyterian lairds and ministers to make them ridiculous, while the young men about town, whom we are meant to admire, speak correct enough English. Perhaps if there had been an assured and powerful literary culture in Scotland, a prose would have evolved, which in aspiring to an ideal educated speech, took in Scottish forms. As it was, Scots became merely a vernacular.

The absence or inoperancy of those institutions that maintained letters in England may go some way to explain the poverty of Scottish letters. There was rarely a court at Edinburgh. No country house attached a literary circle to itself. It is only towards the end of the century that there are hints that Edinburgh might become the sort of city that could support a literary life. There was, of course, a church. Probably, though I cannot judge, the century of Cameron, Forbes, Leighton and Barclay was a distinguished period in Scottish divinity. But the Scottish church did little for letters in comparison with the English and French churches. The common view, indeed, is that an obsession with religion and church politics was too much for literary culture in Scotland. There is perhaps something in the idea that Presbyterian divinity had little to do with literary culture. In 1678 the Presbyterian Alexander Brodie wrote in his diary,

> Mr Massie cam heir. He told me sad things: I That Socinianism is growing ryf: Justification by Christ questiond and denied: Supernatural assistanc of grace or influences of the Spirit not needful: Moraliti is al that is requird in religion: Plato and Seneca of [as] much authoriti as Peter or Paul: Dr Skougal that's dead vented this doctrine: The Bishop his father does not disclaim or discountenanc it: Ther be that inclin to it. (*The Diary of Alexander Brodie*, ed. D. Laing [Aberdeen: Spalding Club, 1863], p. 404)

What lies behind this canard is not a Presbyterian hostility to the study of the classics but a sharp distinction between divinity, the study of sacred literature, and humanity in an old sense of the word, the study of *litterae humaniores*, human letters. For the same reason at the end of the century the Presbyterian, Gilbert Rule, supposes that when Bishop Sage writes of "Christian philosophy", he must mean Christian divinity, and that gives Sage his opening to inform Rule of the many ancient and modern divines who had spoken of a "Christian philosophy", meaning a union of good literature and Christian faith.[1] For Presbyterians of Calvinist views such a union would appear a serious confusion, and although they had good latinists among them like Andrew Melville and Andrew Ramsay, that may explain why they did not take the claims of humane letters seriously enough to produce Barrows and Swifts or Bossuets and

Fénelons, or for that matter Robertsons and Blairs as they did in the next century. But after all the Presbyterians were in power for only thirty-five years of the seventeenth century. They can hardly have repressed vigorous literary urges under Episcopacy. The truth is that there is no simple explanation why Scotland produced so much religious and ecclesiastical writing and so little of real literary value.

Perhaps it is foolish to hope for more. Maurice Lindsay thinks that "the seventeenth century, with its long and bitter periods of religious struggle – family divided against family, maintaining attitudes of bigotry and intolerance – is not an age upon which Scots can reasonably look back with much pride".[2] Perhaps. And yet the political history of this last century of at least partial independence displays a sort of heroic energy, however contracted its sphere. The struggle over church polity was carried on with fierce intransigence. It threw up ambitious designs, the Laudian scheme for the reform of the church as well as the Covenanters'. For a time during the Civil War Scotland tried to play a great role in the affairs of the island. And with the Restoration there was a remarkable development and complication of political life in Edinburgh. But while in England the revolutions of the century are associated with a great critical movement of the mind, in Scotland there is no stirring of literary culture to match the upheavals on the political scene.

Still as I have said, there is in the prose a minor literature of genuine interest. It is taken up with the great affair of national life, the struggle about authority in church and state. That struggle was not, of course, the only thing that interested Scotsmen, but it was what they wrote most about and, even if indirectly, what on the whole they wrote most interestingly about. And so in order to bring out the character of Scottish literary culture it seemed a good idea to focus on that absorbing concern. Moreover, the various pieces shed light on each other, and that, in view of the often special and local form of Scottish concerns, appeared a great advantage. These considerations outweighed the anxiety that a selection about a single topic might exaggerate the narrowness of the Scottish literary effort. I must emphasize that the selection is a literary one. I have not tried, as a historian might, to document controversies or illustrate the course of events. I have tried instead to represent the state of letters in seventeenth century Scotland by what I judged its most interesting prose.

I looked in the first place for passages that made what was going on vivid to the imagination or illuminated the issues and made them humanly intelligible. It is not easy to understand what the struggle over church polity was really about or why it mattered to people so much. The partisan tracts are rarely much help. They are usually plainly written and closely argued, at least in the period of the Civil War, but any sense of principles people might live by is lost in interminable disputation. Nothing came out of the Scottish controversies that takes us, as the debate between Luther and Erasmus on free will does, to the heart of the contention between evangelical Protestantism and human institutions (including the institution of literature). But James Melville's wonderfully circumstantial account of how James VI and his bishops cajoled, brow-beat and suppressed the high Presbyterian leaders in London does, I think, help us to understand what a Presbyterian meant by "Erastianism". And Hugh Binning's sermon on true worship may help us to understand the idea of religion that lay behind the extreme Covenanters' intolerant and intolerable policies, which otherwise look like mere fanaticism.

The sort of writing through which we can most easily enter into the seventeenth century experience is memoirs of the time, a genre ranging from letters and journals with Baillie to histories with Kirkton and Burnet. Here Scottish writers had already attained excellence in the sixteenth century – with Knox's *History of the Reformation in Scotland* and the *Memoirs* of Sir James Melville of Halhill, for example – and here most obviously produced a literature of lasting interest in the seventeenth century. Much of their material will be familiar from nineteenth century historical novels like *Old Mortality* and *Ringan Gilhaize*. But it seems to me the accounts of the men of the seventeenth century are better; they don't soften the harsh outlines of things or make them picturesque, and so they are more lively and serious. It must be said that the frame of ideas among the Presbyterian writers gives them narrow views of events. They saw the Scots as a chosen people. The following passage from Calderwood's *The Pastor and the Prelate* is an elaborate treatment of a favourite theme.

> For as Scotland, albeit far from Jerusalem, was one of the first nations that the light of the Gospel shyned on when it appeared to the Gentils and one of the last that kept the light when the shadowes of the hilles of Rome began to darken the earth, so when the sun came about againe at the Reformation, if this blessed light shyned first upon others, all that had eyes to see both at home and abroade, have seen and sayd, that it shyned fairest upon us, divine providence delighting to supply the defect of nature with abundance of grace and to make this backside of the earth, lying behind the visible sunne, by the cleare and comforting beames of the Sunne of righteousnes, to be the sunnie side of the Christian world. ([No place, 1628], p. 40)

4

This dangerous special relationship of the backside of the earth with God meant that the history of the Church of Scotland, like the history of Israel, could only go the way of backsliding, divine retribution ("The Lord's controversy with the land") and return to the divinely appointed model for church and state. This is a way of reading events one can discern even in a fairly polished historian like Kirkton. Presbyterian memoirs are also much occupied with the constitution of the church. Large tracts of Melville's *True narration* and Calderwood's *Historie of the Kirk of Scotland* are taken up with documenting the establishment and corruption of the true constitution of the church as they saw it.[3] They write then as prophetic and as constitutional historians, but either way they have the sort of ideas that can account for anything, and so they do not inquire into the nature of what was going on nor do they accumulate the sort of weight of political experience that speaks through Clarendon's *History*, for all his prejudices and moral designs. Kirkton with his sardonic analyses of political shufflings is perhaps an exception, but even with him the experience of the world has narrow bounds. What makes up for these limitations is a lively gift for telling a story and a sharp eye for detail. Consider the importance of dinner in Melville's account of the treatment of the Presbyterian leaders in London, how meanly and effectively it was used against them. Or take Baillie's amused picture of himself riding out to war. Melville has in addition a knack of dialogue that is alive to the humorous side even of his venerated uncle's character. Calderwood also has a way with dialogue, but with him it is a coarser, knockabout matter.

Burnet's *Memoirs* are written from a very different point of view. What he has to say about Scottish affairs in the reign of Charles II vindicates Leighton's moderate and conciliatory Episcopal policy, with which he was associated before he left Scotland and became a latitudinarian bishop in the English Church. Burnet's vindication lies in the way he recommends or disparages the men involved. He was a confident and voluminous but rather weak controversialist and his grasp of principles was not very firm. His real passion was for an acquaintance with the world of affairs, which he enlarged by going to England. He was a great gossip and knew everyone he could. And so as a historian he writes as one who knew the chief actors and was privy to what was going on. In this way his views take on a certain authority, which owes nothing to argument, statement of principles or citing of documents.

His knowledge of the world also helps to account for the interest of his portraits. For whatever one thinks of Burnet's judgement (it has been thought malicious and unstable), he has an advantage over every other Scottish historian in his wider experience. Compared

5

with Halifax's portrait of Charles II, Burnet's may be slight, but compared with Melville's picture of King James, it is vastly richer in human likeness. The interest of the portraits has also something to do with their style. Burnet's style varies enormously in the course of his career. Yet as a member of the Royal Society he was conscious of the new ideals in prose and revised the style of his *Memoirs* when he worked them into his *History of My Own Time*, speaking of the pains he took to write clearly in short sentences. The revision is not usually thought an improvement, and Swift had plenty of scope for his waspish annotations. Whatever its faults, though, the style of the portraits in the *Memoirs* and indeed the *History* is very well suited for lively recording. Burnet has arrived at a rough way of jotting things down as they come to him. He gets down those details that suggest the man he is drawing in a way that might have escaped his deliberate judgement and a more polished discursive treatment. In liveliness and immediacy he shares something with the other writers of memoirs in this selection, especially Baillie, not that I imagine he learnt from them.

Scottish historians made a name for themselves in the eighteenth century, and Gibbon is full of elaborate compliments to Hume and Robertson. Clearly Hume is vastly superior to the seventeenth century historians in the art of composition, of subordinating and connecting events to a coherent narrative. Clearly he is in possession of a literary and philosophical culure that goes with a wider outlook on human affairs than they could command and with a mastery of tone, of irony and qualification, that was beyond them. And yet if after reading Burnet and Kirkton, one turns to his account of the reign of Charles II in his *History of England*, one discovers how far they surpass him in giving a sense of what things were like. This is a point I should stress. The trouble with the mass of Scottish prose of the seventeenth century is an inadequate literary culture, and whoever reads far in it may seize too eagerly at the standards Hume so sovereignly represents. In memoirs of their own times, however, seventeenth century writers make up for their shortcomings by the directness and circumstantiality with which they got down people and things.

Memoirs are the most interesting but not the only interesting sort of prose written at the time. Here and there among the treatises, tracts, sermons and essays, there is something that we can recognize as the life of the mind, and where the issues of the time called forth so much that is merely entrenched, dogmatic, fanatical and precipitately dull, that is precious indeed. I don't propose to write an intellectual history of seventeenth century Scotland; for that the reader would best go to G. D. Henderson's *Religious Life in*

6

Seventeenth Century Scotland. Yet some account of the literary culture of the period is necessary to bring out what is remarkable in those pieces that show a critical mind and free intelligence at work, and perhaps the best way to go about that is to take up the business of style.

Some writers are interesting for their style. Of course the interest of a writer's style should be inseparable from the interest of what he says. But fine writing, or at least hypertrophy of literary manner, is typical of one side of the literary effort of the early seventeenth century, and there are good Scottish examples of that. Drummond among Scottish writers most easily lends himself to analysis in terms of Croll's typology of prose written in the vein of art, Mackenzie shows an individual adaptation of the manner of Sir Thomas Browne and Urquhart is one of the most peculiar writers of the century. Of these, Drummond and Urquhart should certainly find their way into any anthology of English prose that set out to illustrate the elaborate and curious styles of the time. But this is to take style in a limiting sense.

Considered broadly, style touches central concerns of literary culture, especially in the seventeenth century when the attempt to arrive at what is truly human has so much to do with notions of how humans should express themselves and with the development of urbane and reasonable discourse. Urbanity, the real not the pinchbeck article, is not just a matter of decorum after all, nor even of sweetness and light. It implies a knowledge of oneself and other men, the sort of sense of what human nature is like that is to be had only from a mature culture. Obviously urbanity is not everything, but it probably covers what is most valuable in the seventeenth century pursuit of literary elegance. And so with English prose the line to trace is a change in the idea of literary elegance, a change from convoluted or ornate or mannered prose to prose that unites plainness and vigour with ease and amenity. I should have liked to trace that development among Scottish writers, only the development is not really there. That lack of development is something we shall have to look into at some length. For one thing it will perhaps suggest why acquiring a literary culture was so urgent a business for Scots of the Enlightenment. More to the point, it will call attention to what was in fact achieved by Scottish writers against the odds in the way of urbane and critical writing.

For the lack of a development of the English sort in Scottish prose there are two reasons. The first (and this is something I shall explain later) is that the critical movement of the mind associated with the development of English prose makes itself felt in Scotland only fitfully. The second (and this is our way in) is that notions of literary elegance are less evolved in Scotland. The departure of James VI broke up his Castalian Band and left the country without the sort of circle in which literary manner is intensely cultivated and intensely appreciated. It left Drummond in the next generation culturally isolated for all his literary contacts. He is one of the most accomplished of those seventeenth century writers whose prose is a work of art. But in him, unlike the best English practitioners, the elaborate mannerism does not express a peculiar energy of apprehension; it shows a refined taste, a good ear and in his political pieces, a cultivated distance from Scottish affairs. A very different sort of writer could turn out a highly wrought piece on occasion by way of flourish, but it will stick out in the middle of plain, serviceable prose. The introductory epistle to George Gillespie's *A Dispute against the English Popish Ceremonies (1637)*, for example, is written in a sententious and patterned style but the body of the work in the staple of Presbyterian tracts, a utilitarian style, the matter divided by heads and the argument closely reasoned. In Scotland, as in England, there was a workmanlike plain style before the development of the new prose of the Restoration. But the plainness was without amenity or any pretension to elegance. In the hands of the controversialists it tended towards dryness, in the hands of the historians towards vernacular raciness. Literary elegance was usually something stuck on.[4]

The new notion of elegance, the cultivated yet natural plainness that comes in with the Restoration, was a rather scrubby growth in Scotland. The country was too backward, perhaps too distressed, to supply the experience of civilization that lies behind the urbanity of, say, Halifax's *Character of a Trimmer*. Rochester thought that "Scotch Civility", like French truth and Hibernian learning was to be found with "Nothing, thou Elder brother ev'n to shade". There are the letters of Sir Robert Murray, president of the Royal Society. But decidedly we shall have to make the most of that exception, and besides he would have learnt his civility abroad. Towards the end of the century there is a great deal of talk of moderation, even among extreme Presbyterians, and a great deal of appealing to what gentlemen think. But we shall not easily find a balanced human temper or a judgement enlarged by a wide experience of the world, and without these things talk of moderation is cant and the appeal to what gentlemen think, snobbishness.

According to Christopher Hill,[5] the pamphleteering of the Civil War period was one of the schools of the new prose. But in Scotland, where the Civil War was less of a social revolution than in England, there was no development of the popular journalistic styles he points to, except perhaps at the end of the century in the prefaces to

Alexander Shields's tracts, written in a pert, brisk manner, which jars with the all too earnest contendings of the actual works. There is a change in the tone and conduct of controversy. But on the Presbyterian side it is a decline not a development.

The controversies between church and state go back to the sixteenth century. Knox's debate with Lethington, recorded of course as a triumph for himself in his *History*, is a good example from the reforming side, and specimens of the monarchical reply may be found in James VI's essays in government, *Basilikon Doron* and *The True Lawe of Free Monarchies.* By the Civil War controversy had become scholastic in method. It is hard to feel that such a method of disputation with its endless division into heads, and answering these heads "by retail" in answers, replies to answers, "duplyes" to replies and so on, its point scoring and logic chopping – that all this could persuade anyone or in fact lead to an intelligent consideration of the issues. But at least it sets out to make a disinterested appeal to the mind and is the product of great mental agility and stamina. Of course asperity comes in and malice, invective and imprecation. But on the whole what is striking is the discipline and trust in rationality the Scottish Presbyterians show in their disputing in this earlier period.

During the troubles of the Restoration period invective becomes more prevalent. But for all its reading of the signs of the times in the language of the Apocalypse and its hate filled imagery drawn from the Old and New Testaments, it sounds peevish and indeed puny. Prophetic invective attains a certain power in the denunciations of popular preachers like Cameron, Walwood and Peden. But the pamphlets of the extreme party are disappointing stuff. Titles such as *Naphtali* (1667), *The Poor Man's Cup of Cold Water* (1678) or *A Hind Let Loose* (1687) may lead us to hope for something bizarre. But their clumsy old-fashioned prose with its windy scolding is hard to attend to. There are, of course, striking passages. In *The Poor Man's Cup of Cold Water,* McWard celebrates Mr. Mitchell as a saint of Samson's type because he tried to murder Archbishop Sharp and was hanged for it: "Samson was a rackel and rough-handed saint ready to pelt the Philistims on all occasions".[6] Here as often the vehemence runs to alliteration. But generally far from enlivening their pages, the zeal or ferocity of the extreme party exhausts itself in turgid and doctrinaire polemic. At the Whig Revolution when the Presbyterian party came to power, their writers make a poor showing, partly no doubt owing to the difficulty of reconciling the principles of a suffering remnant with a moderate constitutional establishment, but partly because the language of moderation and appeals to good sense were not really mastere'd by them and indeed came oddly from them. The

Presbyterians, Rule, Ridpath and Jameson are outclassed by their Episcopalian opponents Crockat, Monro and above all Sage, that very rare thing in this age of controversy, a first rate controversialist.

Generally the Episcopalian side seems to have had the better controversial writers. Even in the scholastic manner of disputation favoured by the Presbyterian divines the Aberdeen Doctors seem to have given better than they got in the debate with the Covenanting commissioners in 1638. On the whole, however, the Episcopalian pamphleteers rely less on the close logical method of disputation, and malice and insolence make Corbet's *Epistle Congratulatorie of Lysimachus Nicanor* (1640) and Bishop Maxwell's *Sacro Sancta Regum Majestas* (1644) more lively reading than Baillie's *Ladensium* Ἀυτοκατακρισις (1640) or Rutherford's *Lex Rex* (1644) from the Presbyterian side. But while malice and insolence are never very far from seventeenth century urbanity, they are not enough. Even in the best period of Episcopalian pamphleteering after the Presbyterian triumph of 1688, one is everywhere conscious of a defective urbanity. *The Scotch Presbyterian Eloquence* (1692) of Crockat (if he is its author) is certainly malicious and insolent. It is also funny and stung the Presbyterians to disgraceful replies. But in the end Crockat's contempt for the ways and speech of his countrymen becomes itself rather contemptible, and the squib seems ill-judged, as his fellow pamphleteer, Alexander Monro, regrets. Monro himself can write temperately and in *An Enquiry into the New Opinions* (1695) with an amusing, though unsustained, affectation of puzzlement.[7] But he is too easily provoked into an undignified scolding, and some of his ridicule is a bit puerile, of a kind effective perhaps with the students of Edinburgh University, where he had been principal, but hardly in cut and thrust with men.

In Sage, however, we have a polemicist of great force and a thoroughly estimable writer. The force of his tracts lies partly in their learning. In *The Fundamental Charter of Presbytery* (1695), he argues against the view that the Scottish Reformation was anti-Episcopal or that Presbyterianism had been the established constitution of the Church of Scotland before the Revolution. These ideas had been put forward by others, but Sage's case is more scholarly. His excellence consists, however, not only in his learning but in his way of arguing. He goes less by appeals to authorities than by examination and analysis of the evidence, and his tracts convey the excitement of a rational inquiry into a state of affairs. Although he is concerned with his method, that is, the orderly disposition of his material, his whole way of reasoning has freed itself from the art of disputation that makes almost all other heavyweight Scottish polemicists of the century so unreadable. Here, one feels, is how a man might reason as distinct from a divine or lawyer. And while he is a skilled debater, never missing an opening and adept at drawing out the absurd implications of an opponent's position, the thrust of his argument and equally its dignity and claim upon our attention are never lost in mere point scoring. Sage's excellence as a controversialist is a matter of temper and tone as well as of force of argument. We are always conscious of a man speaking to us. He writes with indignation of his party's wrongs. Yet he expresses himself not in the prophetic way of the Presbyterian pamphleteers but with the indignation a reasonable man would have to feel in the circumstances as he lays them out. And though he feels wronged, he does not whine but sets out to expose the folly and baseness of his opponents. Above all he keeps his temper and even in his most spirited and aggressive sallies it is not fury but force of mind that seems to carry all before it. Sage is a writer of narrow scope: even his works of patristic scholarship, *The Principles of the Cyprianick Age* (1695) and *A Vindication of the Principles of the Cyprianick Age* (1701) are polemics against the claim that the Presbyterian model might be found in the primitive church. His tone is without subtlety and his loyalties are simple. Yet because he writes as a reasonable man talking to other reasonable men, he strikes us as an urbane writer.

There is admittedly some horseplay with Gilbert Rule in the preface to *The Fundamental Charter of Presbytery*. And if we think of the London wits his humour may appear bucolic:

> There is something delightful in Marvelism,[8] in well humor'd wantonness, in lively judicious drollery. There may be some enormous strokes of beauty in a surprizing banter, some irregular sweetness in a well cook't bitterness. But who can think on drinking nothing but corrupted vinegar? What human patience can be hardy enough for entering the lists with pure barking and whining? With original dullness? who can think on arming himself against the horns of a snail? or setting a match for mewing with a melancholy cat? (n.p.)

The defects of that are obvious, but at the same time it makes an interesting distinction between witty and dull mismatchings and is touched with a lively apprehension of manners. Or take this:

> Master Andrew Melvil, after some years, spent at Geneva, returned to Scotland in July 1574. He had lived in that city under the influence of Theodore Beza, the true parent of Presbytery. He was a man by nature fierce and fiery, confident and peremptory, peevish and ungovernable. Education in him had

not sweetened nature, but nature had soured education, and both conspiring together had trickt him up into a true original, a piece compounded of pride and petulance, of jeer and jangle, of satyr and sarcasm, of venome and vehemence. He hated the crown as much as the mitre, the scepter as much as the crosier, and could have made as bold with the purple as with the rochet. His prime talent was lampooning and writing *Anti-Tami-Cami-Categorias.*[9] In a word he was the archetypal, bitter beard of the party. (pp. 217–18)

That too is overdone. Luckily he could not find a fourth pair of metonymies for monarchy and episcopate. And yet no other Scottish controversialist I can think of is able to enforce an argument, as Sage does here, with an appeal to our sense of character and so of men and manners and what is humanly amiable. In Sage then we can speak of a real, if provincial, urbanity. And this is a remarkable achievement given the state of letters in Scotland and the general run of controversial writing.

I said earlier that it was not very profitable to go about tracing a development of prose in Scotland of the kind to be found in England, for in Scotland notions of literary elegance were not sufficiently evolved. We might be tempted to make much of Sage's urbanity. But Sage stands very much by himself, even among his fellow Jacobite writers. He stands more as an exception than as a representative of a line of development. There is another reason for its being unprofitable to trace a development of prose in Scotland. The development of English prose is associated with a critical movement, with the criticism of vain learning and empty words among such writers as Bacon, Hobbes and Locke, and with the criticism of enthusiasm among Restoration divines. But there is little to show of this current of ideas in the intellectual culture of seventeenth century Scotland. To find it we would have to go to the philosophers of rhetoric of the later eighteenth century, to Blair, Campbell, Smith, Stewart. There the new ways of reasoning and writing that were developed in seventeenth century England were further developed and became the basic discipline of the Scottish Enlightenment. In seventeenth century Scotland, however, the influence of those ideas is tantalizingly desultory.

There is one intellectual field in which Scottish writers spent themselves with great energy and persistence, the field of political thought. Yet here perhaps more than anywhere else an inadequate literary culture and unreceptiveness to the new ideas makes their efforts dull. I have included statements of the constitutional conservative position by Drummond and Napier, for in different ways they are interesting to read. But I have not included anything of the vastly more copious radical Presbyterian writings on the polity, for they are hard to read and hard to understand. The dreary style of Presbyterian polemic has come up already and all Presbyterian political thought was polemical. But more than style and the sort of tone and human temper that involves is at issue here. What above all makes the political tracts intellectually impotent is an authoritarian and uncritical cast of mind and a method of arguing to match. Rutherford's *Lex Rex* (1644) is perhaps the most remarkable example of these writings. Its method of disposing the material under heads, arguing syllogistically and citing authorities in cartloads gets in the way of thought. It tries to build up an irrefragable case instead of conducting an inquiry into the nature of government. It meets objections by hairsplitting rather than considering the case. Locke's treatises on government do not display such formidable argumentative powers, but they engage the mind because speculative inquiry and new ideas are at work. With *Lex Rex* by contrast, a rigid and mechanical way of entrenching a position is proof against inquiry and new ideas.

As for the successors of *Lex Rex*, *Naphtali* (1667), *Jus Populi Vindicatum* (1669), *A Hind Let Loose* (1687), they are generally not argued in Rutherford's scholastic manner, and still there is little in these tracts by way of real inquiry into bases of government. On the contrary their whole effort is bent on making a case for the Covenanting resistance and tying their arguments to authorities that could not be questioned by anyone of their way of thinking. The right to dispose of an unjust prince is clinched with the "Phineas fact", an appeal to the biblical precedent of Phinehas, who pursued and killed an adulterous Israelite with his javelin.[10] The issue of civil liberty will finally turn upon the binding force of the Covenants upon king and nation. These arguments are baffling. They are admittedly the most absurd I could find but they bring out the doctrinaire mentality that makes Presbyterian writing on the constitution of so little permanent value, whatever respect their authors deserve for the risks they took for their principles.

In view of the stir such writings made at the time I have included a passage from Burnet's *Memoirs* summarizing the high Presbyterian line on sovereignty and the right of insurrection. This seemed a painless way of treating the subject. It is only fair to add that Burnet's statement of his own political principles, written before he changed his mind and joined William of Orange, is representative of the not very distinguished political thought that went into Royalist and Episcopalian tracts. In his *Memoirs of the Affairs of Scotland*, Sir George Mackenzie offers this judgement: "Though I give not an account of the fate of great monarchies, . . . the events I relate were the product of as much hate and of as many thoughts in the actors as actions of much greater splendour."[11] Yet in spite of so much hate and thought, seventeenth century Scotland failed to come up with political writing of lasting interest.

Outside this favourite area of intellectual exertion, however, there are pieces of writing with real intellectual force that raise the experience of seventeenth century Scotland to issues that can engage our minds. The finest of these is perhaps Robert Barclay's *Apology* (1678), a work that remained the summa of Quaker belief into the nineteenth century. One may trace Barclay's systematic treatment and his restrained use of syllogistic exposition to his Calvinistic training. But in his writing, as in the writing of his fellow Quaker, George Keith, one is conscious of the operation of new ideas and critical thinking. These have little to do with the critical movement associated with the development of English prose. Though Barclay's writings are informed by wide learning, by his Hermetic reading for example, he had probably little time for literary culture. Yet his radical views on ecclesiastical establishments and the institutional study of divinity enlarge the mind from the narrow issues between Presbyterian and Episcopalian. And clearly it was a free spirit that came to be appalled at the partisan shapes of seventeenth century Christianity. In these respects, at least, there seems a stronger impulse in him towards what Arnold meant by "Culture" than in any other Scottish writer of the century, even though he tried to realize it in an unworldly society.

There are other Scottish writers who are more easily placed in the critical movement of seventeenth century thought. Binning was known at Glasgow as a Baconian, and he comes out with a Baconian thought in his *Treatise of Christian Love* (1651): "The superficial knowledge of nature makes men atheists, but the profound understanding of it makes men pious".[12] Binning was also responsible with Leighton, as Baillie remarks disapprovingly, for introducing "a new guyse of preaching", "a discourse on some common head" instead of "the ordinarie way of exponing and dividing a text, of raising doctrines and uses".[13] The result is an overtly less methodical and vastly more natural sort of discourse. The old way of pulling a text out into many heads is a method of discovery, of finding various matters implied in the text, and even in able hands the result is often forced, much being made of little. With "a discourse on some common head", on the other hand, something has already been found to say on a subject and the arrangement of the material may aim at a natural development of the thought. At least with Binning and Leighton, it seems that the mind, freed from an elaborate method, is able to think and seize upon what is of importance. Baillie also complains that Binning's style is "unscriptural". Binning, that is, does not preach in the language and imagery of the Bible, as Baillie does. What Baillie means, however, when he goes on to talk of a "high romancing style" escapes me as far as Binning is concerned, for while Binning writes with eloquence, his chief aim is obviously lucid and intelligent exposition, and his imagery has clearly been chosen for its aptness and perspicuity, not for its elevation or fancy. I hesitate to call Binning's new way of preaching a Baconian reform of pulpit eloquence. But at least he seems to have been moved to bring a fresh and critical mind to the method and language of preaching and to arrive at a way of discourse in which one can think clearly.

There are others besides Binning one might wish to link with the English critical movement. Leighton and men of his circle like Charteris are to be reckoned for some things among those Restoration divines whose criticism of the language, morals and politics of enthusiasm has a share in the reform of our prose. And Sage with his talk of "clear and distinct ideas" seems to have read his Descartes and perhaps his Locke.[14] Yet all these writers are rather isolated figures. They leave little mark: Binning died at 25; Leighton left the country in despair; Sage's influence went with his Jacobite Episcopalianism. They do not represent a powerful current of ideas at work in Scotland. Indeed they show up by contrast the general poverty of Scottish literary culture. Perhaps the interest of these writers is chiefly historical. They show that the intellectual life of seventeenth century Scotland was not entirely transacted in the fantastic and doctrinaire forms of the political and ecclesiastical controversialists. They show in fact that there were stirrings of what we can recognize as intellectual life in Scotland before the eighteenth century. I hesitate to go further than that. Certainly none of these writers is a thinker of the first rank. But a sermon of Binning's and a piece of Barclay's *Apology* would surely have a place in an ideal anthology of seventeenth century English prose as noble examples of the intelligence of their time.

Without a historical context, the sense of some and the significance of most of the pieces in this anthology would be lost. I have therefore put them together in a historical order so that as far as possible one piece leads on to another and I have supplied a connecting historical narrative usually in the headnotes at the beginning of each chapter. The reader who wants a proper account of the background should go to W. L. Mathieson's *Politics and Religion in Scotland, 1560–1695* and the relevant volumes by Gordon Donaldson and William Ferguson of the *Edinburgh History of Scotland*

and for more specialized studies to David Stevenson's *The Scottish Revolution, 1637–44* and *Revolution and Counter-Revolution in Scotland, 1644–51*, Walter Makey's *The Church of the Covenant* and Ian B. Cowan's *The Scottish Covenanters, 1660–1688*. I have had to prune passages cruelly and leave out many things I would have liked to include, especially among the memoirs. But anthologies should be incomplete. They are meant to start lines of interest not to exhaust them. Those who want a fuller picture should go to Ronald D. S. Jack's very useful *Scottish Prose, 1550–1700*. I also found J. H. Millar's *Scottish Prose of the Seventeenth and Eighteenth Centuries* helpful. He has a sharp eye for interesting passages, quotes liberally and so sends one to the authors.

CHAPTER ONE

THE JACOBEAN SETTLEMENT

The most convenient way of giving the historical background
for this period is in headnotes to Melville and Calderwood.

JAMES MELVILLE or Melvin (1556–1614) was nephew and pupil
of Andrew Melville, the leader of the reforming party in the
Scottish Church. The deposition of Mary Queen of Scots in 1567
had made the Reformation secure. But the reformed church was
governed by "superintendents", who exercised the functions of
bishops, as well as by General Assemblies. The second impulse
of the Reformation in Scotland was to assert the independence of
the national church not only from Rome but from the state. And
since superintendents or bishops could be managed by the king
and indeed fitted in with the government of church and state
under one sovereign power, the reforming party took its stand
on the principle of the parity of ministers. That, they thought,
was essential to keep the "two kingdoms" of church and state
separate. So the *Second Book of Discipline* drew up a scheme
under Andrew Melville's direction for the government of the
church in which bishops were replaced by church courts.
Presbytery was not mentioned by name but emerged as the most
effective of those courts for taking over the bishops' functions
soon after the General Assembly endorsed the *Book* in 1578.

James Melville shared his uncle's ideas about the separate
powers of church and state and was active in furthering his
designs; he became himself one of the Presbyterian leaders.
When his uncle was principal, he was a regent or tutor in classics
at Glasgow University, and when his uncle moved to St.
Andrews, he became professor of Hebrew and oriental languages there. In the struggle with Archbishop Adamson, he fled
to England after his uncle in 1584 and returned and joined with
him in excommunicating the archbishop in 1586. For a time
during the late 1580s and early nineties the Melvillian party were
on top. But in 1596 James began to assert his authority against
their overbearing conduct and got his way at the General
Assembly of Dundee over the return of the exiled Catholic
lords. From that Assembly, Melville dates the decline of the

Church of Scotland. Certainly Melvillian influence was cut back in the following years and bishops were restored. When he became King of England, James was firmly in control of both church and state in Scotland. In 1605 the Presbyterians held a General Assembly at Aberdeen in spite of the king's ban. The government responded by imprisoning and banishing some of the ministers, then summoned eight of the Presbyterian leaders to London for talks with the king and kept them waiting for nearly a year. The passages below show how the king was able to detain them until finally he sentenced them to various degrees of banishment. After that, he went ahead restoring a moderate Episcopacy without coming up against effective opposition. Both Melvilles died in exile.

Melville's *Diary* and this, its continuation, is the most attractive of the Presbyterian narratives. Like his uncle, James Melville was an accomplished humanist and figured in the reform of the universities. But usually his diary is free of humanistic affectations. His literary manner is plain and moderate in tone. It has a way of suggesting that the extravagance or immoderation of the other side is ridiculous. Even in his uncle, a perfervid character seems to amuse him, though of course the humour is sympathetic and more complicated there.

The passages come from *The True Narration of the Declyneing State of the Kirk of Scotland from 1590–1610*, a copy made in 1623 (Edin. Univ. MS. DC.4.10, pp. 1; 80–83, 84–85; 86; 90–91; 95–96; 101–102; 102–103). Except for year dates and "often" on p. 20, which the Wodrow Society edition usefully supplies, emendations, where the manuscript is clearly erroneous or makes little or no sense, are from the Wodrow MS. Quarto XIV in the National Library. I have cut out among other things the documents Melville cites and his reports of what was going on in Scotland. The reader who wants to take in the extent of the crisis should go to the full account in the Wodrow Society edition of *The Autobiography and Diary of James Melvill*.

True Narration of the Declyneing State of the Kirk of Scotland

The aige of the Kirke of Scotland, since scho wes brought out of the darknes of Paprie to the cleir light of the gospell, hes bein now a perfyt jubilie of sevin sevines,[1] from the yeir of hir Lord's incarnation 1561 unto this present yeir 1610;[2] the infancie quhairof wes admirabille, the grouth to hir full perfectioun incomparabill in any kingdome, and so this doolfull decay in this almaist dieing aige most pitifull and lamentabill. Hir infancie most happie, men in all most blissed tyme haiff most excellentlie, boith for the truth and stylle, comitted to wrytt. Hir perfectioun, just, according to the paterne schawin be God to the prophettis and apostelles on the montaines of Sionn, in doctrine and discipline without any mixture from that citie set on the 7 hilles or from the policie of manes braine, hes bein, for sinceritie, truth and libertie, thais mony yeirs, all the kingdomes of Europe with admiration beholding and looking upoun, faire as the morneing, cleir as the mone, pure as the soone in the ey of hir freinds and dreidfull as ane armie feghting undir ane bannar to all hir enimies. And now necessitie is laid upon me, with sorrowfull heart and drouping eyes, to sett doun the declyneing thereoff, quhilk tuik the sensibill beginning at that evil sinod, sevintein day of December, the yeir of God 1596,[3] and haith contenewit from evil to wors unto this present 1610, as the true narratioun subsequent sall mak manifest.

. . .

Fryday, the 19 of September [1606] we come to Kingstoune. Their Mr Johnne Gordoune [Dean] of Salisberrie, directit to wait upon us and dres us the best he could for the purpos, com, salutit and welcumit us. And on the morne he convoyit us to Hamptoun Court, quhair eftir the kingis dinner, immediately we got presens of the king, as sitting yit at his dinner, admitting us verie graciousely to the kis of his hands. And eftir a few words mirrily to Mr James Balphoure[4] and concerneing the gud order takin with the pest at Edinbruche, we wer dimissit with a very gud countenance and went to Kingstoune to dinner with Mr Johnne, our attendar, at his ludgeing. . . .

Mononday, the 22, we wer sent for to conferrence with his Majestie. And being enterit into the chalmer, the hous wes uschit[5] be the Erle of Dumbar and none sufferit to byd thairin but the Scottis counsellouris and the ministers, save only Doctor Montague, Dein of the Kingis Cheppel, wes permittit to stand within to keipe the dore. The king, sitting in his chyre, callit on us to come nere about him and enterit to expon the caus quhairfoir he had writtin for us, almost according to the proclamatione and the tennoure of the lettre sent to us, gathering upe all in end to tuo poyntis, quhairin he wes to be throucht[6] with us for the pice of the Kirk and annent the pretendit Generall Assemblie (so he termit it) hadin[7] at Abirdein and the doeing of thais ministeres ensewing thairupon; the uthir, how thair mycht be ane orderly and piceabill Generall Assemblie keipit to sett all thingis in quyttnes and guid ordure. Now we had agreit amongis our selffis that on sould be spiche man for all, quhilk burdein wes laid upoun Mr James Melvin, and that we sould give no present ansyr but tak all to guid advysement. So the said speiker maid ansyr in thais words: "Pleas your most excellent Majestie, quhen we had resavit your Majestie's lettres, we mett togider at Edinbruche, and reiding the same, we were greatlie rejoyceit to haiff so guid occasioune to sie your Majestie's face and kiss your hand but meikl more quhen we perceivit the purpose of your Majestie's lettres to tend to the intreating the peace of the Kirk of Scotland in that estait quhilk your Majestie left the same and to testifie your Majestie's love and affectioune thairto, according to your Majestie's lettres from tyme to tyme sent to sume of the presbyteries and synods and also to the commissiouneres of the Kirk, and maist ample to your Majestie's honourabill Counsel. So that howbeit divers of us, namely for seiknes and knawin inhabilitie, mycht haif excuisit our selffis, yit we resolvit to come to your Majestie, evir with alacrity and diligence preventing[8] the day appoyntit, least accidentis of wether, or any uthir impediment, mycht haiff impedit. And now finding your Majestie in helth, welfair and hight honoure and testifieing the same thingis to us by your gracious mouth with so favourable countinence towardis us, we can not express our joye and propens[9] dispositioune to serve and plese your Majestie in quhat can lie in us in God. But as concerneing any perticular, your Majestie's lettres beris none, nethir haiff we befoir to this tyme hard of thame. We wald thairfoir maist humbly desyre your Majestie to give us tyme to advyse, and we sall returne with ane answer, the best way we cane.

Thairefter thair wes a guid tyme spent in reassouneing annent[10] the presbyteries sending thair commissiouneres, efter the ressaiveing of his Majestie's commissiounere's lettres for discharging of [the] Assemblie at Aberdein. ... Finaly annent Mr James Melvine's lettre,[11] thais words wes betuixt the king and him: "I hard that ye wreitt a lettre to the Synod of Fyff at Cowper, quhairin wes meikle of Chryst, but lytle guid of the King. Be God, I trow ye wer reavand[12] or mad, for ye speik utherwayis now. Wes that a charitabill judgment of me?" "Sir," sayis Mr James with a low courtessie, "I wes boith seik and sair in body quhen [I] wreit that lettre, bot sober and sound in mynd. I wreit of your Majestie all guid, assuring my selff and the britherine that thais articles, quhairoff a coppie com in my hands, could not be from your Majestie, they wer so strange. And quhom sould I think, speik guid off, if not off your Majestie, quho is the man under Chryst quhom I wisch most guid and honour to?" "But quhair ar these articles?" says the King. "The coppie that com in my handis is at Londone, Sir," said he. So divers of the bisschoppis and commissiouneres, to put end to that, affirmeing befoir the king that thair wer divers coppies, and sume very [often] hard off thais articles, quahiroff ane mycht haiff cume in Mr James' handis, that matter wes laft off. And the king reassouneing againe the first tuo heidis, dimissit to the nixt day for giveing ansyr thairto.

We wer not wel cume to our ludging at Kingstoune, quhen we had a lettre from Mr Alexander Hay, secretary to his Majestie in Scotis effairis, wairneing us in the kingis name to cume to syrmone to morrow in the Kingis Chappel and to dyne in the palice. So Tuysday, the 23 of September, we came tymous[13] in the morneing to Hamptounecourt, quhair we walkit in the gardeine quhill the tyme of sermone; quhair sitting in our place appoyntit in the Kingis Chappel, the king and the quein present with many nobillis, Mr Doctor Butricht[14] prechit on the 13 to the Romans, anent the magistratis auctoritie in matteres ecclesiasticall, all out of Bilsoune's buikis[15] of obedience; quhairinto we assentit, [except] that quhair of ignorance, or of malice, or of boith, he joynes divers tymes the Presbyterie with the Pope, as thought the ane with the uthir had beine joynit in the same judgment together. . . . Efter sermone be Mr Johne Gordoune, our attendant, we wer led to the kingis closet, quhair we saw the royall ceremonie of tuiching of childrein for hailling off sume of the escrolles,[16] commounely callit "the kingis seiknes," and unerstood by the same Mr Johnne his discours in quhat respect and maner the king usit it, to witt, not for hailing (quhilk wes in God's hand), but for prayer and almes towards the poore diseasit and for sume politick reassoune, least omitting the ceremony usit in France by the kingis thairof, he sould thairby losse sume of the substance and title quhilk he hais to the kingdome and croune of France; quhilk respects had maid the king, quho wes alltogider againes it at the beginning, to yeild to the use thairof now.

Thaireftir, we went to diner in the kingis closet and maid guid cheir. Eftir the diner, remembering that [we] wer to be callit *coram*,[17] calling on God, we tak this resolutioune that our appoyntit speiker sould speik, unles that uthir wer comandit by name, and that our said spichman sould declair how we could not judge of the Assemblie at Abirdein. . . .

But by quhat counsellour or in quhat consideratione, I can not tell, the king had takin ane uthir cours, quhilk wes to appel every ane in perticular, that heiring every manis forme of spiche and ansyr, they mycht marke and tak advantage of menis infirmities and formes of behavior for thair purpos. And so admitting divers of the Counsel of England, to witt, the Bisschoppe of Canterbury,[18] placit on the kingis rycht hand, the Erle of Salisberrie, Great Secretar, [the] Erle of Suffolk, Great Chamberlane, and the Erle of Worchester, Maister of the Hous, the Erle of Nottinghame, Admiral, the Erle of North-hamptoune, Lord Knollis, with divers uthiris nobillis, and with thrie or four bischoppis and deanes, standing induris[19] behind the tapestrie, quho now and then discoverit thameselffis, hither also the prines wes brought, standing at his fatheres left hand with all the Scottis nobilis and Counselloris. The king, efter reassouncing of the poynt left at the last day, com in end to be resolvit of this questioune perticularily, quhither the Assembly last haldin at Abirdein wes ane lawfull Assembly or not and the proceiding of thais britherin thairat and eftir, justifiabill, yea or no? "And," he sayis, "I will begine at yow bisschoppis and commissiouneres." Thais wer Mr George Glaidstanes, John Spotiswood, James Law, Andro Lamb, now bisschoppis, Mr James Nicolsoune, Patrik Scharpe, Robert Howy and the Great Commissiouner Lawristoune, quho all ansyrit that they had evir damnit that Assembly and the proceidingis of thais britherine as unlawfull.

And sua it com to us. "Now, Siris," sayis the king, "quhat say ye, and first Mr Andro Melvin?" Quho with meikle law courtessie talkit all his mynd in his awin maner, roundly, soundly, fully and fervently, almaist the space of ane hour, not omitting no poynt he could remember. In end, he refusit to judge of that Assembly for the reassounes afoir sett doun. Mr James Balfour followit at the kingis calling; regraiting hevily uncheritabill and fals delatiounes[20] maid of him, in end to the same effect ansyrit and that uthirwayis he could not sie the peace of the Kirk could be settillit.

The king spendit meikle tyme with thais tuo; and following how the matter went, semit wery and callit Mr James Melvin: "I will not weary your Majestie, quhairfoir pleis yow ressaive my ansyr schort. Thair hes bein meikle tyme about the questioune. Iff it be *in thesi*, sett doun in wrytt, and we sall ansyr as we can; iff *in hypothesi*,[21] your Majestie's demand is anent the presbyteries, senderis and the doeing of thair commissiouneres sent. Annent the senderes, I did schaw your Majestie thair reasoune yisterday; and iff your Majestie judg a fault thairine, let the presbyteries that sent the commissiouneres be punischit, and not the britherine that wer sent be thame. Annent thair doeingis, it is judgit already by your Majestie's Counsell; quhairin I am resolvit with the [panell][22] to obtemperat[23] ethir by obedience or patience. Iff your Majestie judge it by a Generall Assembly of the Kirk, quhilk is all our wisches, I can not prejudge that. And iff your Majestie in the mein tyme will urge me for my judgment of the matter according to my conscience, unles the alledgit wronge done unto thame and givin in by wrtt to your Majestie's Estaitis in Parliament last haldin at Perth be considerit disscussit and rychtly judgit, I wald not for all the world condemne thame; ane coppie of the quhilk wrongis we ar earnestly desyrit to present to your Majestie be thame." And this said, he stoppit to[24] and delyverit thame in the kingis hands. . . . The king red thame all ovir quhill as the rest wer sporting, and with ane angry smyle, said he wes glaid thair wer givin in. . . .

In the end, Mr Andro Melvin, craifting licence on his knies humbly to speik bak again, in his awin maner and friely and plainely, affirmit the innocencie of the guid, faithfull and honest britherin in all thair proceidingis at Abirdein. And thairfoir he recomptit the wrongis done unto thame at Linlithgow,[25] as ane that wes present as ane eye and ear wittnes. And taking him in direct termes to the Advocat, Mr Thomas Hamiltoun, he invyit[26] scharpely againes him, telling him planely and pathetically of his favoring and spaireing of Papistis and craftie, cruel and malicious dealing againes the ministeres of Jesus Chryst, so that he could be no moir againes the saintis of God then he had at Linlithgow. At the quhilk words the king luiking to the archbisschoppes, sayis, "Quhat! Me thinkis he makis him the Antichryst!" And suddentlie, again with ane oath, "Be God, it is the divelis name in the Revelatioune! He hes maid the divel of him, wel-belovit bretherine, brother Johne!"[27] And so cuttitly turneing his back, said, "God be with yow, Siris."

Quhen we wer gone out of the palice a lyttle way towards Kingstoune, Mr Alexander Hay sendis back for us and in the Uttir Court reids a chairge from the king not to returne to Scotland nor to com neir the king, quein and prines [their] courtis without speciall calling for and licence. . . .

Sonday, the 28 September, writtin for be Mr Alexander Hay, we come to court, quhair wes prepairit for us a royall service, with the haill solemnetie of ceremonies in the Kingis Chappel. And Doctor Andreas,[28] then Bischoppe of Exchester, maid the syrmone of the [tenth] of Numberes, on the two trumpettis, thairon a long discours, proving that the conveineing of assemblies and counseles and dischairgeing of the samyn perteinit to christiane kingis and emperoures.[29] And becaus we wer tendit on by no honnest [man] of any countinance to leid us to dinner as befoir, howbeit on tauld us it wes redy in the queine's chalmer as befoir, our braines full of wyne and musick and our stomakes emptie of victuallis, we come home to dyne at Kingistoune. . . .

So on Mononunday, the 29 of that moneth, tymous in the morneing we com. In the morneing, as we wer wairnit, that day was keipit in honour of Saint Michel with strange musick and hie service in the Kingis Chappel; to the quhilk we wer desyrit to come and commandit to bring Mr Andro and James Melvine cheifflly be Mr Alexander Hay at the kingis expres command. The said Mr Alexander, becaus of the great thronge, convoyit [thaim] throucht the secreit passage throw the chapplane's chalmer. Mr James tauld his uncle by the way that it wes to trappe thaim and assay thair patience in cais they wer hard speik or wryt any thing againes that superstitione or vanity. Thair they saw the king and quein offer at the aultar, quhilk wes decorit with tuo bukes, tuo basines, tuo candelstickes. And upon this occasioun, Mr Andro maid the verses for the quhilk thaireftir he was trublit. Thair one of the Count de Vaudemontis[30] cumpenny said in Latine in the heiring of many, "Ego nunquam vidi talem cultum. Nihill hic profecto deest de solemna missa, preter adorationem transubstantiati panis"[31]. . . .

That same day befoir noone, Mr James Melvin, walking in the great hall of the palice, Mr Doctor Montague, Dean of the Kingis Chappel, com by, with quhom Mr James had this conference: "Will it pleas yow, Sir, to be favourabill to us and our caus at the kingis hand?" "I can not," sayis the doctor, "for ye ar againes the stait of our Kirk, that is, of bischoppis, quhilk haith bein fyftein hundrith yeiris in the Kirk of Christ." "Not so, Sir, in this sort of bisschoprick, involvit in civil and worldly effaires *cum tipho seculi hujus.*[32] Such wer niver in the Kirk but sinc the Popes of Roome declairit thamself Antichryst." "Howsoevir," sayis the [dean], "[ye] ar againes our Kirk and bisschoppes." "If ye trubill not us, we trubill not yow." Sayis the deane, "Ye haiff [made] mentioun of our bisschopes to the king and your Parliament." And with this he pulles out of his bosome the protestatioune givin to the Parliament at Perth and poyntit at the place quhair it mentiounit papisticall and angelicall bischoppes. "Ay, the corruptioune of thame," sayis Mr James. "I pray yow, Sir, think ye not that thair is corruptioune in that stait?" "I think thair be," said he, "but ye deny the kingis supremacie." "None that he sould haiff," sayeth the uthir. "Yes," sayeth [he], "that [supremacie that] he sould haiff [in] the ministeriall Kirk, the quhilk athir the Pope, or the Prince, or the Presbyterie must have. The Pope sould not, we say all." "Mr Calvine gives it to the Presbyterie, and soe doe we," sayeth Mr James. "Ay," saith the doctour, "but that is treassoun in England, for the Prince hes it be our lawis." "But not," saith the uthir, "by the lawis of Scotland." "But ye must haiff it sua in Scotland," and sua abruptly went his way.

Tuysday, the 30 of September, we wer bidin to the syrmone againe befoir the kingis moveing from Hamptoun Court, quhair Doctour King[33] maid a most violent invective againes the presbyteries, cryeing to the king, "Doune with thame all!" The quhilk four sermones wer by commandement imprintit soone eftir, as they wer purposely long befoir prepairit and dressit. . . .

The 5 of November, the Parliament of England sat doun againe, quhilk maid us to be excludit againe from all actioun and dealing for our selffis. In the meintyme, we keipit ane honnest tabille and

24

ludgeing hous altogider, quhairunto resortit many honest men and britherin of the best sort. So, haifing comfortabill comoditie of our beinge togidder, we thought it guid to tak to sume guid excercise of the Word and prayer and fasting joynit with humiliatioune on day in the weik, namely, becaus of the dangerous deilling at home, that [the] brither[in] thair mycht be constant that God in mercie wald give unfainyieit repentance to our haill Kirk, baith pastour and peiple, for the lycht estimatioune and fruitles abuse of the gospel, so sincerely continowit so long a tyme in our contrey; and for the quhilk this hevy dissapatioune and danger of great corruptioun wes hanging on, that it mycht pleas God withe his mercifull eye to look doun again unto his awin Sion, to gadder his disperssit [and] to repair the breiches. That exercise continowit about a moneth. Not ceisseing by all occasioune of all our freinds to give in our supplicatioune to the kingis Majestie and use all meines quhat we could for our friedome, the effect we fand wes that one Sonday the 23 of November Mr Alexander Hay come to our ludgeing, sent, as he said, from the king, intimating ane ordinance for wairding[34] of every ane of [us] with a severall bisschoppe, so greitlie wes our remaineing togidder invyed. For boith the king and bisschoppes, namely of Canterbury, had thair spyes, quho under coullour of freindly visitatioune, reportit boith our spiches and actiounes. . . .

This movit us all to great indignatioune and anger, so that [Mr] Alexander wes laid upoun [by all] round about, and in end ressavit[35] his ansyr: if we had committit any cryme, let us be judgit ordinarly and punischit; uthirwayis we would not disschonour God, the king of our callinge, to goe to sic menes housses, but would rethir chuse imprissounement and banischement. We maist humbily besought his Majestie to regaird his awin honour, quho had writtin for us so fairly, the honour of our Kirk and contrie, affirmeing bouldly they wer not guid counselleres had mentiounit that. This and meikle moir wes reportit be Mr Alexander Hay. We hard no moir of that matter till a quarter of yeir was donne. And eftir being mychtily affryeit thairwith we wer fain to breck our socitie, quhilk wes sua invyit. But befoir we severit, we thought it most neidfull that the four syrmounes that we hard at Hamptoun and now ar publischte in prent sould be ansyrit; quhilk travel we committit to thame quho thought thame selffes best disposit for the same. Unto ane of the number[36] we injoynit to nott and mark eligantly all proceidingis for infor-matioune to ane historie, as it mycht pleas God to grant the benefit thairof to the posteritie.

[Sonday], the last of November, Mr Alexander Hay sent a lettre, desyreing in the king's name Mr Andro Melvin and Mr [James Melvin], with Mr Robert Wallace, to come to his chalmer at

Quhithall by ane of the clock. He tould us thair wer certaine verses maid in Latine com in the kingis hand, for the quhilk we wer to be callit befoir the Counsel of England; and soe we wer callit by and bye. Mr Andro Melvine confessit that he had maid such verses, being much movit in his mynd with indignatioune to such vanitie and superstitioun in a chrystiane kirk, under a chrystiane king, borne and brought upe in the lycht of the gospel most sincerely, befoir idollateres to confirme thame in the same and grive the heartes of true worschipperes. And being spokin unto by the Archebissoppe of Canterburie, quho sat uppmost at the counsel table on the rycht, tuik occasioune plainely in his face to tell him all his mynd, quhilk burst out as inclossit fyre in watter. He burdenyit him with all thais curruptiounes, vanities, with profanatiounes of the Sabbath and beiring doun of the true and faithfull pricheres of the Word of God, of setting and holding upp of anti-chrystiane hierarchie and Popish ceremonies. And taking him by the quhyt sleives of his rocket and schaiking [them], in his maner frielie and roundly callit thame "Romishe ragis and a pairt of the Beastes mark." He tauld him further that iff he wes the autor of the buik intitulat *Scotiseing Genevating Discipline*,[37] he estimit him the captaine enimie of all churches reformit in Europe, and would profess him enimie and in all such proceidingis to the effusioun of the last droppe of all the bloud in his body; being uncessantely grivit at his verie heart to sie such a man haif the kingis ere and to sit so hight in that honourabill Counsel et ct. He paintit out also Bisschoppe Barlo[38] for the wrytting of *The Conferrence at Hamptoun Court*, quhairin he sat doun that "the king wes in the Kirk of Scotland, but nocht of it" and uthir such horribile spiches, marvelit that such a one wes unpunischit examplarilie for making the king to be of no religioune, and entering in his syrmoune maid last at Hamptoun, he refutit the same so long as he gat audience and permissioune. But he wes oft interuptit and at last put furth in a place him selff. And Mr James Melvin callit in, quhom the Chanceler[39] usit verie courteouslie with the styles of lairneing, graveitie, godlines, wisdome and truth, feiring the force of that Spirit quhilk he neidit not in useing such charmeing, he schew him how the kingis Majestie had commandit thame off the Counsell to ask him tuo questiounes, not doubting but he would ansyr truely and plainely: first, quhither he had writtine home to Scotland the lait proceidingis at Hamptoun Court betuixt his Majestie and us? He ansyrit that [at] his coming from Scotland, his freinds wes desyrous to be informit of our matteres how they went and sua he had promisit to thame, and for performeing of his duetie, he had writtin all. The Archbissope askit him how he had writtin of justiefieing his awin pairt and condemneing the kingis pairt. He ansyrit nethir by way of justificatioune nor condemnatioun, but by simple way of narratioune. The Erle of Northamptoune insistit on the same poynt, to quhom he said he had ansyrit already. The Chanceler sayis, "He hes ansyrit simpelie and plainely," and sua movit the uthir questioune, if he had sein verses writtin in Latine againes the ornaments of the aulter of the Kingis Chappel? He said he could not ansyr till he saw thame. They gaiff him thame to reid; quho then said he had sein such verses in his uncle's hand eftir the making of thame at Hamptoun Court and knew weil the great greiff and motioun of his mynd at that tyme. They askit if he had givin out any coppies thairof to send thame to Scotland. He said, no, non at all, nethir knew he yit ony givin out by his uncle to any man being on lyff and marvelit how they could come in the kingis hand. So he wes bidin remove, and Mr Robert Wallace wes demandit the same questiounes and ansyrit conforme.

Eftir ane houre's advysement, we wer all callit in togidder; and Mr Andro, eftir a long and grave admonitorie oratioune of the Chancler, Lord Egartoun, that with his learneing and yeires he sould joyne wisdome, gravite, modestie and discretioun, he wes committit to the Deane of Paulis to remain in his custodie dureing the kingis majestie's will; and the uther [tuo] commandit to the custodie [of] thair awin wyse and discreit cariage with a gentill wairneing to tak heid to thair actiounes, spiches and wryttingis.

The purpose of all this wes to snare Mr Andro Melvine, [quhom they knew] to be frie of speich, that they mycht haif sume appeirance of just occasioun to mak him fast, and sua be quyt of his hinder in the prosecutioun of the Episcopall purpose; for soone in the morneing, Mr Alexander Hay com with the warrand and commissioun to put the Counseles decreit in executioun and restit not till he had gottin Mr Andro enterit in the Deane of Paulis hous and custodie, quhair he remainit quhill the moneth of Marche. . . .

Wednisday, the 4 of Marche [1607], Mr James knawing the Bisschoppe of Durhame[40] to be at Durrhames hous and haiffing the officer waiting on him, thought gud to goe to the bisschope to testifie his obedience to the king, but thairwith to perswad and desyre the bischope, iff he wer wyse, to concurr with him in suit to be frie of such a ghaist;[41] and so acummpannieit with Mr Williame [Scott], went to him and tauld him he com to testifie the dispositioun of his heart inclynit and bent allwayis to rander obedience to the kingis Majestie in all thingis dew but thairwith to requeist his Lordschip to joyne with him in supplicatioun and dealing with his Majestie and honorabill Counsel to haif licence to goe home, quhair he had ane honnest calling and vocatioun and familie to attend upoun, and not on uther menis tablis; for he had ever bein accustomit withal to give

27

rather thane to take of any. And truely it was not fitt that he sould be his hostler[42] and he his guest, being sua different in stait and opinioun, the quhilk wauld breid but cauld affectioun; and how unpleasant would the socieite be quhair thair is throughtnes[43] of opiniounes, his wisdome mycht easiely consider; eikand[44] heirto that he was a man subject to manifold seiknes and diseasses and could not truble the hous of a stranger and such a nobill prelat; farder, he being a man professing the cair of saulis, sould tak pietie on many thousand saulis in the Kirk of Scotland that lackit comfort of their persounes[45] reteinit from so long in England.

His ansyr was sillie and confusit, this in effect: that sieing it was his Majestie's and Counselis will, he sould be welcome to his hous; he sould prepair him a chalmer and a gardein, but he behovit to put a gentillman out of his chalmer for his caus, and that his man behovit to be with that gentlemanes man, and sume such triffelingis. Mr James besought him not to doe sua, for he com not to England to displace any gentilman. He thankit God that he had housses and chalmeres of his awin in Scotland, quhairin he wes accustomit to ludge and plesyr gentilmen, and not to displace thame; and thairfoir in that respect and uthires, he would rethir concurr with us in satisfieing king and Counsel, quhairby he mycht be frie of such a burdein. "Weill," said the bissope, but quhat do ye talk of sua many peiple committit to your ministrie and the peiple being the kingis? And haiff ye not your ministerie of him, so that if it pleise the king to withhauld yow and ruel the people uthirwayis, [ye] sould be content?" "We must be content," said he, "and suffer patientlie, but the peiple is the Lordis and thair saulis in the warrison[46] of Chrystis pretious blood; and for our ministerie, in the chairg thairoff we haiff it not off the king nor no pairt thairof, bot of Chryst and his Church, and is much unlyk your bissoprickis quhilk ar the inventioun of man and so givin and takin by man."

By that occasioun, he would haif bein farder at the main poynte concerneing the governement of the Kirk by the king and bissoppes and not by presbyteries and assemblies conveinit without the kingis licence, but he tauld him that would require a gryter tyme. Yit the bissoppe must use sume argument, viz., that he had studeit so many yeiris that could be red or writtin of that matter, he was doctor and had bein sua oft Vice-Chancler of the Universetie of Oxford and such lyk. Mr James said all that concludit nothing; it would be stronger reassounes that would reclaime thame iff they come to the [schooles].[47] So upon promises that we sould come and dyne with him upoun Settirday nixt, we tuik our leive. But befoir Settirday, on quho attendit him and us, quhom he would haiff cautiouner[48] (fursuith) for our coming to dinner, preventit our coming and tauld us my Lord was not provydit for us yit and could not be at hame quhill the nixt weik . . .

The 23 of Apryl wes Saint George day, quhilk wes keipit at court with great superstitioun and vainitie. The report quhairof come to the eares of Mr Andro Melvin, his spirit wes irritat and much incensit within him, as wes Paulis quhen he saw the citie of Athenes ful of idolatrie. On quhilk occasioun he maid the verses following:

> Andreas, Christi divinus apostolus, est qui
> Scotigenis ritus signat apostolicos;
> Armeniis (ut fama) Georgius, haeresiarcha,
> nunc Anglis [ritus signat] apostolicos.
> signa Andreae ergo sunt nobis nulla Georgi
> undique apostolicis nullibi apostaticis.

> Saint Andro, Chrystis Appostle trew,
> Does signe the Scotismenes ritis;
> Saint George, Armenian heresiarch,
> The Inglishmenes delytis.
> Let Scotis men thane hauld fast the faith
> That is holie appostolicke,
> Howbeit that Ingland keipes the cours
> That [is whollie] apostaticke.

Upon the 26 of Appril being the Sabboth day, betymes in the morneing, being foulle, ane of my Lordis Sallisberie his men come to Mr Andro Melvin, lyand at Bow tuo mylis from Londin in Mr Somaris houss, and verie courteousely intreatit [him] in his lord and maisteris name to come to the court at Quhythall to my Lord's chalmer at 9 of the clocke, quhair my Lord wald talk with him; beseiking him to mak no stay, for my Lord would attend his coming. Thairfor, Mr Andro makis him selff readie with diligence, thinking that it wes in freindschippe and that eftir conferrence, he would bid him to dinner. Cuming from his chalmer to our ludging, quhair we nocht being ready, [he] must goe to court and would schortly stay to break his fast; but haifing borrowit the hors of his hoist, postis away to court with his man, eftir his cousine Mr James Melvin had said ane word to him, "Tak heid that your biding to diner be not a new calling befoir the Counsel." Mr William Scot, Mr Robert Wallace and Mr James Melvin followit one fut and taking the first convenient boiteing, com by watter to Westminster, quhair a little efter 11 of the clock, he come to the hous out of the palace to James Archesoune's hous and tauld us how he had waittit [in a gallerie] before [the Earle of] Salisberrie's chalmer sinc 9 a clock, and sieing the erle and all going to diner and he left alone, come to dyne with us. And till the burd wes coverit and the meitt put thairon, he uttirit to us ane excellent meditatioun, quhilk he had walking in the gallerie, on the second psalme, joyneing thairwith prayer, quhairby we wer al much movit acconting the same in place of [our] Sabbothis [foirnoone's exercise]; and sitting doun to dinner, he rehersit his Saint Georgis verses vehemently againes the corruptiounes and superstitiounes of England. Thairfoir his cousine[49] sayes to him, "Remember Ovidis verses:

> Si saperem doctus odissem jure sorores
> numina cultori perniciosa suo."

His ansyre wes in the verses following:

> "Sed nunc tanta meo comes est insania morbo
> saxa demens refero rursus ad icta pedem."[50]

"Weill" sayis his cousine, "eit your dinner, for I sall warrand yow ye salbe befoir the Counsell for your verses." "Weill," sayis he, "my heart is full and boldenit. I will be glaid to haif ane occasione to disburdein it and speik all my mynd plainely to thame for the dishonoring of Chryst and wrack of sua many soulis be the beiring doun the sinceritie and fridom of the gospel." "I warrand yow," sayis Mr James, "they know ye will speik your mynd friely and thairfoir hes concludit to mak that a meines to keip yow from going home to Scotland." "Iff God," sayis he, "hes ony thing to doe with me in Scotland more, he will bring me home to Scotland again. Giff[51] not, let me gloriefie him, quhairever I be. And as I haif said often to yow, cousine, I think God hes sume pairt to play with us on this theatre." We had not half dyneit quhen on comes to him from Lord Salisberie, [to whom he said], "Sir, I waitted longe upon my Lord's dinner till I wes verie hungrie and could not stay longer. I pray my Lord to suffir me to tak a lytle of [my] awin dinner." That messenger wes not weil gone quhill againe comes anuthir, and soone eftir that, Mr Alexander Hay, the Scottish Secretar, telling him that the Counsel wes long sett attending him. At the heiring quhairoff, with great motioun raysing, he prayit, and living us at diner, for we wer expressely chairgit that we come not within the palice, went with Mr Alexander Hay with great commotioun of mynd. This wes sone eftir tuo of the clocke. About 3, on of our men, quhom we sent to attend at the Counsel dore, comes with tearis and schew us that he wes carieit direct from the Counsel by watter to the Tour. We following with dilligence, yit could we not meit with him by the way nor haif access to him. . . .

Mr James insistit be al the meines and credit he had to be licencit to stay at Londin or thairabout but at last wes counsellit by his best freinds to desist and give obedience to the chairge; and provyding for his necessities the best way he could, they resolvit to goe by sie to New Castle. The day they wer depairtit they come to thair chamber Mr Snape, Mr Balmefurd, parochineres, with Mr Corsbey, a guid brother, apothecarie of calling, quho brought with him in his oxter[52] a great bag of monie, as meikle as he could weill carie; Mr Snapp shewing us that some guid christianes, perceiving our long detentioun at Londin unprovydit for be the king, had maid a collectioun for defraying of thair chairges and carrieing thame haime, understanding that they tuo wer left to outred[53] for thame selffis and the rest of thair britherine, quho wer gain away befoir. They thankit thame and all the guid britherin, but tauld thame that they would haiff non of thair money; not that they despysit thair charitabill liberalitie, for the quhilk they praissit God, but pairtly to esschew offence and pairtlie for conscientious consideratioun. The offence wes a common bruit[54] and opinioun amonges the peiple of England that all Scottish men come hither to begg and purse upe thair money and carie it away with thame; quhilk wes none of our eirrand, quhilk had sufficient to live on according to our callingis at haime and wantit not credit to outred our selff out of all expensses thair. To the conscience, that considering the great number of godly britherin, lairnit and honnest men of thair awin ministerie, quhilk [had] thair families bereft of thair livingis and mantinence, and charitie in this last aige of the world growing cold, we caryit a dispositioun of hart rather to procure sume helpe to thame out of our awin countrie for as poore as it wes nor to be burdeinabill and to intercept that quhairoff the bestowing wes neidfull to thair awin. The quhilk thair constant refusall with such reassoun they heightly commendit and gloriefieit God thairffoir. And so convoyit with a guid number of godly britherin at the Tourstaires, we tuik boitting the 2 of Julie and devallit[55] towardis our schippe with verie sorrowfull heartis becaus of him we left behind us in this danger and of the dissipatioun[56] of the money guid britherin so firmely joynit togidder in Chryst.

James was successful in settling a moderate episcopacy on the Scottish Church. But after some years in England, impressed by the way they ordered matters there, he began to press for further reforms. He wanted to draw the Scottish Church closer to the English model in liturgy. Here his moves aroused an opposition he found it wise to yield to in the end.

He began in 1614 by ordering the celebration of communion at

Easter. Other orders involving the feasts of the church followed, and the drafting of a new service book. Moderate liturgical reform might have gone down, but James's plans went too far for his bishops, let alone the rank and file. He wished to impose Five Articles touching kneeling at communion, private communion, private baptism, confirmation and the church Calendar. These were first put to the Assembly at St. Andrews of 1617, which stalled, then to the packed Assembly of 1618 at Perth, which passed them. Yet though James insisted an issue should be made of obedience to the Five Articles, in practice they were scarcely enforced. The attempt to put them into effect stirred up scenes like those Calderwood records in the passages below and it went against the temper of the Scottish bishops under Archbishop Spottiswoode to risk the peace of the church for the sake of a symbolic conformity. James himself, though continuing to demand enforcement of the Articles, realized the trouble a revised Scottish service book would make and let that project drop.

DAVID CALDERWOOD (1575–1650) was a voluminous controversial writer on the Presbyterian side. In 1608 he was involved in a protest against the bishops' interference with elections to the General Assembly and was confined to his parish of Crailing and excluded from membership of the church courts. In 1617 his protests against the king's management of the church ended in one of those remarkable Presbyterian interviews with the king. He was expelled from his charge, imprisoned and banished to Holland. He returned to Scotland in 1625. His defective temper kept him from playing a leading part in covenanting politics, but his partisan energies, which had already found outlet in pamphleteering against ceremonies, were now taken up with compiling a *Historie of the Kirk of Scotland* tracing a renewal of the church at the Reformation and various corruptions and renewals of its constitution since. There are three versions: the original compilation, of which half is missing, lies in manuscript in the British Library; a digest of that in further manuscript volumes in the British Library was edited by Thomas Thomson for the Wodrow Society in 8 vols., 1842–49; a further digest was published in 1678. The first digest from which the passages below are taken (Add. MS. 4739 ff. 350–51) is still very much a compilation. Into it have gone earlier accounts such as Melville's, transcribed rather than summarized. And however useful to the professional historian, the documents that interrupt the narrative make the *Historie* daunting for the general reader. The scenes of confrontation with the authorities come over best. There Calderwood's acerbic temper expands and becomes lively as he renders angry exchanges and comic disorder.

The Historie of the Kirk of Scotland

The Communion celebrate in Edinburgh eftir the Popishe Forme

The Communion was to be celebrate upon Easter day, the 28 of March [1619]. To allure manie to come to the kirk, the ministers of Edinburgh offered them libertie to sitt, stand, or kneele, as they pleased and dealt with some in particulare, bot few wes moved with the offer. The inhabitants of [the] toun went out at the ports in hundreths and thousands to the nixt adjacent kirks. These who did communicate either kneeled not, or if they kneeled, were of the poorer sort, who lived upon the contribution and kneeled more for aw nor for devotion, or were members of the Secrete Counsel, or of the Colledge of Justice. Some were deceived with the offer of the ministers, for when they come, the ministers used all the meanes they could to caus them kneele. Some were dashed and kneeled, bot with shedding of teares for greefe. Cold and graceles were the communions, and few were communicants. The chancelour, the president and other lords of Secrete Counsell and Session, except Sir George Areskine, Lord Innerteill, and Sir James Skeene of Currihill and sundrie advocats communicate in the Great Kirk. Sir William Nisbitt, Provest of Edinburgh, absented himself, resolved not to communicate kneeling. Mr Patrick[57] efter sermone inveighed against these that scarred[58] at the communion for kneeling in the act of receiving the sacramentall elements. Mr Patrik, after he had given thanks and blessed the breade and his college, Mr Andro Ramsay,[59] satt doun in their knees. First he received himself and then he delivered to Mr Andro. Therefter Mr Patrik delivered the breade to the communicants, and Mr Andro followed with the wine. Mr Patrik challenged some persons for not meaning to kneele, bot a sillie handmaid stopped his mouth. There were fewer comunicants in the Colledge Kirk, yit the most part kneeled not. The Communion wes celebrate this same day in the Abbay Kirk, the West Kirk and in the kirk on the north side of the bridge of Leith, efter the old forme, whereunto the inhabitants of Edinburgh resorted in great numbers. Yit wes there great confusion and disorder in manie kirks be reason of the late innovation. In some kirks, the people went out and left the minister alone; in some, when the minister wold have them to kneele, the ignorant and simpler sort cryed out, "The danger, if anie

33

be, light upon your owne soule, and not upon ours." Some, when they could not gett the sacrament sitting, departed and besought God to be judge betweene them and the minister. It is not to be past over in silence how that when Johne Lauder, minister at Cockburnspeth, wes reaching the breade till one kneeling, a black dogge start up to snatche it out of his hand. . . .

Contention in the Session of Edinburgh

The session of the kirk of Edinburgh being conveened upon the first of Aprile, the baillie, Alexander Clerk, complained that he wes forced through the absence of the deacons to caus other honest men serve at the tables. Mr Patrik Galloway said it wes not sufferable that they sould sitt in that place and be disobedient to the session, "They will have teachers, everie man according to his owne humour." One answered, "Nay, Sir, there is none heir that will be disobedient." "Yes," said Mr Galloway, "Johne Meine heir." Jhone Meine answeired, "Sir, I shew my reasons the last day." "Man, ye will be an Anabaptist,"[60] said Mr Galloway in a threatning and disdainfull maner. "I hope in God to keepe myself als long from being an Anabaptist as your self," said Jhone Meine. "What! are ye comparing your self to an old father of the kirk?" said Mr Sydserfe.[61] "He sould not rule as a lord over his brethren," said Johne Meine. "What say ye, will ye say that we are lords over you?" said Mr Sydserf. "Yes, Sir," said Johne Meine, "what will ye call it, if this be not a lordlie governement to command us in this maner?" "Sir, ye must goe to Flanders," said Mr Galloway. "Is not that tirannie?" said Jhone Meine. "What say ye, is there tirannie heir?" said Mr Sydserfe. "Yes, Sir," said Jhone Meine, "I pray you give it another name if it be not tirannie to a kirkman to take upon him to banishe men and send them to Flanders." Jhone Byris, bailyie, father-in-law to Mr Sydserfe, start upon his feete and said to Jhone Meine, "Ye are farre in the wrong. Ye may hold your toung verie weill." Mr Patrik Galloway sayeth to Johne Meine, "Ye must not sitt heir in this place if ye will not obey us. Ye must be putt out." "I will not be displaced," said he, "be noe particular man. Let them putt me out that putt me in heir, and I sall not cummer[62] you. As for anie particulare man, I will not acknowledge their discharge."

The nixt session day, which wes the 3 of Aprile, Alexander Clerk renewed the former complaint that there wes none to serve at the tables in the Old Kirk till they sent doun to the Colledge Kirk for some of their number to helpe. Jhone Inglis, merchant and skinner, answeired, "Ye know they were ay readie before, bot this novation is the occasion of men's unwillingnes now. Men cannot serve contrarie to their mynd." Mr Struthers[63] said, "Johne, we thought somthing of you before, and now we know what is in you." Then Bartle Fleaming said, "Think ye men will serve contrare to their conscience?" Mr Struthers said, "Barthole, we thought somthing of you before. Now we count nothing of you. Barthole, hold your peace. When ye are stillest ye are wysest." Then said Jhone Meine, "This is a strange thing. Ye will have us to serve whither it be reasone or not." "Sir, lett us alone," said Mr Galloway. "I suffered eneugh of you last day. I say to the, man, thou art a verie Anababtist." Mr Struthers said "What, Sir! know ye the office of a deacone? I will examine yow presentlie," and with that he turneth him to him. "Yes, Sir, I trow I know somthing," answeired Johne Meine. "What is it?" said Mr Struthers. "To serve the tables," answeired Johne Meine. "What is the caus ye doe it not then?" said Mr Struthers. "Becaus," said the other, "ye have left Christ's institution, for ye will be wiser then Christ in setting doun a better forme of your owne." Mr Struthers cryed out, "O horrible blasphemie! O horrible blasphemie!" Mr Thomas Sydserfe sayes, "If ye sould serve, wherefor have ye left us?" Jhone Meine answeired, "We left yow not till ye left the trueth." "What!" sayes Mr Thomas, "call ye us apostates? I think ye sould be compelled to make it goode. Ye may als weill take us to the Mercate Crosse and choppe our fleshe and bones together like meate for the pott as to persecute us this way with your tounges, calling us apostats and saying we have left the trueth." "Aggredge[64] it as ye please," answeired Johne Meine. "Know ye," said Mr Struthers, speaking in a proude and loftie countenance, "the Sixt of the Acts, what the word "deacon" means? Know yow the Greek word?" and againe, "Know yow the Greeke word? I say, man, ye are our servants." And then scorning, he said, "We know nothing. We must goe doun to Johne Mein his booth and buy books and get a lesson from him and Jhone Logan. They will learne us what we sall doe." Barthole Fleaming rose up to speike. Mr Struthers said to him, "Have ye redd the Sixt of the Acts? Ye sould serve at the tables. Ye think your selfs verie wise. Wold to God we had als meikle wisdome amongst us all foure as everie one of yow thinks ye have." Barthole taketh out a New Testament out of his pocket and sought the words. Then he said, "We served ay before till ye come in and tooke our place over our heads and wold serve your selfs." In the meane time, the ministers were ever commanding silence. Mr Patrik Galloway taketh up the roll of the names of the elders and deacons, which wes lying upon the boord, saying, "I sall keepe this. The king's Majestie sall be informed. There cannot be a king in the countrie if this be suffered." Then Mr Patrik Henrisone, clerk, craved the roll to call

35

the names that they might know who wold serve and who wold refuse. Mr Galloway answeired, "Ye sall not gett this. I sall keep it. The king sall be informed." Yit he delivered the roll and badd the clerk call the names "that we may see who will refuse" and caused marke the names of the refusers.

When Johne Meine wes called, in a great rage he cryed thrise, "Put him up there! put him up there! put him up there!" Jhone Meine answeired, "We know now who are our persecutors." Yit they were so moved that none heard him, except these who were not speaking themselfs. Then Alexander Clerk, baillie, said, "Hold your tounge. There is too much spoken. I comand yow silence, Sir." Johne Meine answeired, "Ye may not command me silence in this place." "What say ye, Sir?" said the baillie, and with that start up on his feete and said, "I command yow silence." "Ye may not command me silence in this place," answeired Johne Meine. "What say ye, Sir?" said Alexander Clerk, "may not I command yow silence? I command yow silence." Jhone Meine answeired, "Sir, ye may not lawfullie command me silence in this place. Ye are but a sessioner heir, Sir. Ye may not raigne over us." "What say ye, Sir?" said Alexander Clerk. "I sall let yow witt, Sir, I am more then a sessioner. Ye are bot a verie false knave." Efter a litle advisment, he said, "Ye are but a gouke, Sir. I sall fasten your feete, Sir." Johne Meine answeired, "I can beare all that, Sir, and all that ye can doe to me, and more to, Sir. Bot I will not hold my toung so long as they (meaning the ministers) speake to me." "My joy, Johne, hold your toung," said Alexander Clerk. So endit that session.

CHAPTER TWO

THE CIVIL WAR

Since the career of ARCHIBALD JOHNSTON OF WARISTON (1611–63) is so involved in the history of the Civil War, it will be best to sketch the two together.

James had enough sense of the country not to provoke a revolution with his designs for the church. But Charles's government was out of touch with Scotland and managed even well-conceived projects in so high-handed and maladroit a way that they aroused widespread resentment and fears for the constitution. He upset the nobility, into whose hands much of the old church possessions had passed, with his equitable measures to settle the endowment of the church by means of a commutation of tithes, and he upset them further by making Archbishop Spottiswoode chancellor in 1635 and by his use of bishops as government officials. These and other sectional discontents entered into the general exasperation with the government that Charles's liturgical policy provoked. On his visit to Scotland in 1633 he ordered the wearing of surplices on the strength of his prerogative. Further reforms of a high-church Laudian sort followed, and in 1637 the new Scottish prayerbook, largely modelled on the English one, came out, its use also ordered on the authority of the king's prerogative. Presbyterianism suddenly revived with opposition to the royal control of the church.

The great fear was that Charles in his arbitrary way would undo the Reformation. Rioting broke out in Edinburgh, petitions came in for the withdrawal of the liturgy and with them crowds of petitioners, and the agitation grew as Charles met the crisis with peremptory and unyielding proclamations. In early 1638 opposition was sufficiently organized to frame a manifesto, the National Covenant, and put it to the country. In some parts, it was received with the popular enthusiasm Wariston records in his diary, and it was sufficiently general or ambiguous to bring many sorts of opposition together. For although it was drafted by Alexander Henderson and Wariston, who were to become leaders of the Covenanting party and for whom the idea of a Covenant was of a nation bound under God to uphold a Presbyterian church polity, still the Covenant itself did not actually repudiate Episcopal government, and while it bound those who signed it to defend the religion of the country as it had been before the recent innovations, it bound them at the same time to defend the authority of the king – contradictions or ambiguities that gave opponents of the Covenant a chance to score, as the Aberdeen Doctors did in debate with the covenanting commissioners, but also at least for a time allowed the Covenant to draw together men of very different principles, constitutional conservatives like Montrose as well as radical Presbyterians like Wariston and Rutherford. So the Covenant had a sufficiently broad appeal to serve as a national bond of resistance. In the Bishops' Wars of 1639 and 1640 when Charles advanced to invade and force Scotland to submit to his policies, the Scots were able to meet him with a Covenanting army far more effective than his unenthusiastic levy and impose their terms on him.

The aristocracy took charge of this first stage of the Scottish revolution and clerical radicalism was suppressed. The bishops were expelled and the high Presbyterians held in check. Nevertheless, the Presbyterian church party supplied much of the drive and the organisation behind the revolution, even at this stage. Here Wariston was a shaping spirit. He was a lawyer, whose ability, energy and religious intensity made him one of the leaders of the theocratic high Presbyterian wing of the Covenanters. For him, the day on which the lairds and the nobility subscribed in Greyfriars Churchyard to the National Covenant, which he had helped to design, was "that glorious mariage day of the Kingdome with God" (*Diary*, I, 322). As clerk to the Glasgow Assembly of 1638, he produced the lost minutes of the General Assemblies since the Reformation, which seemed to authorize the proceedings. At the making of the treaties concluding the Bishops' Wars, he was one of the negotiators on the Scottish side. And he went as one of the Scottish commissioners to the Westminster Assembly, whose deliberations were supposed to come up with a Presbyterian constitution and forms of worship and doctrine to be adopted by the English and Irish, as well as Scottish, churches and so fulfill the undertakings of the Solemn League and Covenant of 1643, to which the English Parliamentarians had bound themselves as the price of bringing the Scottish army into the war against the king.

The Covenanters, however, had already begun to divide

among themselves. For though Wariston's grand designs for a covenanted Britain were shared by other radicals like Rutherford, they were at odds, not only with the feudal views expressed by Napier and Drummond, but also when it came to the crunch with the moderate Presbyterianism of men like Baillie who had no quarrel with a church controlled by the upper classes. These divisions came out once the Covenanters joined with the English Parliamentarians against the King. First Montrose, holding that the moderate constitutional aims he had bound himself to fight for had been achieved, raised an army for the king against those he now considered subverters of the kingdom. But though he won all his battles on this campaign except the last one, he did not draw a large part of the country with him. Then in 1647 a great split occurred among the Covenanters, which was to persist with extraordinary rancour. The quarrel was over supporting the king. But neither side was republican, and the real issue was whether to press the Covenants as the absolute frame of government or to make some compromise with what remained of the old royal and feudal constitution. The king had fallen into the hands of the English Army, whose Independency in religion and republican politics went against the Scottish plans for England. The moderates among the Scots entered into an Engagement to restore the king in return for a trial establishment of Presbyterianism in England for three years. This scant allowance for English wishes in the matter of religion was still too much for the high Presbyterians, and in the disarray following the defeat of the Engager army at Preston, they seized power, passed the Act of Classes of 1649 excluding those who had taken part in the expedition into England from office and purged the clergy of those who had not preached against the Engagement. In the radical party opposed to the Engagement, Wariston was a leading figure.

The radicals in their detestation of the Engagement with the king had sided with the English Army, but on the news of his execution enough of them were prepared to take up the cause of Charles II, provided he took the Covenants and repudiated his parents' offences against the true religion. That brought Cromwell up into Scotland. The Scots got together an army purged of officers who had gained experience under the Engagement and were routed at Dunbar (1650). And now it was the moderates' turn. In the face of Cromwell's army and the remonstrances of the high Presbyterian party, they crowned Charles at Scone, rescinded the Act of Classes and dispatched another army into England, unpurged this time and including even cavalier "malignants" like Sir Thomas Urquhart, yet equally unsuccessful. The defeat at Worcester (1651) was crushing.

The English Army, which occupied the country, put an end to Covenanting schemes for Scotland as well as England, moderate and theocratic alike. The two clerical factions, Resolutioners and Remonstrants (or Protesters as they came to be known after 1651) hated each other more than the Army, but under military rule they could not force their views on each other. Cromwell played on their divisions, winning the cooperation first of some of the Protesters, later of the Resolutioners. Meanwhile the Scottish Parliament was joined with the English into a Parliament of Great Britain.

Wariston, who had been accused of betraying the country after the battle of Dunbar and had long held aloof with the more uncompromising Protesters from cooperating with Cromwell's government, was at length induced to accept the office of lord clerk register in 1657. From 1658 he sat in the House of Peers in London, often acting as president of the Council of State. At the Restoration he fled the country but was brought back and tried and condemned to hang in Edinburgh. He broke down at his trial and made a very miserable spectacle. By the time of his execution, however, he had pulled himself together sufficiently to reaffirm his Protester principles on the scaffold and die with composure.

Wariston has two distinct literary characters, legalistic and enthusiastic. The outpourings of the diary come strangely from the able legal mind that helped to draw up the National Covenant and write *The Causes of the Lord's Wrath* (1653). This double character was, however, frequent with the writers of his party. The first passage from the *Diary* deals with a private rapture, the second with the public rapture accompanying the taking of the National Covenant. They bring out the enthusiastic temper behind Covenanting politics. Later writers of an anti-enthusiastic type such as Charteris have some hard hitting things to say about the religion of Wariston and those like him, its sensationalism, unsteadiness, self-seeking, self-deception. But it is possible to prefer Wariston's grossness with its extravagant energies to Charteris's meagreness. And there is something uncommonly painful in Wariston's realization in later years that his unusual appetite for God could not resist Cromwell's appeals to his ambition. For all its stretches of canting, self-centred devotion, the *Diary* can sometimes make us wish to think that even within the narrow scope of Covenant politics,

> Desire of Power, on Earth a Vitious Weed,
> Yet, sprung from High, is of Caelestial Seed:
> In God 'tis Glory: And when men Aspire,
> 'Tis but a Spark too much of Heavenly Fire.

Text: folio volume of Wariston's Diary, 1637–39, ff. 5v–6; 30, Mellerstain archives. Apart from one minor correction and details of punctuation, my text does not differ from what is given in *The Diary of Sir Archibald Johnston of Wariston*, Vol. 1, ed. George Morison Paul (Edinburgh: Scottish History Society, 1911), pp. 251–53; 327–28.

Wariston's Diary

Ane exstasie

On Sunday, 23 Apryle [1637], in my auin chalmer it pleased the Lord to comunicat himself fully to my saule as I was mooved to wryt it at lenth to Mr. David Dick,[1] for to stand as ane testimonie against myselth in neu afflictions or tentations. Betuixt 3 hours and six at night in my auin chalmer, quhyle I was walking al alone and meditating on the nature, essence, naimes, attributs, words, works of a Deitie, my quhol body took a schuddring, and extream coldness seased on al my joints especyaly on the roots of my haire, quhilk stood al steave,[2] bent up fra the croun of my head; my eies stood brent open,[3] never closing, albeit rivers of tears ran doun my scheaks; my tounge strokin dumb; my hands at will now reatched out as it wer to receive a Deitie, nou glasped in as it were to inclose and imbraice a Deitie receaved. This was the temper of my body, quhyl in al this tyme my saul was transported out of myselth and fixed upon the immediat vision and fruition of ane incomprehensible Deitie, lyk lightnings glauncing in at a windou; first his nature in general, then the Unitie in Trinitie, Trinitie in Unitie, then his attributs of justice, mercie, pouer, presence, wysdom, treuth, then his works al in order, first of creation, then of election, of redemption, of justification, of sanctification, of aeternal glorification and condemnation, every an after uther, then the application of al to my auin saul, wer obversant[4] and presented to my mynd. At the glaunce of every on after another the schuddring wakned, my haire bended and a neu rusch of tears gusched out. Thir glaunces wer presented and went by lyk spectacles on a theatre quhyl my saul was crying without utterance, "Deitie, Deitie, I adore, I adore, I adore." Quhyl my saul ran somtymes upon the contemplation of a Deitie, my thoughts wer in a confusion and som sort of fear. Bot quhen it ran upon the conception of the Trinitie and especyaly of the second person as clothed with our humain nature, my sight was mor clear and sense mor sueat. Then my saul was as it wer separated from my body and so united as to be maid on with him. In the tuinkling of ane eie, befor I wist, behold the catologue of al my sins doone eyther befor or since my calling presented to my memoire and mynd distinctly, clearly, particularly, quhairat I begoud to trimble, my saul ever crying without utterance, "God's mercie, God's mercie, God's mercie." On a sudainte, quhyl I am thus praying, behold a neu rool[5] of al God's favors and blissings, outward, inward, of his providence or indulgence on saul, body, or affairs old or recent, quhairat my saul revived crying, "Haleluya, Haleluya." Or ever I wist againe, behold a thrid of al my present wants, desyres, necessities, wisses, hoopes, prayers, quhilk I was commanded from within to summe up in a compend, quhilk my saul did, calling, "Fayther, glorifie thyselth in my lyfe and death and thy servant after both. Fayther, graunt thou mercy to my miserie and graice to my graicelesnes. Fayther, give thyselth to me and taik myselth to the that thou may be myne and I may be thyne, as thy spouse sayeth in hir song." I thought at this tyme that my Jesus took my heart in his hand and knet[6] it and wrapped it within the heart of God, so that I found God as it wer within my heart posessing and filling al the hirnes[7] and holes thairof, and I fand my heart and saul within the heart of God contemplating, adoring, imbraicing his inmost bouels, and turning, yea quheeling, itselth aboot as it wer within his armes to see perfytly his inward pairts. I could not then conceave, far les nou expres hou persuading and persuaded I was by present reflecting thoughts on my present contemplation that God was myne, yea fully myne, and I was his, yea totally his, that he was myne with al his blissings and follouers, and I was his with al my infirmities and burdens. Al the night thairafter, yea evin this morning quhyl I am wryting this doun, the stampe of yesternight's impression cleaveth fast to my saul, and my thoughts, desyres, desyres hytherto both sleaping and walkning, ar as unsatiable, as unexpressable. The Lord God opin my eies by a second sight to seie[8] his favor, aime and end, with my use of this od seie[9] of transporting motions, quherby in so inexpressable a bountiful maner and measure, he comunicateth himselth to dust, yea to sinful dust and asches, and maiketh me forced to acknouledge his Son's prayer to haive bein heard and his auin promise evin heir to be verefied in my person, in that I haive bein maid on with him and he on with me. The Lord maiks me to apprehend that this clear day wil haive a dark night, and this faire calme wil haive ane foul storme. The Lord give me the right use of this and praepaire me for that, and let this stand for a testimonie against myselth of consolation in neu walknings of mynd and of conviction on my yeeldings to subsequent tentations.

Communion and the Covenant

On Sunday, the 18 day of Merch, 1638, after motion in your[10] familie prayer ye went to Rothau,[11] heard Mr. J. Hamilton follou out his text verry sensibly. Ye went with sense to the second taible[12] of the morning service; got motion and tears at the taible; ryde presently away with your familie and Riccarton,[13] conferring on the sermons til we came to Currie, quhair Mr. Jhon Chairtres, minister, was reading the 28 and 29 Deuteronomy, quhilk he pressed in his exhortation. He preatched on 17 Genesis, 1 *v.*, "I am thy alsufficient God; walk thou befor me, and be perfyte." After sermon, being a solemne fast day apoynted for subscription of the Covenant, he read it al over again as he had doone the Sunday of befoir. He syne explained to the people al the pairts of it. Thairafter, to schau his warrand for seiking, and thairs for giving, ane oath at the renovation of the Covenant, he pressed the 10 ch. Nehemiah *v.* 28 and 29, "Al the rest of the people, thair wyves, sons, and daughters, every on haiving knouledge and understanding; they claive to thair brethren, the nobles, and entred into a curse, and unto ane oath to walk in God's lau"; and the 2 Chronicles ch. 15 *v.* 12, "And they entred into a covenant to seek the Lord God of thair faythers with al thair heart and al thair saule; that quhosoever would not seek the Lord God of Izrael sould be put to death, whither great or small, man or woman. And they suare unto the Lord with a loud voyce, with schouting, trumpets, and cornets. And al Judah rejoyced at the oath: for they had suorne with al thair heart, and sought him with thair whol desyre; and he was found of them: and the Lord gaive them rest round about"; quhairof applyed verry weal every word. Yet in al this tyme thair was no motion nor tears in any of the congregation. Bot immediatly thairafter at his lifting up of his hand and his desyring the congregation to stand up and lift up thair hands and sueare unto the aeternal God and at thair standing up and lifting up thair hands, in the tuinkling of ane eye thair fell sutch ane extraordinarie influence of God's Sprit upon the whol congregation, melting thair frozen hearts, waltering thair dry cheeks, chainging thair verry countenances, as it was a wonder to seie so visible, sensible, momentaneal[14] a chainge upon al, man and woman, lasse

43

and ladde, pastor and people, that Mr. Jhon, being suffocat almost with his auin tears and astonisched at the motion of the whol people, sat doune in the pulpit in ane amazement, bot presently rose againe quhen he sau al the people falling doune on thair knees to mourne and pray, and he and thay for ane quarter of ane houre prayed verry sensibly with many sobs, tears, promises and voues to be thankful and fruitful in tym coming. Honor and prayse be to the naime of the aeternal God, quho only can work wonders and maiks us daylie seie wonders, as this a pryme remarquable on, quherby he testifyed from the heavens this work to be his auin work, his real reentrie in the Covenant with his people, his acceptance of thair offer, his reservation of ane work of mercie for the congregations of this land, albeit personal plauges schal light upon particular persons.

SAMUEL RUTHERFORD (1600–61) was a minister and a prolific controversialist on the high Presbyterian, or Protester, side of the Covenant. The headnote to Wariston's *Diary* will supply the general background. Under the bishops, he refused to conform and in consequence was removed from his parish of Anwoth and confined to the strongly Episcopalian Aberdeen in 1636. Deprived of his pulpit, he carried on his spiritual exhortations by letter. With the Covenanters' takeover, he was appointed professor of divinity of St. Mary's College, St. Andrews, and entered into the controversies of the time, defending the Presbyterian system against Independency in tracts such as *A Reasonable and Temperate Plea for Paul's Presbytery* (1642) and the right of the people to elect and depose their kings in *Lex Rex* (1644). He went as one of the Scottish commissioners to the Westminster Assembly. Milton mentions him in a sonnet as one of those who taught the Presbyterian party in the Long Parliament "To force our consciences that Christ set free/And ride us with a Classic Hierarchy", with, that is, a Presbyterian hierarchy as rigid as an Episcopal one. In 1651 Rutherford was made Rector of St. Andrews but as a Protester found himself isolated from his colleagues. Unlike Wariston, he did not go over to Cromwell. At the Restoration, *Lex Rex* was publicly burnt, and Rutherford would have been tried for treason if illness and death had not prevented his appearing before Parliament.

Like Wariston, he has a double character as a writer. I have spoken in the Introduction (p. 13) of his character as a controversialist, of his dialectical agility, his impenetrableness. It is only fair to add that the introductions to some of his tracts are written with vigour and eloquence. His character as preacher and letter writer is an enthusiast's. According to "a friend", "In the pulpit he had a strange utterance, a kind of skreigh, that I have never heard the like. Many a time I thought he would have flown out of the pulpit when he came to speak of Jesus Christ" (A. A. Bonar, ed. *Letters of Samuel Rutherford* [Edinburgh: Oliphant, 1891], p. 5). The style of his letters is more bizarre than the style of his sermons, so densely figurative that it is hard to know what he means. It may be that his obscurity was an apt medium for spiritual intimations his readers would catch at. And still Rutherford's enthusiastic style has flashes of real imaginative power. It is idiosyncratic and rough, but its exuberance has affinities with the baroque manner of the poets of the Thirty Years' War, or indeed of the Catholic and Anglo-Catholic poets, Crashaw and Beaumont, or Benlowes for that matter.

The letters below show the sort of spiritual pressure the covenanting clergy might exert. The first, written during the events leading up to the National Covenant, to John Campbell, Lord Loudoun, one of the aristocratic opponents of Charles's policy, is an unusually violent piece of tumultuary prose for a Scottish writer at this time. The second was written to John Fenwicke, an English puritan, who suffered under the bishops and who had many contacts with the Covenanters and was with them at Duns Law. It speaks of Rutherford's extraordinary hopes of the Covenant and shows how the plight of the individual soul might be read into the times. For in comforting this English sympathizer, Rutherford talks about the events in Scotland in a way that suggests deliverance from his troubles, spiritual and political, is at hand. The letters, like Wariston's *Diary*, bring out the spirit at work behind the controversies and legalistic forms of high Presbyterian politics.

Their style conveys Rutherford's radical temper: the commotion of the short syntactical units and riddling figures goes with spiritual and political upheaval. The moderate Presbyterian, Baillie, by contrast, expresses his sense of being involved in a divinely inspired movement in a much more conventional style of religious exalation: the periodic sentences of the first part of his letter to Spang (pp. 54–55) would be thuriferous if they were more polished.

Rutherford's letters were first published in 1664 in the collection, *Joshua Redivivus* (pp. 410–12, 504–9), which enjoyed a remarkable esteem. Concerning its rating as a devotional classic by Rutherford's party, the Quaker, George Keith, has some sensible observations in *The Way Cast Up* (1677), pp. 4–15.

To my Lord Lowdoun

Right honourable and my very worthy Lord.

Grace, mercy and peace be to you. Hearing of your Lordship's zeal and courage for Christ our Lord in owning his honourable cause, I am bold, and I plead pardon for it, to speak in paper by a line or two to your Lordship, since I have not access any other way, beseeching your Lordship by the mercies of God and by the everlasting peace of your soul and by the tears and prayers of our mother church to goe on as ye have worthily begun in purging of the Lord's house in this land and plucking down the sticks of Antichrist's filthy nest, this wretched Prelacy and that black Kingdom, whose wicked aims have ever been, and still are, to make this fat world the onely compass they would have Christ and religion to sail by and to mount up the man of sin, their godfather the Pope of Rome, upon the highest stair of Christ's throne and to make a velvet church, in regard of parliament-grandour and wordly pomp,[15] whereof alwayes their stinking breath smelleth, and to put Christ and truth in sack-cloth and prison to eat the bread of adversitie and drink the water of affliction. Half an eye of any not misted with the darkness of Antichristian smoke may see it thus in this land. And now our Lord hath begun to awaken the nobles and others to plead for born-down Christ and his weeping gospel. My dear and noble Lord, the eye of Christ is upon you; the eyes of many noble, many holy, many learned and worthy ones in our neighbour churches about are upon you. This poor church, your mother and Christ's spouse, is holding up her hands and heart to God for you and doeth beseech you with tears to plead for her husband, his kingly scepter, and for the liberties that her Lord and King hath given to her, as to a free kingdom that oweth spiritual tribute to none on earth as being the free-born princess and daughter to the king of kings. This is a cause that before God, his angels, the world, before sun and moon, needeth not to blush. O what glory and true honour is it to lend Christ your hand and service and to be amongst the repairers of the breaches of Sion's walls and to help to build the old waste places and stretch forth the curtains and strengthen the stakes of Christ's tent in this land! O blessed are they who, when Christ is driven away, will bring him back again and lend him lodging! And blessed are ye of the Lord. Your name and honour shall never rot or wither in heaven, at least if ye deliver the Lord's sheep that have been scattered in the dark and cloudy day out of the hands of strange lords and hirelings, who with rigour and cruelty have caused them to eat the pastures troden upon with their foul feet and to drink muddy water, and how have spun out such a world of yards of indifferencies in God's worship[16] to

46

make and weave a web for the Antichrist that shall not keep any from the cold, as they minde nothing else but that by the bringing in of the Pope's foul tail first upon us (their wretched and beggerly ceremonies) they may thrust in after them the Antichrist's legs and thighs and his belly, head and shoulders, and then cry down Christ and the gospel and up the merchandise and wares of the great whore. Fear not, my worthy Lord, to give your self and all ye have out for Christ and his gospel. No man dare say who ever did thus hazard for Christ that Christ payed him not his hundred fold in this life duely and in the life to come, life ever lasting. This is his own truth ye now plead for, for God and man cannot but commend you to beg justice from a just prince for oppressed Christ and to plead that Christ, who is the king's Lord, may be heard in a free court to speak for himself,[17] when the standing and established laws of our nation can strongly plead for Christ's crown in the pulpits and his chair as law-giver in the free government of his own house. But Christ shall never be content and pleased with this land, neither shall his hot fiery indignation be turned away, so long as the Prelate, the man that lay in Antichrist's foul womb and the Antichrist's lord bailiffe, shall sit lord carver in the Lord Jesus his courts. The Prelate is both the egge and the nest to cleck[18] and bring forth Popery. Plead therefore in Christ's behalf for the plucking down of the nest and crushing of the egge, and let Christ's kingly office suffer no more unworthy indignities. Be valiant for your royal King Jesus, contend for him; your adversaries shall be moth-eaten worms and shall die as men. Christ and his honour now lieth upon your shoulders; let him not fall to the ground. Cast your eye upon him who is quickly coming to decide all the controversies in Zion, and remember the sand in your night-glass will run out. Time with wings will flye away, Eternity is hard upon you, and what will Christ's love smiles and the light of his lovely and soul-delighting countenance be to you in that day when God shall take up in his right hand this little lodge of heaven, like as a shepherd lifteth up his little tent, and fold together the two leaves of his tent and put the earth and all the plenishing of it into a fire and turn this clay-idol, the god of Adam's sons, into smoke and white ashes! O what hire and how many worlds would many then give to have a favourable decreet of the Judge! Or what moneyes would they not give to buy a mountain to be a grave above both soul and body to hide them from the awsom looks of an angry Lord and Judge! I hope your Lordship thinketh upon this and that ye minde loyalty to Christ and to the king both. Now the very God of peace, the only wise God, establish and strengthen you upon the rock laid in Zion.

Aberd. Jan 4.   Your Lordship's at all obedience in
1638.   Christ, S. R.

To his very dear friend John Fennick.

Much honoured and dear friend,

Grace, mercy and peace be to you. The necessary impediments of my calling have hitherto kept me from making a return to your letter, the heads whereof I shall now briefly answer. As I.[19] I approve your going to the fountain when your own cisterne is dry. A difference there must be betwixt Christ's well and your borrowed water, and why but ye have need of emptiness and drying up as well as ye have need of the well? Want and a hole there must be in our vessel to leave room to Christ's art; his well hath its own need of thirsty drinkers to commend infinite love, which from eternity did brew such a cellar of living waters for us.

Ye commend his free love, and it's well done. Oh if I could help you, and if I could be master-conveener to gather an earth-full and an heaven-full of tongues dipped and steeped in my Lord's well of love or his wine of love, even tongues drunken with his love, to raise a song of praises to him betwixt the east and west end and furthest points of the broad heavens! If I were in your case (as alas! my dry and dead heart is not now in that garden) I would borrow leave to come and stand upon the banks and coasts of that sea of love and be a feasted soul to see love's fair tide, free love's high and lofty waves, each of them higher then ten earths, flowing in upon pieces of lost clay. O welcome, welcome, great sea! O if I had as much love for wideness and breadth as twenty outmost shells and spheres of the heaven of heavens, that I might receive in a little flood of his free love! Come, come, dear friend, and be pained that the King's wine cellar of free love and his banquetting house (O so wide, so stately! O so God-like, so glory-like!) should be so abundant, so overflowing, and your shallow vessel so little to take in some part of that love. But since it cannot come in you for want of room, enter your self in this sea of love, and breath under these waters and die of love and live as one dead and drowned of this love.

But why doe ye complain of waters going over your soul and that the smoke of the terrors of a wrathfull Lord doeth almost suffocate you and bring you to death's brink? I know the fault is in your eyes, not in him: it's not the rock that fleeth and moveth, but the green sailer. If your sense and apprehension be made judge of his love, there is a graven image made presently, even a changed God and a foe-God, who was once "when ye washed your steps with butter, and the rock poured you out rivers of oyl" (Job. 29.6), a friend-God. Either now or never let God work. Ye had never since ye was a man such a fair field for faith, for a painted hell and an apprehension of

48

wrath in your Father is faith's opportunity to try what strength is in it. Now give God as large a measure of charity as ye have of sorrow. Now see faith to be faith indeed if ye can make your grave betwixt Christ's feet and say, "Though he should slay me, I will trust in him. His beleeved love shall be my winding-sheet and all my grave-cloaths. I shall roll and sowe in my soul, my slain soul, in that web, his sweet and free love. And let him write upon my grave, 'Here lieth a beleeving dead man, breathing out and making an hole in death's broad side, and the breath of faith cometh forth through the hole.'" See now if ye can overcome and prevail with God and wrestle God's tempting to death and quit out of breath, as that renowned wrestler did: (Hosea, 12, 3) "And by his strength he had power with God. (*v.* 4) Yea he had power over the angel and prevailed." He is a strong man indeed who overmatcheth heaven's strength and the holy One of Israel, the strong Lord; which is done by a secret supply of divine strength within, wherewith the weakest being strengthned, overcome and conquer. It shall be [a] great victory to blow out the flame of that furnace ye are now in with the breath of faith. And when hell, men, malice, cruelty, falshood, devils, the seeming glooms of a sweet Lord, meet you in the teeth, if ye then as a captive of hope, as one fettered in hope's prison, run to your strong hold, even from God glooming to God glooming, and beleeve the salvation of the Lord in the dark, which is your onely victory, your enemies are but pieces of malitious clay; they shall die as men and be confounded.

But that your troubles are many at once, arrows come in from all airths, from countrey, friends, wife, children, foes, estate and right down from God, who is the hope and stay of your soul, I confess is more and very heavy to be born. Yet all these are not more than grace; all these bits of coals casten in your sea of mercy cannot dry it up. Your troubles are many and great, yet not an ounce weight beyond the measure of infinite wisdom; I hope, not beyond the measure of grace that he is to bestow; for our Lord never yet brake the back of his childe nor spilt his own work. Nature's plastering and counterfit work he doeth often break in sheards and putteth out a candle not lighted at the Sun of righteousness. But he must cherish his own reeds and handle them softly: never a reed getteth a thrust with the Mediator's hand to lay together the two ends of the reed. O what bonds and ligaments hath our chirugion of broken spirits to binde up all his lame and bruised ones with! Cast your disjoynted spirit in his lap, and lay your burden upon one who is so willing to take your cares and your fears off you and to exchange and niffer[20] your crosses and to give you new for old and gold for iron, even to give you garments of praise for the spirit of heaviness.

It's true in a great part what ye write of this Kirk, that the letter of religion onely is reformed and scarce that. I doe not beleeve our Lord will build his Zion in this land upon this skin of reformation. So long as our scum remaineth and our heart-idols are keeped, this work must be at a stand, and therefore our Lord must yet sift this land and search us with candles. And I know he shall give and not sell us his kingdom:[21] his grace and our remaining guiltiness must be compared, and the one must be seen in the glory of it and the other in the sinfulness of it. But I desire to beleeve and would gladly hope to see that the glancing and shining luster of glory coming from the diamonds and stones set in the crown of our Lord Jesus shall cast rayes and beams many thousand miles about. I hope Christ is upon a great marriage and that his wooing and suting of his excellent bride doeth take its beginning from us, the ends of the earth. O what joy and what glory would I judge it if my heaven should be suspended till I might have leave to run on foot to be a witness of the marriage-glory and see Christ put on the glory of his last married bride and his last marriage-love on earth, when he shall enlarge his love-bed and set it upon the top of the mountains and take in the elder sister, the Jewes, and the fulness of the Gentiles! It were heaven's honour and glory upon earth to be his lackey, to run at his horse-foot and hold up the train of his marriage-robe-royal, in the day of our high and royal Solomon's espousals. But O what glory to have a seat or bed in King Jesus his chariot, that is bottomed with gold and paved and lined over and floored within with "Love, for the daughters of Jerusalem!" (Canticles. 3.10). To lie upon such a King's love were a bed next to the flower of heaven's glory.

I am sorry to hear you speak in your letter of "a God angry at you" and of "the sense of his indignation", which onely ariseth from suffering for Jesus all that is now come upon you. Indeed apprehended wrath flameth out of such ashes as apprehended sin, but not from suffering for Christ. But suppose ye were in hell for by-gones and for old debt, I hope ye ow Christ a great summe of charity to beleeve the sweetness of his love. I know what it is to sin in that kinde; it is to sin out, if it were possible, the unchangeableness of a Godhead out of Christ and to sin away a lovely and unchangeable God. Put more honest apprehension upon Christ. Put on his own mask upon his face, and not your vail made of unbelief, which speaketh as if he borrowed love to you from you and your demerits and sinfull deservings. Oh no! Christ is man, but he is not like man; he hath man's love in heaven, but it is lustered with God's love, and it is very God's love ye have to doe with. When your wheels goe about, he standeth still. Let God be God and be ye a man and have ye the deserving of man and the sin of one who hath suffered your welbeloved to slip away, nay, hath refused him entrance when he was knocking till his head and locks were frozen. Yet what is that to him? His book keepeth your name and is not printed and reprinted and changed and corrected. And why but he should goe to his place and hide himself? Howbeit his departure be his own good work, yet the belief of it in that manner is your sin. But wait on till he return with salvation and cause you rejoyce in the latter end. It is not much to complain, but rather beleeve then complain, and sit in the dust and close your mouth till he make your sown light grow again. For your afflictions are not eternal; time will end them, and so shall ye at length see the Lord's salvation. His love sleepeth not, but is still in working for you. His salvation will not tarry nor linger, and suffering for him is the noblest cross that is out of heaven. Your Lord had the waile[22] and choice of ten thousand other crosses beside this to exercise you withall, but his wisdom and his love wailed and choosed out this for you, beside them all; and take it as a choice one, and make us of it, so as ye look to this world as your step-mother in your borrowed prison. For it is a love-look to heaven and the other side of the water that God seeketh. And this is the fruit, the flower and bloom growing out of your cross, that ye be a dead man to time, to clay, to gold, to countrey, to friends, wife, children and all pieces of created nothings, for in them there is not a seat nor bottom for your soul's love. O what room is for your love, if it were as broad as the sea, up in heaven and in God? And what would not Christ give for your love? God gave so much for your soul, and blessed are ye if ye have a love for him and can call in your soul's love from all idols and can make a God of God, a God of Christ, and draw a line betwixt your heart and him. If your deliverance come not, Christ's preference and his beleeved love must stand as caution and surety for your deliverance till your Lord send it in his blessed time. For Christ hath many salvations, if we could see them, and I would think it better born comfort and joy that cometh from the faith of deliverance and the faith of his love then that which cometh from deliverance it self. It is not much matter, if ye finde ease to your afflicted soul, what be the means, either of your own wishing, or of God's choosing. The latter, I am sure is best and the comfort strongest and sweetest. Let the Lord absolutely have the ordering of your evils and troubles, and put them off you by recommending your cross and your furnace to him, who hath skill to melt his own metall and knoweth well what to doe with his furnace. Let your heart be willing that God's fire have your tin and brass and dross. To consent to want corruption is a greater mercy then many professors[23] doe well know, and to refer the manner of God's physick to his own wisdom, whither it be by drawing blood, or giving sugared drinks that cure sick folks without pain, it is a great point of faith, and to beleeve Christ's cross to be a friend, as he himself is a friend, is also a special act of faith. But when ye are over the water, this case shall be a yesterday past an hundred years ere ye were born, and the cup of glory shall wash the memory of all this away and make it as nothing. Onely now take Christ in with you under your yoke, and let patience have her perfect work, for this haste is your infirmity. The Lord is rising up to doe you good in the latter end. Put on the faith of his salvation, and see him posting and hasting towards you. Sir, my employments being so great hinder me to write at more length, excuse me; I hope to be mindfull of you. I shall be obliged to you if ye help me with your prayers for this people, this College and my own poor soul. Grace be with you. Remember my love to your wife.

St Andrews Feb. 13.   Yours in Christ Jesus,
1640.   S. R.

ROBERT BAILLIE (1599–1662) was, like Rutherford, a covenanting minister, academic and controversialist, but of more moderate views, siding with the Engagers and later the Resolutioners against the high Presbyterian party (see headnote to Wariston for background). Just as he never accepted the divine right of Presbytery, so he was reluctant to condemn Episcopacy in principle, his objection being rather to the claims of the Laudian party to a divine right of bishops and to what he saw as their corruption of the Reformed Church. Though he refused to recommend the Book of Canons and Prayer Book of 1637 from the pulpit, he tried to temper the doctrinaire abjuration of Episcopacy in the Glasgow Assembly of 1638. And still the tone of his anti-Laudian tracts, in spite of his moderate theoretical position, is rather intemperate, and he vigorously supported the armed defence of the Covenant. He was chaplain to his patron Eglinton's regiment in the First Bishops' War of 1639 and was with the army again in the Second Bishops' War of 1640. In 1642, he was appointed professor of divinity in Glasgow, and he went as one of the Scottish commissioners to the Westminster Assembly. The following years are the main period of his pamphleteering, not only against the Scottish Laudians, Corbet and Bishop Maxwell, but also against Independency. At the Restoration his fellow Resolutioner, Lauderdale, offered him a bishopric, which he declined, but he accepted appointment as Principal of Glasgow University.

The most interesting parts of Baillie's *Letters and Journals* are the records of events he was involved in, which he wrote, not as a diary but as letters to keep correspondents like his parishioners of Kilwinning or his cousin, William Spang, minister of

Campvere in Holland, informed about the politics of the Covenant. As these were passed around, they must have done something of the work of a party newspaper, keeping sympathisers with the movement in touch. Baillie was concerned that the Covenant should appear in the right light as part of the general advance of the Reformation cause. He was also a great recommender of sound men for influential positions. But as well as being party man and journalist, Baillie is an agreeable letter writer. He obviously enjoyed the wheels within wheels of the work he was engaged in, and at the same time he communicates his excited and solemn feeling that the hand of God is behind it all. He is an eager observer on his adventures with the army or later at the trial of Strafford in London. In the extracts below from a letter written during his soldiering in the First Bishops' War, his amused picture of himself as man of war, his attention to the details of meals and good order in the camp and his easy and familiar way of recording these things give his friend something of himself.

The *Letters and Journals* were edited for the Bannatyne Club by David Laing in 3 volumes (Edinburgh, 1841–42). The text below is based on MS X 15 b 3/1, ff. 178v–180; 181v–182; 182v–183; 187–188, in New College Library, Edinburgh, a copy corrected in places by Baillie himself.

To William Spang, September 28th, 1639.

Coosin,

Ye have heir the rest of my papers concerning the Assemblie of Glasgow, also ye will find about yow a letter of myne, the 12 of Februar, giving yow ane account of our affaires till that tyme. The accidents of our land this 7 moneths bygone hes beene verie many and verie strange. I doubt if the providence of God sheltering a poore church from imminent ruine with a power, wisdome, goodnes, clearlie divine hes ever in any land shyned so brightlie as in ours thes dayes. The hand of our God hes now well neir led us all downe from the stage of extreame danger that we may all goe about in our old security, everie one his owne neglected affaires, with a mutuall amity and a most universall joy.[24] Our prince is brocht off so well as may be and much more honouriblie then any could have dreamed from the persewing the reveng of inraged churche men, who wold nether indure to amend their crymes nor suffer the censure of their obstinacie. Our state is secured from the wrathe of our misinformed prince, from the armes of our neighbor kingdomes and a strong faction among our selfe. Our church hes gotten a full purgation and

53

hes cast furth freelie all the corruptions that did infect either doctrine or discipline. We are putt in possession of Generall Assemblies and Parliaments according to our mynd, the soveraigne medicines against the sudden returne of such mortall deseases amongst us. The Canterburian faction in our land,[25] which with full sailes was hayling us all away to Rome for our religion, to Constantinople for our policie, who was not carefull much to cover their intention to have our church presentlie popishe and our state slavishe alone that they themselfes might have their desyred honour, wealthe, pleasure, whatever displeasure thairby could come to God, or disgrace to thair prince, or ruine to their countrey – that faction is now brocken, lying in the pitt of shame and povertie in a strange land, pitied by none, helped by verie few, and that bot in such a measure as to their proud and prodigall stomacks bring rather ane incresse of byting and tormenting disdayne than any sweetnes of a present relieffe, or ground to expect a redres to their miseries in any following tyme. We by the favor of our God and grace of our king are putt in such a condition that thes of our néighbors, who in all Europe were beholding the theater of our yle thir bygone yeres with the eye of compassionat pittie and ane heart affrayed not with the farre prognostications, bot the imminent appearances, of our woefull calamities, or els according to their contrare interesse were gazing with ane eye kendled with ane overjoyeing hope to sie the long envyed prosperitie of our happie ylands change to thes confusions that micht open a faire port to carrie in the charet of their great goddesse on earth, the Pope and Catholick king[26] to reigne in our church and state, and by this new accresse[27] of impire be much furthered in erecting that Fyft Monarchie,[28] which the Jesuits hes beene long hatcheing for their darleinge, the Spanishe king, had not the puritanick Calvinists especiallie in Brittayne, layed hitherto fome straes[29] in thair way; thes our neighbors, I say, will now reape the fruit of their former affections, either by thair sweet congratulations to partake in our present rejoyceing in our God and humble thanksgiveings to our king, or els by turneing thair back and hyding thair face being confounded at the breckneck of thair expectations, bitterlie to regrat the returne of our peace, thair ancient eyesore and mayne ground of desperation, ever to gett the airmes of thair empyre one inche inlarged; yea to be amazed with feares leist the evanishing of thair best devysed plotts heir into wind and reike be a divine presage of the downefall of all thair cunning contrivements oversea and of the redemption of the churches abroad from that oppression quhairwith their tyranous feet hes long treade them downe.

The severall peaces of this heavenlie worke, which God hes begun and perfected by the noble spirits of many brave men among us, fitted excellentlie with gifts correspondent to the extraordinarie exigents of the tymes, I wishe ye had them well descryved. They could serve our freind for verie good purpose to be matterialls for his latine storie,[30] quhairin I hope he will goe on, not onlie becaus that declaration will be a full apologie to stoppe the mouth of all his calumniators and a certayne meane to procure to him the readie patrocinie of the best in this land to answer ever for him, and that hotelie against all who wold heirefter for any bygone mistaks move thair tongue against his fame, bot speciallie becaus the continuance of that discourse wold be a good office towards his native countrey, to which he is tyed both becaus he hes begun and is well approven for his labure and is tollerablie well furnished with all parts neidfull for that taske. I sall be glade for my pairt to send to yow for his use all the information comes to my hands.

The secreitt wheiles wherupon this wark hes runne are all within the curtayne where the lyke of me winnes not. I heir that thes who hes beene prime workers hes lykewayes beene diligent wrytters of all the proceidings. Thair comentars, when they come to the publick view, I perswade my selfe, will give great contentment to all mynds who are inclyned towards a laudable curiositie to understand and behold all the strings of that muntoure;[31] that sieing the motion goe on by the counterpassing of so many small wheells, everie one runneing on their owne axell, he may be ravished with the strenth of the first mover and delyted with the sight of the skill of the great engyner, whose hand hes framed the first great wheelle and hes sett all together with such a mutuall dependance that the whole multitude of all thair countermotions works together for no other end then to bring the palme[32] about to thes precise lynes which the artificers wills at such tymes to be poynted at. Bot in the meanetyme the world of comon witts, who are contented to behold the outsyde without deiper inquirie, careing for no more then in thair way to looke upe to the hand upon the houre, being impatient to interrupt thair privat adoes by any laborious searche into the causes of the motion and wayes how publick affaires hes beene caryed throughe (the most of the world consisting of such simple and blunt spirits) must not be disapoynted. But quhill our noble agents gett leasure from the importunitie of thair laborious actions, which yett is not ended, to give a sight of thair wryttings, quhairin to such noble mynds as thair own they may be pleased to give a view of all the convoy of this great effaire, I wishe our freind were going on in his playne, short and simple way to lett strangers oversea behold that face of matters which the blindest among us hes seene this whyle bygone and much admired. For his service and better furtherance, I sall goe on quhair I left with thes passages which now comes to my mynd. Ye sall have them in that shape that they were presented to the eye of us, the comon people, and in that order quhairin they stand in a verie weake memorie some moneths efter thair passing by.

The suplication[33] which we decreed in the Assemblie of Glasgow to be sent to the king could heardlie be gotten presented. Howsoever, many wold have ventured to have gone with it, though thair head sould have gone thairfore. Yet understanding the increasse of the king's wrath and the danger thair was, even in peaceable tymes, for any subject to play the ambassador or capitulator with the prince quhen he did not call for, or his Councell did not send up, which by law and his declared will is apoynted to be his onlie informer in highe poynts of state, also hearing oft words from court of great spyte against the verie lyves of most of our nobles, gentrie, ministrie who were able to agent our bussines, it wes resolved that none of note or parts sould goe up without greater assurance for thair returne then could for that tyme be expected; and withall a gentleman of the Marquis of Hamilton's[34] acquaintance, Mr. George Winrame, undertooke on all hazards to delyver to the Marquis the suplication and upon his refusall, to give it to the king himselfe. He was no worse then his word, as indeid some of our faire undertaking statesmen thairefter did prove. He went to court, shew to the Marquis his eirand; his Grace acquainted the king, who was pleased that the suplication sould be receaved, so his Grace tooke it and on his knee did read it to his Majestie in the Councell. The best answer then it gote was the Scottish proverbe, "When they have brocken my head, they will putt on my coule." However, the gentleman stayed many weekes for ane answer, bot receaved none. He did us good offices thair, thought his letters, which were lyke to be sighted, were full of greate feares and Englishe braggs, yett diverse of his more secrit ones shew so long as he remained thair the true estate of the court, which was not verie terrible.

We in the meane tyme went on with our effaires, held the committies apoynted by the Assemblie. Many ministers who remayned obstinat in scandals were deposed at Edinburgh, St. Andrewes, Dundie, Irwine and elsquhair, how justlie, the reports of thes committies' diligence to the late Generall Assemblie at Edinburgh did declair; where before the king's commissioner, all the deposed ministers who pleased were heard to plead, and all of them who kythed[35] penitent for thair misdemeanor wer receaved.

The Councell of England after long advysement, permitted the king (I wold have said, consented to the king's desyre) to enter in a course of warre against us. The first assurance we had of this conclusion was the oath exacted of our nation at court of renunceing the Assemblie and our band, promiseing also the king thair full asistance, when ever he requyred it, against us. The nixt was the king's lettir, published for all the shyres, the 26 of Januar, comanding all the nobles and gentrie of England to attend his royall standart at Yorke against the first of Apryle, where he was to goe to the border to oppose the Scottes thair, who were to invade England. And the thrid was the comission, which the Marquis of Hamilton's man caryed to the north for the Marquis of Huntley to be lewetenant to the king in thes pairts with great authority.

Thir alarmes putt us out of all doubt of our enemies' intention quicklie to sett upon us. Our first care was to send in a true Information to England of all our purposes. We had some moneths befor given to that nation account in print of all our former proceidings, to thair good lyking. We then in a printed sheet or two labured to cleare ourselfe of all sclanders, especiallie of that vyle calumnie of our intention to invade England, or to cast of our duetifull obedience to our prince.[36] This peace, as wes thoucht old Durie's hand cheifflie,[37] did us good service, for it satisfied so fullie the hearts of that nation that our adversaries, being extremlie galled with our successe, moved the king to make that pitifull Declaration of the 27 of Februar, where we are, contrare to all reason and law, declared in all the churches of England the foulest traitors and rebels that ever breathed.[38] Bot at once we lost nocht by that most injurious dealing, for our innocency was so well remonstrat in print by thes three or four most dayntie sheits of Mr. Henderson's that we over all England began to be muche more pittied then befor and our inraiged partie, the bishops, to be the more detested.[39]

Our nixt care was to have all our mynds cleared of the lawfulnes of our defence. No man doubted more of this then my selfe; yea, at my subscryving of the Covenant, I did not dissemble my contrare resolution, for I had drunken in without examination from my master Cameron[40] in my youth that slavishe tenet, that all resistance to the supreeme magistrat in any case was simplie unlawfull. Bot setting my self to diligent reading and prayer for light in that question, which the tymes requyred peremptorlie to be determined without delay, I fand many doubts lowsed, especiallie by Bilson, Grotius, Rivet and the Doctors of Aberdeene, who were alleadged to be most opposed to that tenet.[41] Being fullie cleared in my owne mynd, as my fashion is I held not long in my resolution. At our meiting in Edinburgh, being so desyred, I gave out that sheit or two, which I gave yow, for which I gote many thankes, of the lawfulnes of our defence by armes. My Lord of Cassils, who had drunken of the same fontayne with me, by his obstinat refusall to joyne in any course tending to a forcible resistance, did give great offence to verie many. Nothing was more hinderfull to us then that gracious man's exemple, withdrawing from the rest on meere conscience. When he was given over of all as desperat, I tooke him in hand and left him not till at last, by God's grace, he became as franche in the defence of his countrey as any of his neighbors. Diverse papers went then abroad upon this question, some quhairof was not voyd of scandall, especiallie one of a prettie scholler, Mr. G[illespie], bot to rashe a youth in his determinations, if I conceave him right, in many things.[42] To helpe this inconvenient it was layd on Mr. Hendersone, our best penman, to drawe up somewhat for the comon view. He did it somewhat against the hair[43] and more quicklie then his custome is, so it was not so satisfactorie as his other wrytts. For this cause, though read out of many pulpitts, yett he wold not lett it goe to the presse; but one of our deposed ministers wold ease him of that expensse. Mr. Corbett, to whom I had obteined favor in our comittie at Irwin and had moved him under his hand to passe from his declinator[44] of the Generall Assemblie and joyne in our Covenant in all things so farre as I went my selfe, yett upon some splene, as it seemes, or rather rashenes in some of his brethren of the Presbytrie of Dumbrittayne,[45] he is putt to the subscryving of the Assemblie's declaration, farre besyde our mynd; which not being willing to doe, he flees away to Ireland; and thair to shew his repentance of what I had moved him to wreitt, he will putt himselfe in print in the Deputie's hand[46] in a refutation of Mr. Hendersone his Instructions, with so little matter and so muche spytefull venome as no man wold ever have conceaved to have beene lurking in his heart against all our proceidings. We have thought him unworthie of a reply and are content with our advantadge, that my Lord Deputie permitts to goe out under his patronage that desperatt doctrine of absolut submission to princes, that notwithstanding of all our lawes, yett our whole estate may no more oppose the prince's dead, if he sould play all the pranks of Nero, then the poorest slave at Constantinople may resist the tyrannie of the Great Turke. We are confident that our sweet prince will not faill to doe justice upon all who countenances such tenetts that strykes at the roote of his just and lawfull soveraignity, if the tymes were so peaceable that Parliaments could gett, in a deduced[47] processe, represented to his eye the state-undermyneing plott of that faction.

When we had done diligence to enforme our neighbors of England and make sure the courages of all our freinds at home, in the thrid place, we tooke course for a reall opposition to our enemies. . . .

[The Covenanters prepared for war.]

Certainelie our daingers were greatter then we might let our people conceave, bot the trueth is we lived by faith in God. We knew the goodnes of our cause; we were resolved to stand be it upon all hazards whatsoever; we know the worst, a glorious death for the cause of God and our dear countrey.

Always we resolved no longer to be ydle. In all the land we apoynted noblemen and gentlemen for comanders, divyded so many as had beene officers abroad among the shyres, putt all our men who could beare armes to frequent dreillings, had frequent both publick and privatt humiliations befor our God, in whom was our onlie trust. Everieone, man and woman, incouraged thair neighbors. We tooke notice at Edinburgh of the names, disposition, forces of all who joyned not with us in covenant, apoynted that in one day the Castle of Edinburgh, Dumbartane and all the cheiffe adversars sould be assayed; that with diligence, Montrose, with the forces of Fyffe, Angous, Perthe, Mernes, with the advyse of Leslie[48] and sundrie of his officers, sould goe and take order with Huntley and Aberdeene; that Argyle sould sett strong guards on his coasts; that Leith sould be fortified. It pleased God in all this to give us extraordinary successe. Leslie in ane efternoone went up quietlie with the noblemen to the Castlegate of Edinburgh, caused the towne companies to follow them in armes under the walls, parleid a litle with the constable; who being much more unwilling to rander[49] then was expected, yea peremptor not to rander, at once efter a dry fairewelle and playne upgiveing, everyie one returneing to his owne company, a pittard[50] is sett to the utter gate and is blowne up. Axes and hammers and ramming leddirs are aplyed to the inner gate. The walls are scaled with so much the greater courage that amazement had so seased on all the sojors within that none of them durst so much as drawe a sword. So in halfe ane houre that strong peace is winnit without a stroke. So farre were the keepers frie of all trasone or collusion that the constable's first retreat was to the king, quhair yett we have not heard of any punishement inflicted upon him. That night the noblmen supped in the hous. Thairefter great care was had by the generall and Crowner Hamilton[51] to bettir much the old fortifications and putt to many new ones at ane hudge expence of moneyes. We thocht it a great mercie of God that a peace of such importance was caryed without any harme either gotten or given and tooke it for a happie praesage of the whole effaire. . . .

[Various other "defensive" measures were taken.]

Thus in a short tyme by God's extraordinar helpe, we cutt the mayne sinewes of our adversars' hopes; all the strenths of our land came in our hands; no man among us, bot thes that swore they were stout freinds; all otherwayes disposed, both nobles, gentrie, ministers, were gotten away to our professed enemies, and the whole countrey putt in such ane order and magnanimitie that we fand sensiblie the hand of God in everie thing goeing before us; so all feare of humane force was cleane banished away, and a pregnant hope raised in the heart of all the faithfull of a happie conclusion of this divine worke. This mervellous successe detracted nothing of our great desyre to give in all humility full satisfaction to all the reasonable comandements of our gracious prince. The counsellers that remayned offered to come up all of them to his Majestie for to give him much more true information of our proceidings then yett he had receaved. Whill that motion was bot closelie intertayned, they layd it upon one of thair number, my Lord Orbistoun,[52] to goe from them to represent on all hazards the justice and necessitie of our actions. This man undertooke much to speake verie freelie, as he had done before in the countreye's quarrell. Bot quhen he came to Yorke, he gote no hearing, so farre as we could learne. For all this, another was sent, my Lord Carmicheall,[53] whose audience in that cause was no greater. The king's honour was now ingadged; his rage was increassed by his disapoyntment in all his designes among us; he was on his way; thair was nothing now able to divert him from persewing of us with fyre and sword bot the God of heaven. Of this celestiall diversion we did never despare, hoping still that the goodnes of God wold never permitt so gracious a prince to defyle his hands in the blood of so loving subjects for no cause at all bot thair opposition to that corruption and tyrannie [they] were bringing under the colour of his name, both into church and state.

[The Covenanters levied an army to meet the invading army of the king and encamped on Duns Law. David Stevenson, *The Scottish Revolution 1637–44* (Newton Abbot: David and Charles, 1973), p. 150–51, tells us that in fact the covenanting army was desperately short of horsemen and provisions and that "Baillie's belief in the existence of adequate supplies for the future is an indication of the success of the Covenanters' propaganda."]

It wold have done yow good to have casten yor eyes athort our brave and rich hill, as oft I did with great contentment and joy, for I, quoth the wren, was thair among the rest, being chosen preacher by the gentlemen of our shyre, who came late with my Lord of Eglinton. I furnished to halfe a dozen of good fellowes muskets and picks[54] and to my boy a broad sword. I caryed my selfe, as the fashion was, a sword and a couple of Dutch pistols at my sadle, bot, I promise, for the offence of no man, except a robber in the way, for it was our part alone to pray and preache for the incouragement of our countreymen, which I did to my power most cheirfullie. Our hill was garnished on the toppe towards the south and east with our mounted canon, well neir to the number of fortie, great and small. Our regiments lay on the syds of the hill, almost round about. The place was not a myle in circle, a prettie round rysing in a declivitie without steepnes to the hight of a bowshott, on the toppe somewhat playne, about a quarter of myle in lenth and as much in breadth, as I remember, capable of tents for 40 thowsand men. The crowners[55] lay in kennous[56] lodges, high and wyde; thair captaynes about them in lesser ones; the sojours about all in hutts of timber, covered with divott or stray.[57] Our crowners for the most part were noblemen: Rothes, Lindesay, Sinclair, had among them two full regiments at leist from Fyfe; Balcarris, a horse troupe; Lowdon, Montgomerie, Areskin,[58] Boyd, Fleming, Kircubright, Yester, Dawousie,[59] Eglinton, Cassils and others either with whole or halfe regiments. Montrose regiment was above 15 hundred men in the Castle of Edinburgh; himselfe was expected, bot what deteined him ye sall heir at once.[60] Argyle was sent for to the treatie of peace, for without him none wold mint[61] to treat. He came and sett up his tent in the hill, bot few of his people with him. It was thocht meitt that he and his sould lye about Stirling in the heart of the countrey to be alwayes readie in subsidies for unexpected accidents; to be a terror to our newtralists, or bot masked friends; to make all without din marche forward, leist his unkannie trewesmen sould light on to call them up in thair reire;[62] alwayes to have ane eye what either the north, or the shippes, or the west, or our staill host sould mister[63] of helpe. It was thocht the countrey of England was mor affrayit for the barbarietie of his hillanders then of any other terror. Thes of the Englishe that came to visit our campe did gaze much with admiration upon thes souple fellowes with thair playds, targes and dorlachs.[64] Thair was some companies of them under Captayne Buchanan and other in Areskin's regiment. Our captaynes for the most pairt barons or gentlemen of good note, our lewetenants almost all sojors who had served over sea in good charges, everie companie had flieing at the captayne's tent dore a brave new colour stamped with the Scottishe airmes and this ditton,[65] *For Christ's Crowne and Covenant*, in golden letters. Our generall had a brave royall tent, bot it was not sett up. His constant guard was some hunders of our lawers, musketers under Durie and Hope's comand,[66] all the way standing in good airmes with cocked matches befor his gate, well apparelled. He lay at the foot of the hill in the castell with Baylie, his serjant major or lewetenant generall. That place was destinat for Almond,[67] in whose wisdome and valour we had bot too much confidence. Yett in the tyme of our most neid, the grievousnes of his gravell, or the pretence of it, made him goe to France to be cutted. Alwayes quhen he came thair, it was found he neidit no incision, so he past to his charge in Holland, quhair to us he was as dead in all our dangers.

The councells of warre were keeped daylie in the castle, the ecclesiastick meitings in Rothus' large tent. The generall with Baylie came nichtlie for the setting of the [watch] on their horses. Our sojours were all lustie and full of courage, the most of them stout yong plewmen, great cheirfulnes in the face of all. The onlie difficultie was to gett them dollors or two the man for thair voage from home and the tyme they entred in pay; for among our yeomen, money at any tyme, let be then, uses to be verie scarse. Bot once having entered on the comon pay, thair sixpence a day, they wer galliard.[68] None of our gentlemen was any thing worse of lying some weeks together in thair cloake and boots on the ground, or standing all nicht in airmes in the greatest storme. Whyles, through storme of weather and neglect of the comissaries, our bread wold be to long in cumeing, which made some of the eastland sojours halfe mutine. Bot at once order being taken for our victwals from Edinburgh, East Louthian and the countrey about us, we were answered better then we could have beene at home. Our meanest sojors was alwayes served in wheitbread, and a groat wold have gotten them a lambe legge, which was a dayntie world to the most of them. Ther had beene ane extraordinarie crope in that countrey the former yeir. Besyd abundance which still was stollen away to the Englishe campe for great pryces, we wold have feared no inlaick[69] for litle money in some moneths to come. Mairch and Tividaill[70] are the best mixt and most plentifull shyres both for grasse and corn, for fleshes and bread, in all our land. We wer much oblished to the towne of Edinburgh for moneyes. Harie Rollock by his sermons moved them to shake out thair purses. The garners of non-Covenanters, especiallie of James Maxwell and my Lord Winton, gave us plenty of wheitt. One of our ordinances was to sease on the rents of non-Covenanters, for we thocht it bot reasonable fra they sydit with thes who putt our lyves and our lands for ever to feile,[71] for the defence of our Church and countrey to employ for that caus (quhairin thair entres was as great as ours, if they wold be Scottish men) a pairt of thair rent for one yeir. Bot for all that, few of them did incurre any losse by that our decreit, for the peace prevented the execution.

Our sojours grew in experience of airmes, in courage, in favour daylie. Everie one incouraged another. The sight of the nobles and thair beloved pastors daylie raised thair hearts. The good sermons and prayers morning and even under the rooff of heaven, to which

thair drummes did call them for bells, the remonstrances verie
frequent of the goodnes of thair cause, of thair conduct hitherto by a
hand clearlie divyne, also Leslie his skill and fortune made them all so
resolut for battell as could be wished. We were feared that emulation
among our nobles micht have done harme when they sould be mett
in the feilds, bot such was the wisdome and authoritie of that old,
litle, crooked souldior that all, with ane incredible submission from
the beginning to the end, gave over themselfe to be guyded by him,
as if he had beene Great Soliman.[72] Certainelie the obedience of our
nobles to that man's advyses was as great as thair forbears wont to be
to thair king's comands. Yet that was the man's understanding of
our Scotts humors, that gave out not onlie to the nobles, bot to verie
meane gentlemen, his directions in a verie homelie and simple
forme, as if they had beene bot the advyces of thair neighbor and
companion. For as he richtlie observed, a difference wold be used in
comanding sojours of fortune and of sojours voluntars, of which
kynd the most pairt of our campe did stand. He keeped daylie in the
Castle of Dunce ane honorable table for the nobles and strangers
with himselfe, for gentlemen wayters[73] thairefter at a long syde
table. I had the honor by accident one day to be his chaiplayne at table
on his left hand. The fare was as became a generall in tyme of warre,
not so curious be farre as Arundail's[74] to our nobles – bot ye know
that the Englishe sumptuositie both in warre and peace is despysed
by all thair neighbors. It seemes our generall's tables was on his owne
chairge, for so farre as yitt I know, neither he nor any noble or
gentleman of considerable rent gote anything for thair charge. Well I
know that Eglintoun, our crowner,[75] intertayned all the gentlemen
of note that were with him at his owne table all the tyme of our
abode, and his sonne, Montgomrie, keeped with him verie oft the
chieffe officers of his regiments; for this was a voyage quhair we were
glad to bestow our lyves, let be our estates.

Had ye lent yor eare in the morning, or especiallie at even, and
heard in the tents the sound of some singing psalmes, some praying
and some reading scripture, ye wold have beene refreshed. True,
thair was swearing and cursing and brawling in some quarters,
quhairat we were greaved. Bot we hoped if our campe had been a
litle setled, to have gotten some way for thes misorders, for all of any
fashion did regraitt and all did promise to contribut thair best
indevoirs for helping all abuses. For my selfe, I never fand my mynd
in bettir temper than it was all that tyme fra I came from home till my
head was agayne homeward, for I was as a man who had taken my
leave from the world and was resolved to die in that service without
returne. I fand the favor of God shyning upon me, and a sweet,
meek, humble, yet strong and vehement spirit leading me all along.

63

Bot I was no sooner in my way westward efter the conclusion of peace than my old securitie returned.

JOHN CORBET (1603–41) was a minister and pamphleteer on the Episcopal side (see above, p. 58). He was deprived of his charge of Bonhill in 1639 for refusing to subscribe to the acts of the Glasgow Assembly and took refuge in Ireland where he wrote the anti-Covenanting tracts, *The Ungirding of the Scottish Armour* (1639) and *The Epistle Congratulatorie of Lysimachus Nicanor* (1640); the latter, Baillie thought the work of Bishop Lesley or Bishop Maxwell and answered in a postscript to his *Ladensium* *ΑΥΤΟΚΑΤΑΚΡΙΣΙΣ* (1640). In Ireland he obtained the living of Killalan and Balintubride, but in the Irish rising of 1641 against the English was "hewed to pieces in the very armes of his poore wife" (Baillie, *An Historicall Vindication of the Government of the Church of Scotland* [1646], p. 2).

Scorn and malice are things that Corbet has in common with Bishop Maxwell, the other considerable Episcopalian controversialist at this time. But the sustained irony of *The Epistle Congratulatorie of Lysimachus Nicanor of the Society of Jesu to the Covenanters in Scotland, wherein is Paralleled our Sweet Harmony and Correspondency in Divers Material Points of Doctrine and Practice* is unusual in Scottish polemical writing and is managed ingeniously. The pretence that the Jesuits are on the Covenanters' side is not only meant to rile the Covenanters and inspirit the bishops' party; it is meant to make a serious point that in political principles the high-flying Presbyterians were at one with the Jesuits in urging the claims of the kingdom of Christ against the claims of Charles I, or whoever the sovereign magistrate might be. Corbet was certainly not the first or the last to make something of this coincidence of opposites (see for example, Dr. Buckeridge in Melvill's *Diary* [p. 21], or Drummond of Hawthornden in his notes to |*ΣΚΙΑΜΑΧΙΑ*: "a puritaine is a jesuiticall Protestant; and a Jesuite is a puritanicalle Papist"). It was an idea especially popular with those who, like Corbet, held that the true Protestant Reformation should be the work of the king establishing the right order of things against the tyranny of churchmen. But in addition to putting forward the serious thesis that Presbyterian and Jesuit politics agree, Corbet means to embarrass the Covenanters. They were pledged to maintain the authority of the king. And so Corbet's harping on high Presbyterian principles is an unpleasant reminder to them of the inconsistency of their aims and to the moderates among them of the extreme courses they might find themselves committed to. All this is managed with a sort of horrible playfulness. In the pamphlet as a whole, the analogy between Presbyterian and Jesuits is often laboured and obvious, but in the passages below Corbet turns it with something of Swift's unsettling way of coming at his victim from an unexpected quarter. The extracts from the *Epistle* are from pp. 14–15; 20–22; 33–34; 59–60. Footnotes in square brackets are Corbet's marginal notes.

The Epistle Congratulatorie of Lysimachus Nicanor

Rebellion for such an important businesse against a king cannot bee disloyaltie, and they that have not followed your course justly deserve excommunication and banishment. Athanasius was but too silly a man, being under the tyrannie of Constantius, the Arrian hereticke, that did not incite the people to rebellion, or to promove the designes of the emperour's brother, who was orthodoxe and worthier of the crown. . . .[76]

This man was too fearefull, but you were of another spirit, encouraging the people and dehorting them from "being afraid of shadowes";[77] yea, your priests were good patterns to the rest to follow. There was one of them,[78] who is worthy (if you could permit images) to have his statue ingraven in marble to eternize him to the world's end, who went so stoutly to the camp upon his horse with two carabins at his sadle, two pistols at his side with a broad Scottish sword. Those five weapons were like unto David's five smooth stones which he tooke out of the brooke to kill Goliah with. This David no doubt would have killed five English at the first encounter with his five deadly weapons and would have returned with triumph, saying with Paul "I have fought a good fight" (2 Tim. 4.7), for "should such a man as he flie?" (Nehem. 6.11). But if any shall produce the canons of divers generall councels ordaining clergie men that beare arms to be degraded and put from their place and that of Davenant, "Christus gladium verbi promittit, non ferri: fugam suadet, non pugnam" (Christ promiseth to his pastors the sword of the word, and not the sword of iron; he perswades to flie, but not to fight),[79] the answer is easie: those generall councels, though not *in toto*, yet *pro tanto*, are like your 6 generall or nationall councels which you have condemned because they were against you,[80] and Davenant is a bishop and so your adversary. . . .

I say then, if you shall receive such a charge from your king [to appeare before him to plead your cause], you should not obey (for in your sense, that is to betray the royall prerogative of your king Jesus Christ) but returne the answer of Core, Dathan and Abiram with ingemination, "We will not come, we will not come" (Num. 16.12,

65

14); or your lords, lay elders, may return that of Jeremy, "We are lords, we will no more come unto thee" (Jer. 2.31). And if your king will not be content with your answer, prosecute your begun course with all diligence and earnestnesse. Having begun in the spirit, end not in the flesh, but go on with that which they call disorders till you get the king in your power, and then he shal know what subjects you will be. If the people of one citie falling in sedition for matters of religion so prevailed and passed all power of resisting that Anastasius the emperour was fain to come to an open place without his crown and by heraulds to signifie to the people that he was readie with a very good will to resigne the Empire into their hands,[81] how much more may you, who have many cities, by continuing your courses force your king to resigne his crown of Scotland? And howbeit the people of that citie seeing the emperor in so pitiful a case were moved with the spectacle and changed their minds and besought the emperour to keep his crown and promised for their parts to be quiet, yet do not you so till your king shall performe all your demands.

From that which hath been done by you and repeated by me, I see other two errours banished, which I conjoyn for brevities sake lest my epistle should encrease to a treatise, viz. that the king is no more to be president nor supreme governour in causes ecclesiasticall. It is the folly of your divines to make the moderator of your Assemblies to be unto the king or his delegate in Assemblies as the chancelor in the Parliament is to the king or his deputy in Parliaments. But I extoll your courage, who now conclude with us, "Ad regium officium pertinet, ut legibus et edictis suis eam fidem teneri quam sacerdotes tenendam docent, etc." (It's the duty of kings by their lawes and edicts to cause that faith to be kept which the priests teach should bee kept).[82] For the spirit of the prophet is subject to the prophets. But is Saul also among the prophets? Is it true, that the Anticovenanter sayes, that in your ecclesiasticall judicatories called 1 sessions, 2 presbyteries and 3 synods, there wil be in the first sometimes twelve, sometimes sixteene, in some places 24 lay elders for one priest? secondly, in your presbyteries, lay elders of equal power and number? thirdly, in your synods as many lay elders with their assessors as there is priests? all which lay elders have as great power in matters of doctrine and discipline as the priests themselves to judge and passe definitive sentence, etc? But I trust it is not so, for I heare that they are offended to be called lay elders and will be called ruling elders and ecclesiasticall persons, and so I doubt not but they have received orders from you. And therefore seeing ecclesiasticall persons among you have the managing of church affaires, the civil magistrate must be content to execute what you decree, neither ought he to judge otherwise then you judge, neither can he hinder you to make lawes in the Church. For as Stapleton sayes very learnedly with you, "Oves non possunt judicare pastores" (Let the sheepheards judge of the sheep, who must follow them as Christ's sheep heard his voyce and followed him).[83] Therefore you have most valiantly shaken off that yoke of the king's supremacie in causes ecclesiasticall and at the Crosse of Glasgow proclaimed to the world (against the king's Proclamation for raising the Assembly)[84] that your Assemblies are the supreme judicatorie in all causes ecclesiasticall, and since supreme, it's independent from the king; and your reason is good, for that which is superiour cannot be subject to that which is inferiour. Now (as Bellarmine also sayes) "regimen ecclesiasticum sublimius est politico" (the ecclesiasticke government is higher then the politicke), for "principatus politicus institutus est ab hominibus et de jure gentium; at principatus ecclesiasticus est a solo Deo et de jure divino" (the politicke government is institute by men and of the law of nations, but the church government is from God alone and of divine institution.)[85] Therefore you conclude right that the king hath no more power to appoint officers in the Church then you have power to appoint officers of state for this court. . . .

From this sweet harmonie in the preceding points, especially of your independent power in church matters, there followeth another parallel by way of consequence, viz. that you may excommunicate your king if hee doe not obey the acts and constitutions of your Assemblies. Thus you threatned King James and his Councell, both, with excommunication if he would not execute your acts of your Assemblie; and good reason, seeing it is the supreme judicatory and the king is a sonne of your Church, from whom he ought to take the meaning. And if hee bee refractarie, why may not the Assembly excommunicate him, as Ambrose did Theodosius? And as I have said already from your Travers[86] of your government, "Huic disciplinae omnes principes etc" (There is a necessity that all princes and monarchs should submit their scepter and obey this discipline). It's your chief commander in the camp royall, Thomas Cartwright,[87] being asked whether the king himself might be excommunicated, answered, "That excommunication should not bee exercised upon kings, I utterly mislike," and so do we also. Yea, albeit they be not heretickes themselves, yet if they doe not punish such as their pastors commands them, they may be excommunicate. "Potest ac debet pastor regibus jubere ut puniant haereticos, et nisi fecerint, etiam cogere per excommunicationem" (The pastor may and ought to command kings to punish hereticks, and if they do it not, even to compell them with excommunication),[88] but especially "si sit haereticorum vel schismaticorum fautor, receptor, vel defensor" (if hee be a favourer, receiver or defender of hereticks and schismaticks).[89] If your bishops be such men, is not this your king's fault? Your fault is that you use but too much lenity in not ascending from the myter to the crown. For this may stand very well with your tenent and ours, though protestant divines disclaim it; for your Buchanan teacheth you that not only it is lawfull to excommunicate princes, but that they should both despose him and destroy him, for he sayes, "Ministers may excommunicate princes, and he being by excommunication cast into hell is not worthy to enjoy any life upon earth."[90] But truly Knox and Buchanan are more rigid then we are herein, for howbeit we grant that it's lawfull to excommunicate kings, yet wee hold it not necessary that upon excommunication either deposition or killing should follow. Indeed by our common tenent it will follow that excommunication is an antecedent to deprivation or killing, but we do not hold that deprivation or killing of princes is a necessary consequent or effect of excommunication. For (say we) "quando talis effectus adjungitur, non est effectus ipsius excommunicationis, sed specialis poena simul cum excommunicatione imposita" (when such an effect is joyned to excommunication, it's not the effect of it, but a speciall punishment imposed with it).[91] But it's wonderfull to see the wide difference between this our tenent and yours and that which Protestants hold, for they make the power of the supreme magistrate architectonicke and subject unto it all power civill and ecclesiasticall. . . .

Paul writing to the Romans sayes, "Let every soul be subject to superior powers." "Paul," saies [Buchanan], "writes this in the infancy of the Church. There were but few christians then, not many of them rich or of ability, so as they were not ripe for such a purpose. . . . The Apostle did respect the people he wrote unto, and his words are not to be extended to the body or people of a commonwealth or whole city." And he tels us in this case, if Paul were alive and did see wicked kings raigning in christian commonwealths, Paul would say that he accounted no such for magistrates. He would forbid all men for speaking unto them and from keeping them company. He would leave them to their subjects to be punished, neither would he blame them if they accounted no such longer for kings.[92] And as Bellarmine sayes, . . . "Such a king by the consent of all may, yea ought to be, deprived of his dominion. If this in old times was not done, the cause was because they had no strength."[93]

But now the times are changed. Haec aetas alios mores postulat (this age requireth other manners). Spare not big words, tell the head it's sick, presse the people to armes too, strike the basiliske[94] veine, since nothing but that will cure the plurisie of your estate. Your strength is great, yea, so great that you professe your selves invincible "if you keepe unitie and veritie;"[95] that is the doctrine which I congratulate.

Certainly you have an invincible generall, your head, Lesley. And as there is great union between us in doctrine and practice, so I perceive a great similitude between both our generals, our Ignatius Loyola and your Lesley. As for their birth, I cannot compare them, for neither Maphaeus nor Ribadeneira nor Valderana nor Becanus nor any that writes his life tels us who were his parents; so that it seems "pater Ignatii fuit dubii generis et mater communis generis" (Ignatius's father was of doubtful parentage and his mother of the common people).[96] As for his life, we deny not the truth, for as our own writers say of his childhood, "satis constat eum in pueritia profanos admodum hausisse spiritus" (it is certain, that in his childhood he drew in very prophane spirits). And "in adolescentia, militiae ac vanitati sese dedit" (in his childhood, he gave himself to wars and vanity, being ready to serve any man for his pay), so that our Ribadeneira caleth him "vanitatis vile mancipium" (a vile slave of vanity).[97]

But at Pompeiopolis being couragiously fighting, his leg was sore wounded, and it was good for him, for "accepto hoc luculento vulnere, ad Deum conversus est" (having gotten this great wound, he was converted to God, and his leg was amended).[98] But yet, "non nihil claudicavit, sed honeste, et quod ambulandi moderatione tegeretur" (he halted a little but decently and which he might hide by the moderation of his walking)[99] and become the founder and generall of our holy society. All this hath hapned to your generall, in his childhood, youth-hood, in his wound, in his halting, in his conversion and becomming generall of your holy society. But from the halting of both our generals, the Anticovenanters draw an ominous conclusion that wee are like Israel in the daies of Elias, halting betweene God and Baal and running crooked courses. But notwithstanding of our halting, they shall find that we can run and give them matter enough to worke on.

ARCHIBALD NAPIER, 1st Baron Napier (1576–1645), son of the inventor of logarithms, was a successful political servant of James VI and Charles I. His constitutional ideas were based on his experience as a politician, his earliest pieces probably dating from about 1633 when the unrest occasioned by the reform of the tithes, in which he had had a hand, evidently moved him to set down some of his thoughts on government. He is the theorist of a moderate constitutional conservatism. His ideas failed, however, to make an influential party among Scottish politicians at the revolution. Only his brother in law, Montrose, to whom he had been tutor, acted effectively on his ideas, but as a soldier not as a politician.

The only copy of the "Letter about the Soveraigne and Supreme Power" the late seventeenth or early eighteenth century Wodrow MS. Quarto XL, ff. 3–5, in the National Library, gives Montrose as signatory, but Napier seems to have been the author. One finds not only the same ideas and intellectual style, but even the same phrasing, as in Napier's other political writings. Ideas are easily passed on; Napier's thought probably influenced Drummond's *Irene*. But style and phrasing are another matter, and if Montrose actually wrote the "Letter", we should have to suppose that Napier's mind exerted an extraordinary influence over his former pupil's. Mark Napier, who edited the "Letter" in his *Memorials of Montrose and his Time* (Edinburgh: Maitland Club, 1848), 2, 43–53, did suppose such an influence, but David Stevenson's suggestion (*The Scottish Revolution*, pp. 225–27, 365–66) that Lord Napier wrote the "Letter" and that somehow it was attributed to Montrose is more plausible.

It is natural to wish that Montrose were the author of this sober and vigorous essay on government, for without it, it is not so easy to dismiss Gilbert Burnet's remark that he had "taken upon himself the port of a hero too much and lived as in a romance" (*History of My Own Time*, I, 53). And yet it is not unreasonable to think that Montrose shared the moderate constitutional principles Napier sets out. It is true that Montrose fought with the Covenanting army in the Bishops' Wars, and that is hardly consistent with the principles of the "Letter". Still like most of his class, he was alarmed by Charles's management of Scotland, his disregard of aristocratic interests, his use of bishops in the government of the country. Napier himself disliked the influence of the bishops and at first chose rather to moderate than to oppose the Covenanting resistance to Charles. But sometime about 1640, when it began to look as if the Covenant was being used to further the interests of the magnate Argyll and the high Presbyterian faction, he expressed his constitutional misgivings in the "Letter", going so far as to maintain that passive obedience to a tyrannical sovereign was preferrable to the tyranny of subjects. About the same time Montrose with other nobles actively engaged himself to resist the tyranny of subjects by the Cumbernauld Bond and entered into a correspondence with the king. When these intrigues came out in 1641, the Covenanters imprisoned Montrose and, though he had not signed the Bond, Napier along with him.

Napier had to pay a second time for his association with Montrose. In 1644 when the Covenanting army was in England with the Parliamentary forces, Montrose took command of an army of Highlanders and Ulster Macdonalds, and Napier was again imprisoned. In spite of an amazing series of victories, Montrose was unable to hold the country for the king. Lowland royalists would not join him or his Gaelic host, and he could not keep chieftains like Huntly in his camp. His army melted from him, and what was left was easily overcome by the Covenanters at Philiphaugh. Napier, who had been rescued from prison by his son after the victory of Kilsyth, joined Montrose on his flight into Atholl but died there of a fever.

That Napier's ideas of temperate government should lie behind Montrose's career is a paradox. Yet though many were troubled by the lengths to which the Covenanters were taking resistance to the king, the constitutional conservatives mounted no effective political opposition, and when it came to action, Montrose had to draw his support from the anarchic royalism of chieftains like Macdonald and Huntly. That and the heroic spirit with which he died have perhaps made his political designs look more rash, and in a limiting sense, more cavalier, than they were.

Letter about the Soveraigne and Supreme Power

Noble Sir,[100]

In the letter you did me the honnour to send me, you move a question in two words, to give a satisfactory answer to quhilk requires works and volumes, not letters; besides the matter is soe sublime and transcendent a nature as is above my reach and not fitt for subjects to medle with, if it wer not to doe right to soverainge power in a time quhen soe much is said and done to the disgrace and derogation of it.

Nevertheless to obey your desire, I will deliver my opinion: 1. concerning the nature, essentiall parts and practise of the supreme power in government of all sorts; 2dly. I will show quherein the strenth and weakness thereof consists and the effects of both; 3dly. I will answer some arguments and false positions mentioned by the impungers of royall power, and that without partiality and as breifly as I can.

Civil societys, soe pleasing to almighty God, cannot subsist without government, nor government without a soverainge power to force obedience to lawes and just command, to dispose and direct private endeavours to publick ends and to unite and incorporate the several members into one body politick, that with joynt endeavours and abilitys they may the better advance the publick good.

This soverainty is a power over the people, above whilk there is none upon earth, whose acts cannot be rescinded by any other, instituted by God for his glory and the temporall and eternall happiness of men.

This it is that is recorded soe oft by the wisdome of antient times to be sacred and inviolable, the trewest image and representation of the power of almighty God upon earth, not to be bounded, disputed, medled with at all by subjects, who can never handle it, tho never soe warrily, but it's thereby wounded and the publick peace disturbed; yet it's limited by the lawes of God and nature and some lawes of nationes and by the foundamentall lawes of the country, quhilk are these upon quhich soverainge power itself resteth, in prejudice of quhilk a king can doe nothing, and those also quhich secure to the good subject his honnour, his life and the propriety or his goods.

1. This power (not speaking of those who are kings in name only and in effect but *principes nobilitatis* or *duces belli*,[101] nor of the arbitrary and despotick power, quhere one is lord and all the rest slaves, but of that quhich is soverainge over free subjects) is still one and the same in points essentiall quhere ever it be, whither in the person of a monarch, or in a few principle men, or in the estates of the people.

The essentiall points of soveraignity are these: to make lawes, to creat principle officers, to make peace and warr, to give grace to men condemned by law and to be the last to quhom appellation is made. There be others to[o] quhilk are comprehended in those set down, but because majesty doeth not soe clearly shine in them, they are here ommitted.

These sett down are inalienable, indivisible, incommunicable and belong to the soveraigne power privativly[102] in all sorts of government. They cannot subsist in one individuall body, or in one body composed of individuityes, and if they be divided amongst severall bodyes[103] there is noe government, as, if there wer many kings in one kingdome, there should be none at all; for quhosoever should have one of these wer able to crosse their proceedings who have all the rest, for the having them negative and prohibitive in that parte to him belonging might render the acts of all the other invalid, and there should be a superiority to the supream and ane equality to the soverainge power, quhilk cannot fall in any man's conceit that hath commone sense. In speech it's incongruity, and to attempt it in act is perniciouse.

The [mixt][104] government, then, delineated by some otherwise learned and wise men is a mistaking; that quhich deceives them, that in all sortes of estates they who have the supreme power doe sometimes cast the care of publick business upon officers and commissioners during their pleasure, quhich may be superseded or recalled or calld to ane accompt at their pleasure.

Having in some measure expressed the nature of supream power, it shall be better knowen by the universale practise of all nations in all their several sorts of concernment, as weel republicks as monarchys.

The people of Rome, who wer masters of policy and warr too and to this day are made patterns of both, being ane estate popular did exercise without controlment or opposition all the forenamed points essentiall to supreme power. Noe law was made but by the people, and tho the senate in parliamente did propone and advise a law to be made, it was the people that gave it sanction, and it received the force of law from their command and authority, as may appear by the respective[105] phrazes of the propounder, "quod faustum felixque sit vobis populoque Romano, velitis jubeatis".[106] The people used these imperative words *esto, sunto*,[107] and if it were refused, the tribunes of the people expressed it with a *veto*. The propounder or adviser of the law was said *rogare legem* and the people *jubere legem*.[108] The election of officers was only made by the people, as appears by the ambitiouse buying and begging of suffrages soe frequent among them upon the occasions. Warr and peace was ever concluded by them, and never denounced but by their *feciales*[109] with commission from them. They only gave grace and pardon, and for their last refuge, delinquents and they who wer wronged by the sentence of judges and officers *provocabant ad populum*.[110]

Soe it was in Athens and at this day among the Swissers and Grissons,[111] the estates of Holland and all estates popular. In Vinnice, quhich is a pure aristocracy, laws, warr, peace, election of officers, pardon and apellation are all concluded and done *in conciglio magiore*,[112] quhilk consists of principle men who have the soveraignty. As for their *pregadi* and *conciglio di dieci*, they are but officers and exercers of their power, and the Ducke[113] is nothing but the idol to quhom ceremonies and complement is adressed without the least part of soveraignty. Soe it was in Sparta, soe it's in Luca, Genoa and Ragusa and all aristocraties, and indeed cannot be otherwayes without the subversion of the particular government. If then the lords in republicks have that power essentiall to soveraignty, by quhat reason can it be denyed to a prince in whoes person only and privatively resteth the soverainge power and from quhom all lawfull subaltern power, as from the fountain, is derived?

2. This power is strong and durable quhen it's temperat, and it's temperat quhen it's posessed with the essentiall parts foresaid and

73

used with moderation and limitation of the lawes of God and nature and the fundamentall lawes of the country. It's weak quhen it's restrained of the use of these essentiall points, and it's weak also quhen it's extended beyond the lawes quhereby it's bounded, quhich could never be any time endured by the people of the western parts of the worlde and by those of Scotland as litle as any, for that quhich Galba said of his Romans is the humor of them all: "nec totam libertatem nec totam servitutem pati possunt",[114] but a temper of both. Unwise princes endeavour the extension of it, rebelliouse and turbulent subjects, the restraint. Wise princes use it moderatly, but most desire to extend it, and that humor is fomented by advice of courtiers and bad counselours, who are of a hasty ambition and cannot abide the slow progresse of riches and preferments in a temperate government. They persuade the arbitrary with reflexion on their own ends, knowing that the exercise thereof shall be put upon them, quhereby they shall be able quickly to compasse their ends, robbing thereby the people of their wealth, the king of the people's love deu to him and of the honnour and reputation of wisdome.

The effects of a moderate government are religion, justice and peace, flourishing love of the subjects towards their prince, in whoes hearts he reings, durableness and strenth against forraigne invasions and intestine sedition, happiness and security to king and people.

The effect of a prince's power too farr extended is tyranny from the king if he be ill, or if he be good, tyrannie or a fear of it from them to quhom he hath intrusted their managing of publick affaires.

The effect of the royall power restrained is the oppression and tyrrany of subjects, the most feirce, insatiable and insupportable tyranny in the worlde, quhen every man of power oppresseth his neighbour without any hope of redresse from a prince dispoyled of his power to punish oppressors.

The people under ane extended power are miserable, but most miserable under the restrained power. The effects of the former may be cured by good advice, satiety in the prince, or fear of infamy and the penns of writters, or by some event quhich may bring a prince to the sense of his errors; and quhen nothing else can doe it (seing the prince is mortall) patience in the subject is a soveraigne and dangerless remedy, who in wisdome and deuty is obliged to tollerate the vices of his prince as they doe stormes, tempests and other natural evils, quhich are compensate with better times succeding.

It had been better for Germany to have endured the encroachments of Ferdinand and after his death rectifyed them before they had a new election than to have brought it to desolation and shed soe much christian blood by unseasonable remedies and opposition.[115]

But quhen a king's lawfull power is restrained, the politick body is in such desperate estate as it can neither endure the disease nor the remedy, quhich is force only; for prince's lawfull power is only restrained by violence and never repaired but by violence on the other side, quhich can produce nothing but ruin to prince or people, or rather, to both.

Patience in the subject is the best remedy against the effects of a prince's power to far extended, but quhen it's too farr restrained, patience in the prince is soe farr from being a remedy as it formeth and encreaseth the desease, for patience, tract of time and posession makes that quhilk was at first robbery by a body that never dyes at last a good title, and the government comes at last to be changed.

To procure a temperate and moderate government, there is much in the king and not a litle in the people, for let a prince never command soe weel, if there be not a correspondent obedience, there is noe temper. It's not the people's part towards that end to take upon them to limite and circumscribe royall power (it is Jupiter's thunder quhilk never subject handled weel yet) nor to determine what is deu to a prince, what to his people. It requires more than humane sufficiency to goe soe even a way betwixt the prince's prerogative and the subjects' priviledge to content both or be just in itself, for they can never aggree upon the matter; and quhere it hath been attempted as in some places it hath, the sword did ever determine the question, quhich is to be avoyded by all possible means. But there is a fair and justifiable way for subjects to procure a moderate government, incumbent to them in deuty, quhilk is to endeavour the security of religion and just liberty, the matter on quhich the exorbitancy of a prince's power doth work, quhilk being secured, his power most needs be temperate and run in the even channell. But it may be demandit, how shall the people's just libertys be preserved if they be not knowen, and how knowen if not determined to be such? It's answered, the laws contean them, and the parliaments, quhilk ever have been the bulwark of subjects' libertys in monarchys, may advise new lawes against emergent occasions quhich prejudge their libertys and soe leave it to occasion and not prevent it by fools' hast, in parliament quhilk breed contention and disturbance to the queit of the estate. And if parliaments be frequent and rightly constitute, quhat favourite counselour or statesman dare misinforme or mislead a king to the prejudice of the subjects' liberty, knowing he most answer it upon perrill of his head and estate at the nixt enseuing parliament and that he shall putt the king to ane hard choice for him either to abandon him to justice, or by protecting him, displease the estates of his kingdome; and if he should be soe ill advised as to protect him, yet he doeth not escape punishment that is branded

75

with a mark of publick infamy, declared enimy to the state and incapable of any good amonst them.

3. The perpetuall cause of the contraversys between the prince and his subjects is the ambitiouse designs of rule in great men, vailed with the plausible and speciouse pretext of religion and the subjects' libertys, seconded with the arguments and false positions of seditiouse preachers: 1. that the king is ordeaned for the people, and the end is more noble than the mean; 2°. that the constitutor is superior to the constituent; 3°. that the king and people are two contrarys like two scales of a ballance – quhen when the one goes up the other goes down; 4°. that the prince's prerogative and the subjects' priviledge are incompatible; 5°. quhat power is taken from the king is added to the estates of the people. This is the language of the spirits of division quhilk walk between the king and his people to separate them quhom God hath conjoyned, quhilk most not passe without some answer to shew upon quhilk sandy grounds these gyants who war against the godds have builded their Babel.

To the first:– It's treu that the treu and utmost ends of men's actions, quhilk is the glory of God and felicity of men, is to be preferred to all means directed thereunto. But there is not that order of dignity amongst the means themselves or midd instruments compounded together. If it wer soe and a man wer appointed to keep sheep, or a nobleman to be tutor in a law to a pupile of meaner quality, the sheep shold be preferred to the man and the puple to his tutor.

To the second:– He that constituteth soe as he still reteaneth the power to ranverse his constitution is superior to the constituted in that respect. But [if] his donation and constitution is absolute and without condition, divolving all his power in the person constituted and his successors, quhat before was voluntary becomes ever after necessary. It is voluntary to a woman to chuse such ane one for her husband and to a people, quhat king they will at first; both being once done, neither can the woman or the people free themselves from obedience and subjection to the husband and the prince quhen they please.

To the third:– In a politick consideration, the king and his people are not two but one body politick, quhereof the king is the head; and soe farr are they from contrariety and opposite motions as there is nothing good or ill for the one quhilk is not just soe for the other: if their ends and endeavours be diverse and never soe litle excentrick, either that king inclyneth to tyranny or that people to disloyalty; if they be contrary, it's mere tyranny or mere disloyalty.

To the fourth:– The king's prerogative and the subjects' priviledge are soe farr from incompatibility as the one can never stand unless supported by the other. For the soveraigne being strong and in full posession of his lawfull power and prerogative is able to protect his subjects from oppression and mentean their libertys intire; otherwise, not. On the other side, a people enjoying freely their just libertys and priviledges menteaneth the prince's honnour and prerogative out of the great affection they cary toward him, quhilk is the greatest strenth against forraigne invasion or intestyne insurrection that a prince can possibly be possessed with.

To the fifth:– It is a new fallacy, for quhat is essentiall to one thing can never be given to another. The eye may lose its sight, the ear its hearing, but can never be given to the hand or foot or any other member; and as the head of the natural body may be deprived of invention, judgement or memory and the rest of the members receive noe part thereof, soe subjects not being capable of the essentiall parts of government properly and privativly belonging to the prince, being taken from him, they can never be imparted to them without change of that government and the essence and being of the same.

Quhen a king is restrained from the lawfull use of his power and subjects can make noe use of it, as under a king they cannot, quhat can follow but a subversion of government, anarchy and confusion. Now to any man that understands these things only the proceedings of these times may seeme strange and may expostulate with us thus, "Noblemen and gentlemen of good quality quhat doe ye mean? Will you teach the people to put down the Lord's annoynted and lay violent hands on his authority to quhom both you and they owe subjection and asistance with your goods, lifes and fortunes by all the lawes of God and man? Doe ye think to stand and domineer over the people in ane aristocratick way, who owe you small or noe obligation? It's you under your natural prince that gets all imployment pregnant of honnour or profite in peace or warr. You are subjects of his liberality; your houses decayed, either by merite or his grace and favour are repaired, your honnours annexed to his authority, without quihilk you fall in contempt. The people, jealouse of their liberty quhen ye deserve best, to shelter themselves, will make you shorter by the head, or serve you with ane ostracisme. If their first act be against kingly power, their nixt will be against you: for if the people be of a feirce nature, they will cutt your throats, as the Switzers did; if mild, you shall be contemptible, as some of ancient houses are in Holland, quhere every burgomaster is the better man, your honnours, life, fortunes stand at the discretion of a seditiouse preacher. And you, ye meaner people of Scotland, who are not capable of a respublick for many grave reasons, why are you induced by spetiouse pretexts to your own heavy prejudice and detriment to be instruments of others' ambition? Doe ye not know quhen the monarchicall government is shaken, the great ones strive for the garland with your blood and your fortunes, quhereby you gain nothing but instead of a race of kings who have governed you two thousand years with peace and justice and have preserved your libertys against all domineering nations, shall purchase to your selves vulturs and tygres to reign over your posterity and your selves shall endure all these miserys, masacres and proscriptions of the triumvirate of Rome, the kingdome fall again into the hands of one who of necessity must, and for reason of state will, tyrannize over you, for kingdomes acquired by blood and violence are by the same means enterteaned. And you great men, if any such be among you soe blinded with ambition, who aim soe high at the crown, doe you think we are soe farr degenerate from the vertue, valour and fidelity of our treu and lawfull soveraigne, soe constantly enterteaned by our ancestors, as to suffer you with all your policy to reigne over us? Take heed you be not Aesop's dogg and lose the cheese for the shaddow in the well. And thou, seditiouse preacher, who studys to put the soveraignty in the people's hands for thy own ambitiouse ends as being able by thy wicked eloquence and hypocrisy to infuse into them quhat thou pleases, know this, that this people is more incapable of soveraignty than any other knowen. Thou art abused like a pedant by the nimbler witted noblemen. Go, goe along with them to shake the present government, not for thy ends to posesse the people with it, but like a cunning tennis player lets the ball goe to the wall, quhere it cannot stay, that he may take it at the bound with more ease.

And quhereas a durable peace with England, quhilk is the wish and desire of all honest men, is pretended, surely it's a great solecisme in us to aim at ane end of peace with them and overthrow the only means for that end. It's the king's majesty's soveraignty over both that unites us in affection and is only able to reconcile questions among us quhen they fall. To endeavour then the dissolution of that band of our union is noe wise to establish a durable peace but rather to procure emnity and warr betwixt bordering nations, quhere occasions of quarrell is never wanting nor men ever ready to take hold of them."

Now, Sir, you have my opinion concerning your desire and that quhilk I esteem truth set down nakedly for your use, not adorned for publick veu; and if the zeal of my soveraigne and country have transported me a litle to farr, I hope you will excuse the errours proceeding from soe good a cause of

Your humble servant,
Montrois

WILLIAM DRUMMOND of Hawthornden (1585–1649) is the only Scottish writer of the seventeenth century who really achieved the status of man of letters. He was the son of an official at the court of James VI and was able to make contacts with men of the king's old literary circle like Sir William Alexander and Sir Robert Aytoun. The appearance of his celebratory pieces, "Teares on the Death of Moeliades" (1613) on Prince Henry and "Forth Feasting" for James's visit to Edinburgh and of the editions of his *Poems* of 1614(?) and 1616 led to contacts with English writers. Drayton wrote to him. Jonson visited him at Hawthornden, and Drummond took down his views on the literary scene. His library was well stocked, and he took pains to assimilate and improve on what could be learnt from the European masters of late petrarchan modes. His religious poems *Flowres of Sion* came out with his prose meditation, *A Cypresse Grove* in 1623.

The political upheavals of Charles's reign drew a number of squibs from him as well as serious pieces. In politics he was a constitutional conservative with sensible views on religious toleration and the folly of coercion. Like Napier and Montrose, he feared Charles's innovations and equally the tyranny of subjects, especially clerics. But he kept out of political trouble. He prudently subscribed to the Covenant and Solemn League and Covenant ("Give me a thousand covenants, I'll subscrive/Them all"). And while he wrote anti-covenanting papers like *Irene* (1638) and *ΣΚΙΑΜΑΧΙΑ* (1643), he did not publish them. They circulated in manuscript, though, and he had to clear himself with Covenanting committees.

Drummond's poetry is very skilful with certain aesthetic effects, usually expressing a refined melancholy – he loved to be sad. He can, however, be fairly boisterous in his satirical verse. His prose is an elaborate affair. His arguments proceed through a stately unfolding of figures, broad antitheses and sententious observations. No other Scottish writer of the century approaches his mastery of cadence. Among his political writings, *Irene* is the best example of his manner, but it has already been anthologized in this series in Robert H. MacDonald's edition, *William Drummond of Hawthornden: Poems and Prose* (1976). *ΣΚΙΑΜΑΧΙΑ* is less polished and worked over, and perhaps for that reason conveys more urgency. The ideas are less general and more closely applied to what was going on, and Drummond makes good use of his historical reading to characterize the state of a country overrun by clerical politics.

The fight with or for a shadow the Greek title speaks of was the business of the Cross Petition. In 1642 a letter had come to the General Assembly from the English Parliament raising the possibility of religious conformity between the two nations, a project whose results were to be the Solemn League and Covenant and the Westminster Assembly. But meanwhile the letter drew from Charles a declaration warning his Scottish subjects against these overtures. From the radical side, a petition came to the Privy Council that the appeal from the English Parliament should be published, from the constitutional moderates, A Cross Petition that the Council should do nothing to endanger the king's authority or the peace of the country. Drummond wrote in defence of the Cross Petition after it had been denounced by the General Assembly.

ΣKIAMAXIA was edited by Bishop Sage in *The Works of William Drummond* of Hawthornden (Edin., 1711). The text I have used is National Library of Scotland MS. 2058, ff. 260–64; 265–66; 269–73; 275–76; 297–300; 302–5.

ΣKIAMAXIA

Amongst all the sortes of people upon the face of the earth, christianes should be of the most mild, peaceable disposition, humble, gentle, mercifull, bountifull and charitable not onlye to those of their own beleefe, but to such as are without and to all men in generall. Amongst all christianes these who beare a publike charge in the Church of God and who are advanced to teache and governe his people should be eminent, as in their place, in these christian vertues and in the practises of everye pious dutye towards all men; they should not be lifted up with pryd, double-tongued, strikeres, brawleres; of these hollye endeveures glorye ariseth to God and peace to men. So soone as these who beare a publike charge in the Church and should be examples and precedents of holinesse to others beginne to breathe great matteres alltogether estranged and contrarye to their vocation and strive to prostrate princes and people to their good wills and pleasure, would prescribe lawes to all men, as if they were their subjectes, confound hollye and profane thinges together and in stead of the mild doctrine of our maister, Jesus Christ, and of being embassadoures of the glad tydinges of salvation, become herauldes of warre, of preacheres turning souldeurs and for gownes delighte to glance in steele and armes, then everye thing turneth upside down; divisiones, discordes, tumultes not onlye arise and multiplye in kingdomes but in evrye cittye, nay allmost in evrye familye. The fire and the aire out of their naturall places make not more horrible shakinges of the bodye of the earth than these men doe of the politicke bodyes of kingdomes and comonwealthes, confounding the inhabitants of the world. The late bloudye warres of Europe can witnesse this; the fearfull distructiones of this isle represente this unto us as in a mirrouer; and if the mercyes of almightye God were not inexpressable towards us, these men would yet bathe us in our own blood, involving us in most incivill warres amongst our selves.

If small thinges may be adjoyned to great, latlye what a small sparke would these men blow up in a bonfire, what a little brooke make swell to a great lake to overflow and drown this miserable countrey! The king's Majesty, being driven through the ambition of some persones by the force and violence of rude and tumultuous assemblyes from his cittye of London and his House of Parlement *ne in colluvione rerum majestatem suam contumeliae offerret*,[116] after the authors of those combinationes had sent a declaration to his subjectes of Scotland to afford them speedye and powerfull assistance, raise armes for their defence against him, sent a letter to the lordes of his Privie Councell of Scotland declaring the injust proceedinges of this oligarchike power against his royall persone and kinglye office and of the equitye of his taking of armes for the vindicating his crown and state from the implacable malice of those men, recommending to the lordes of his Privie Councell that this letter should be communicated and published to all his loving subjectes. His Majesty's most reasonable command was no sooner obeyed when some men, whose ease and rest is onlye amidst factiones and warres, who never find their accountes and reckninges right nor any saftye for their persones but in the trouble of the state of the kingdome (being like surgeones and sextones, who thrive and waxe more wealthye by the death and plague of the common people) umbrageouslye and with simulate devotione stirre some yonge noblemen and gentlemen ignorant of their hid and misterious intentiones, with a number of the credulous clergye, to assemble and gather together from sundrye partes of the countrey and present to the commissioneres appointed by the king's Majesty and his Parlement of Scotland for conserving the articles of the treatye[117] for the establishing of the peace betweene the two kingdomes a supplication for publishing the declaration of the pretended Parlement of England[118] to the subjects of Scotland also, that the Parlement's declaration and the king's letter should come forth together with equall power, credit and authoritye amongst the king's subjectes of Scotland.

This forme of proceeding, how specious so ever in the outward pretences of religion, seeming tumultuous and scandalous and the verye same which was practised by the oligarchye of the Parlement at London in suborning the multitude and making them give in those petitions to the Parlement which some of themselves had long before limned to the life and formed and which in effect dissolved the bodye of that great counsell and his Majesty's honour and authoritye being wounded in that declaration, some noblemen and gentlemen to whom his king's honour had ever beene deare, out of feare of his Majesty's interest and of their fore-sight of imminent dangeres to the state of thes kingdom, gave a petitione to the commissioneres for the treatye of peace. . . .

No sooner was this petition presented to the commissioneres when some of the clergye of contentious and stormye dispositiones, men grown haughtye of their place and arbitrarye power as being commissioneres of the Generall Assemblye, object, protest and supplicate against it, and not content to have had all satisfaction offered to them and to have obtained what they most required of the commissioneres for the treatye of peace, neither respecting the good and honest meaning of the noblemen nor their places nor some of their former services done in the late troubles, as if they would raise trophes of their victoryes when it had beene better to have covered woundes of shame with a vaile of silence, not onlye published a declaration against their petitione but against their persones and (which no Papist would ever have done except in the porche of a church) caused, as if it had beene a new evangele and authenticke scripture to abuse the credulitye of the poore people, read it with all solemnitye thorough most of the kirkes of this kingdome, verifying that *immoderata potentia non diu manet intra justas metas.*[119]

It is strange the commissioneres of an Assemblye should publish a declaration upon that which the whole bodye of an Assemblye would hardlye justifye to be honest and equitable, except they should be brought to beleeve that the churches cannot erre and what they publish should have the power of the Word wryten and what they call abomination in the Church of Rome to approve in their own church as orthodoxe doctrine. Generall Councels have beene contrarye one to another and so have Generall Assemblyes, as the Councell of Constantinople and Councell of Nice contrarly sayes.[120] All men are lyers in their wordes and sineres in their workes. A great favourer of churchmen said the Church had the keyes of authoritye given her but not the keyes of knowledge, which, if true, she may manye wayes erre, especialye when she midleth with matteres which are not with in her horizon. And thus with out heresie, her declarationes maye suffer an answer. To have power to publish declarationes and to suffer none to replye unto them and answer them is to deprive a commonwealth of her libertye. Libertye of life ceaseth when libertye of speech ceaseth. Manye would withold themselves from doing evill if they were assured to heare thereof thereafter.

The Declaration consisting of observationes and animadversiones gives out a sentence condemnatorye against our petition: that it is no thing but a secret plot and subtle undermining of all the present designes of this kirke and kingdome for unitye of religion and all the worke of God in this land, and although it maye seeme but an errour in the doing, yet doth it implye contempt, usurpation and division, and being winked at, may be the cause of much disturbance and confusion in these tymes. . . .

The matter is . . . taxed that our petition . . . is to overturne the verye foundation of all your endevoures for the worke of reformation. Wee desire you, bretheren, to expresse in more plaine and easier termes what great foundationes of reformation and principall aymes of yours wee have endevoured to overturne. Wherin have wee offended by setting down Brownists, Separatistes,[121] schismatikes, Papistes and overpassing prelates? Is our advice evill that wee desire wee should not prescrive lawes to our neighboures? Yee will saye that yee intend a reformation of the governement of the Church of England and a conforming of it to the governement of the Kirke of Scotland, to which wee seeme to be dissonant. This, bretheren, is our desire; to this wee would contribute our diligence and best endevoures, so it might be peaceablye brought to passe and without troubling the state of our neeghbour countrey. But to these honest intentiones of ours and to this great change, what if the king's Majesty and such of the nobilitye, gentrye and commones of England who are of his opinion shall oppose and will not suffer the governement of their church to be altered? – it being after their opinions more conforme to the monarchicall governement of the state than our Presbyteriall, which is more conforme to the governement of a republike and cantoned townes; for where equalitye is, a monarchie is hardlye maintained, and *consueta longo tempore etiamsi deteriora insuetis minus molesta esse solent.*[122] Will yee arise in armes? Will yee imbrue your hands and swordes in the blood of those for whom Christ hath shed his and stirre up his Majesty's subjectes to a civill warre against him, ay, and whilst hee abolish his Episcopall governement [and our Presbyteriall be embraced][123]? And for this cause will yee hazard your lives and fortunes, fight it out to the last man in both kingdomes? Wee thinke this ayme and foundation neither agreeth with faith nor reasone, and if yee preach this doctrine to a good people, wee thinke that yee give them serpentes for fish and stones for bread; since the wrath of man worketh not the righteousnesse of God (Jacobus, cap. 1, v. 20). It is written God shall persuade Japhet to dwell in the tentes of Sem, not one word of fighting. Did our Lord Jesus Christ and his apostles propagate their religion by pikes and musketes? Where find yee it is lawfull for christianes to establish their religion by armes? It is an especiall maxime of state amongst the Turkes to determine and establish deade religione by armes. The Church should be planted by the spirituall sword not by the materiall. The soules of men being spirituall substances, lead and iron will not worke upon them. The remedye of armes is not that which wee should seeke after to amend their diseases and infirmityes. Spirites are not overcome save by reasone. They will not be constrained and forced to beleeve but by persuasiones. This will be to tyrannize over the consciences, which in the beginning of the Reformation in Germanye and France by all Protestantes was cryed out upon and condemned as tyrannicall and antichristian. But though it wer lawfull to propagate relligion by armes, where find yee it lawfull to shed christian bloud for the externall forme of the governement of the Church? All the world knowes that monarchye, optamacye[124] and populare governement (making the men who beare these charges good) ar all good in state. And why may not these same sortes of governementes, being limited, be receaved in any christian church? All formes not corrupted are good, and none can discern what is best save by what is possest since everye change is dangerous. . . .

Doe yee thinke it is small matter to give not onlye occasion but a cause and subject sufficient to make a schisme in the true Protestant relligion (for the religion professed in England these fourescore yeeres hath ever beene by all Protestant churches in Europe acknowledged such) and that it is lawfull now, when this religion is so impaired, weakened and brought under in the other kingdomes of Europe, to embrue our handes in our own bloud and fight whether the professoures[125] thereof shall be governed by some few good men and well chosen of our selves, which is optamacye, or by the lawes and directiones of manye, which is democracye? Man getteth not that mischeefe but what hee seeketh and buyeth with his own foolishnesse. Bretheren, these tymes require other thoughtes. Take a view of the map of the earth. There yee shall find that the kingdome of Scotland is not all the earth and that England and it together make but an isle. But being so blissed and contented as yee are by your late reformation, why would yee involve your selves in the debates and quarrelles of another kingdome? Yee are men of great faith if yee beleeve the Parlement of England will receave relligion from us (for this in the politikes' consideration is holden a servitude) and establish our Presbyteriall governement in their church. Neither have they promised any such matter by their returne to the commissioneres of our Generale Assemblye, but onlye they desire some godlye and learned divines of our church to be sent to them, by whose advice an uniformitye in church governement maye be obtained (which seemes to import they have an intention to alterre our presente governement) and a more easye passage made to the setling of one confession of faith, one lyturgye, one cathechisme; and heere yee are to fight for religion and governement at least of the Church, which but yet is *in fieri*.[126] By too much trust in bladderes wee may put our selves in hazard of sinking under watter, the old law must be our guyde till the new be made – faire pretextes, till by our meanes these men have brought fordwards their own endes and intentiones, and sufficient to besotte these who would ever have religione new trimmed and dime by some powder of projection[127] the eyes of the rud Scot, as wee were wont to be stiled by those men. . .

If the king doth adore any other God, any other Christ, but what hee should, if hee aspire to any other heaven, embrace any other creed, any other baptisme, if hee be an idolater, if an heretike, if a despiser of God and man, let us take armes against him. If hee be an oppressour, if hee hath embrued our scaffoldes with innocent bloud, if hee hath dishonoured our wyves, ravished our daughters from out our armes, robbed us of our richesse, land and possessiones, let us take armes against him. If hee hath denyed the poorest man justice, if hee hath not granted us more than any, nay, than all his predecessoures did before him, let us take armes against him. But if hee be more devote than the most relligious of his subjectes, if hee be more free of the great vices of his kingdome than any of his subjectes, if hee hath laboured to maintaine the free Protestant relligion to the outermost of his power, if hee hath never wronged any man in his estate or persone, if hee be the best man of all his dominiones and *vere magnus quia bonus*,[128] why should wee whisper of taking armes against him? Why should wee not arise in armes for him? Let the most malitious of this new oligarchye tell what hath hee done why they will not sufferre him to raigne, to live after that forme of governement and obedience in which his father, Queene Elizabeth and Edward the Sixth raigned and lived. What hath a people had to make them happye which was not enjoyed, saftye from being oppressed by any at home, peace with those abroad, plentye evrye where. There is not a greater wickednesse than when benefaites are turned against him of whom they are receaved.

Wee are accused that wee could not be moved to parte from our petition nor to acknowledge our errroures, either in the matter of the petition or manner of the petitioning. Belike that is not right and just which is trulye right and just but that which yee discrive and decree so to be. Doth the essences of thinges change after your appointmentes? Make an act against the ebbing and flowing of the seas and that our winteres be not so long or our summeres so cold, and when yee are obeyed, wee shall beleeve you. Let the two petitiones be matched and conferred together and then shall it appeare which of them hath most reasone and where the erroures are scattered in matter or the forme of petitioning. Our petition is for our native king, to whom wee have sworne fidelitye, that hee suffer neither in his honour nor authoritye. Your petition is for a number of men who have combined themselves together against him, raised armes to make him suffer not onlye in his honour and authoritye but who are daylye endangering his royall persone, as their canon and musket balles discharged so neare unto him can testifye. Our petition is for the preservation of that peace and libertye wee have so graciouslye by the mercye of almightye God obtained and enjoye and not to make our selves umpires of neighbour debates, involve our selves in new disorders, making other men's cases our querrells. Your petitione is for the endangering of our peace and libertyes by marrying the quarrelles of men who for their own interest, pretend religion for altering the ancient governement of a stranger country. Our petition is that the true Protestant relligion, so sorely wounded in this isle, maye recover strength and power, herisyes maye be punished or suppressed, shismes taken away, the king maye be obeyed, brotherlye love continued between the two nationes, justice executed, the strong not oppressing the weake, the guiltye the innocent, the people maye enjoye their own in quietnesse and not be longer thralled with the grievous burthenes of insolent men and oppressoures. Your petitione is that the Protestant relligion maye yet receave more deadlye woundes by mutuall discordes and batailles for the externall forme of the governement of the Church, that the proceedings of the pretended Parlement be allwise approved, the kinge's proceedings, how just so ever, condemned, the strong maye keep under the weake, the guiltye, the innocent, a faire way may be given to rebellion in these naughtye dayes, warres may continue, souldeoures and men, whose miserable fortunes at home maye turne them to any mischeefe abroad, be made rich, the more peaceable sort of honest people become indigent and beggeres, neither having to intertaine their poore lives nor to provide for their miserable childrene, whilst the whole monnyes of the kingdome shall be taken up under pretence of the publike charges, everye man's estate taxed to hold up your utopian communwealth, bloudie cut throtes, as your apostle in his storie nameth them, be intertained and this isle become a scorne to the transmarine nationes abroad . . .

For conclusion yee leave the matter and take you to the persones, whom it appeares yee hated more than the action of petitioning. These yee distinguish in malignantes and incendiaryes and in not malignantes and not incendiaryes, whom yee saye are unequallye yoaked against your own worke, which yee call the worke of God, unlesse yee understand the terrible warre which yee are to raise amongst us, for yee know *non est malum in civitate quod non facit Dominus;*[129] or is this, as yee name manye a seditious and nonsense declaratione, the work of God? or as your Declaration, when it was read in the kirkes, was the hollye word of the blissed Trinitye? Presumptuous church men have proven often worse than the foxes of Samson. They but burnt the corne when the feildes were whit for the harvest, but these have brunt up whole townes, male and female and children and old men, guiltye or not guiltye, holy or prophane, makinge . . . all under the law of their spoyle and licence, dyed the whit feildes in bloud, turning them in a Golgotha as in our own country the Battaille of Pinkye can testifye.[130]

Incendiarye and malignant are wordes of the language of Babell, and wee retorte them upon the first petitioneres and those men who are ever making all thinges new but turne them still worse and worse, whilst they have no boundes nor limites to their novationes, the glosses of roving heades being infinit. The names of Guelfes and Gibilines[131] in Italye, the names of Huguenot, Ravilliack, Papillard[132] in France brought forth most cruell and terrible massacres, and if the mercyes of God be not unmeasurable exceeding towards this isle, by all likelihood the names of malignant, incendiarye, roundhead, puritane shall work little better heer. By you these men are called incendiaryes and malignants who would reestablish the king in his throne and have justice executed upon rebelles, who oppose to a vast arbitrarye power of taxing the poore people, spoyleing the country, turning all upside down by new magistracyes and novationes. *Sublata justitia quid aliud sunt regna quam latrocinia?*[133] A king that doth not punish rebelles shall never during his raigne keep his subjectes in peace nor enjoye himselfe any quietnesse. To save the life of a malefactour is to take the lives of the good men and to offend God and the commonwealth.

There are no such incendiaryes as these men who strive to anticipate the conflagration of the world by the destructiones of states and raising of discordes and disobedience not onlye in evrye countrye but almost everye citye and familye. And these men are presumptuous, ignorant and hypocriticall churchmen, who not keeping themselves within their own vocationes and limites (bussye bodyes!) doe assume the power of kinges and emproures to governe states, use an arbitrarye power, first over the consciences, than upon the persones, goodes and fortunes of men. Plotteres they are of civill warres, fire brandes and matches of communwealthes, and all under pretence of relligion. The least noyse of an hammer must not be heared in the temple of God. But these men have filled the Church of God with lowd alarmes, clashing of bloudye weapons and groanes of dying men. . . .

These are they that set at variance the mightye potentates of the earth, who otherwise perhaps would sit down in an happye peace. They are they that rend whole kingdomes, distracte people, dissolve societyes, nourish faction and sedition, lay waste the most flourishing kingdomes and turne the richest cittyes to dust and rubbish. These men have assasined kinges amidst their armyes, poysoned an emprour by the verye sacrament.[134] Out of ambition to governe, they ruinated the christiane Empyre of the East and have done litle better with the Empyre in the West. They have set all Europe latlye in combustion (is not a church man the Antichrist?). They have turned men's estates so desperate that the living at this tyme envye the dead and manye wish they had never cume in this world to be partakeres of the barbarous dissentiones amongst christianes, who are spirituall brotheres and should live in amitye together; when now any christian shall live in greater saftye amongst the Turkes, Jewes, infidelles than hee can live and drive out this miserable span of mortalitye amongst men professing one Jesus Christ with him; the christian relligion being brought by these men to conflict in outward showes and ceremonyes, rites, songes, springes,[135] bablinges, tautologyes regarding rather *sonantia quam solida*[136] and disputationes of more labour than profit and in an ambition to live backward to the relligion of Rome and what remaines being blind obedience for insurrectiones against princes, tumultes, murtheries, plundering all men who thinke not their thoughtes, have not the like desires, judgementes and opiniones, brothers publishing declarationes one against another, fighting first by pennes then by pikes and musketes to the great affrightment of all that are not of the faith, especiallye of the Jewes, who will rather keep their auncient rites than be partakers of our dissentiones; when pure relligion is this: "to visit the faitherlesse and widowes in their affliction and to keep himselfe unspotted from the world" (James cap. 1, v. 27), "for this is the message which yee heard from the beginning, that wee should love one another" (John, First Epistle, cap. 3, v. 11), "not as Cain who was of that wicked one and slew his brother," and "this commandement have wee from him that hee who loveth God loveth his brother also" (cap. 4, v. 21). . . . "Onlye by pryd commeth contention" (Proverbs cap. 13, v. 10). There is more pryd to be found under a monke's cowle and a broad jesuiticall hate than under the fairest creasted healmes and the richest diademes of princes. They terme themselves free and are so indeed in as much as they are not subject to reasone, a people who see no thing but faultes, because they seeke after no thing else. They fill countryes with calumnyes and at last with slaughtered men.

From the violence and rage of those men and their *sapientia phrenetica*,[137] allmightye God preserve all kinges and potentates and evrye good christian and well affected subject and grant the kinges of Great Britaigne heroicke, true fortitud and power to bring under all rebelles and hypocrites, who under the maske of devotion would cast them out of their royall thrones and turne the church governement and state in an anarchye and confusion.

SIR THOMAS URQUHART of CROMARTIE (1611-60) was an eccentric and dilettante and still a man of genuine intellectual accomplishments. He studied at Aberdeen and completed his education with a Grand Tour, which by his own account he carried off with some of the éclat of his hero, the Admirable Crichton. On the outbreak of the First Bishop's War he joined the Royalists of the North East, who drove the Covenanters before them and for a time held Aberdeen until Montrose ousted them. He then went on a visit to London, was knighted by Charles and published his dreadful *Epigrams, Divine and Moral*. He returned in 1647 to his tower of Cromarty, where he carried on with his studies and succeeded in spite of the persecutions of his creditors and the local Covenanters in bringing out his *Trissotetras,* an ingenious but impenetrable system of trigonometry. On the news of the execution of Charles, the Royalists of the North rose again and Urquhart with them. Although the Covenanting Parliament declared him a rebel and a traitor, he was able to join the Scottish army of 1651, got together to place Charles II on the throne. For some reason he took his papers along with him in a trunk. The trunk was lost in the defeat of Worcester, or so he tells us in ΄EKΣKYBAΛAYPON, and with it his schemes for the benefit of mankind and the results of his studies. He himself was captured and imprisoned. Although he was granted parole, his estates were forfeit unless he could prove to the Commonwealth authorities that he deserved exceptional consideration. His literary output of the following years with its remarkable self-advertisement was meant to prove how exceptional he was. ΠANTOXPONOXANON (1652) traces the descent of the Urquharts through princes of Greece from Adam. ΄EKΣKYBAΛAYPON (1652) and again *Logopandecteision* (1653) outline his project for a universal language. Even his wonderful translation of the first two books of Rabelais (1653) was also perhaps meant to prove his worth to the authorities. But his efforts were in vain. He went abroad and according to the family story died of a fit of laughter when he heard of the Restoration of Charles II.

'ΕΚΣΚΥΒΑΛΑΥΡΟΝ, *Or the Discovery of A most exquisite Jewel, more precious than Diamonds inchased in Gold, the like whereof was never seen in any age* is in part an advertisement for his scheme of a universal language, in part a *Vindication of the honours of Scotland from the Infamy whereinto the Rigid Presbyterian party of that Nation out of their Covetousness and ambition most dissembledly hath involved it.* To this part belong the accounts of eminent Scots including the justly famous one of the Admirable Crichton and an attack on the Presbyterian party from which the passage below is taken (pp. 234–52). It is easy to point to the features of Urquhart's fantastic style, its logofascination, self-parody, elaborate yet headlong syntax, its desemboguing of learning, but it is not so easy to know how to take it. Some of these features are admirably suited to his translation of Rabelais, but they make his tracts curious reading. The earlier seventeenth century had a taste for literary self-display and learned buffoonery. One can see that in Burton's *Anatomy of Melancholy* and one can see Swift making it look foolish in *A Tale of a Tub.* But Urquhart's genuine freakishness and extraordinary love of words make him hard to place.

There is a selection of other parts of 'ΕΚΣΚΥΒΑΛΑΥΡΟΝ in Richard Boston, *The Admirable Urquhart* (London: Gordon Fraser, 1975) and also in R. D. S. Jack's *Scottish Prose, 1550–1700.* Urquhart assumes the name of Christianus Presbyteromastix and explains that he had adopted this pseudonym so that with the precedents of Virgil and Scaliger in mind he can talk of himself in the third person.

'ΕΚΣΚΥΒΑΛΑΥΡΟΝ

It doth suffice him that the main ground of all his proceedings is honesty, that he endeavoreth the prosecuting of just ends by upright means. And seeing the events of things are not in the power of man, he voluntarily recommendeth unto providence the over-ruling of the rest. He hath no prejudicate principles, nor will he be wedded to self-opinions.

And yet, as I conceive it, he believeth that there is no government, whether ecclesiastical or civil, upon earth that is *jure divino* if that divine right be taken in a sense secluding all other forms of government save it alone from the priviledge of that title; those *piae fraudes*[138] and political whimsies being obtruded upon tender consciences to no other end but that without expense of war they might be plyable in their obedience to the injunctions of the vice-gerents of the law, meerly by deterring them from acting any thing contrary to the will of the primitive legislator for fear of celestial punishment.

As for pacts and covenants, it is my opinion that he thinks they are no further obligatory, and consequently being annihilated, no more to be mentioned, much less urged, when the ground whereupon they were built or cause for which they were taken are not in vigour to have any more influence upon the contracters; for *idem est non esse et non operari; non entium nullae sunt affectiones;* and *sublato fundamento tolluntur et omnia quae illi superstruuntur.*[139]

I am confident the consistorian[140] party will be so ill pleased with the freedom of this expression that they will account him a malignant or a sectary that hath penned it. Therefore in my conceit, to use their cavilling idiom, a malignant and independent wil better sympathize with one another then either of them with the Presbyter, whose principles how consistent they are with monarchy, or any other kind of temporal soveraignty, let any man judge that is versed in the story of Geneva, the civil wars of France and Bohemia and history of Queen Mary of Scotland, although what hath been done by the Kirkists these last dozen of yeers had been altogether buryed in oblivion, that nothing had been known of their unanimous opposition by the Presbyterian armies at Dunslaw, Newburne, Marstonmoor and Hereford to the late king's designes, crowned by his own imprisonment at Newcastle and Holmby and that after proclaiming Charles the Second at the market-cross of Edenburgh king of the three realms of England, Scotland and Ireland, that they had wounded him and shed his blood in the persons of the peerage of Huntely[141] and Montrose had been utterly forgotten.

What gallant subjects these Presbyterians have been, are for the present and will prove in times coming to any kinde of secular power, you may perceive by King James his *ΒΑΣΙΛΙΚΟΝ ΔΩΡΟΝ*, the late King's *ΕΙΚΩΝ ΒΑΣΙΛΙΚΗ* and this young King's *ΒΑΣΙΛΙΚΟΣ ΑΔΥΝΑΣΤΗΣ*;[142] they to basilical rule, or any other temporal soveraignty, being in all its genders, and that at all occasions, as infectious as ever was the basilisk's[143] sight to the eye of man.

For of a king they onely make use for their own ends, and so they will of any other supreme magistracie that is not of their own erection. Their kings are but as the kings of Lacedemon, whom the Ephors presumed to fine for any small offence, or as the puppy-kings,[144] which after children have trimmed with bits of taffata and ends of silver lace and set them upon wainscoat cupboards besides marmalade and sugar cakes, are oftentimes disposed of, even by those that did pretend so much respect unto them, for a two-peny custard, a pound of figs, or mess of cream.

Verily, I think they make use of kings in their consistorian state as we do of card kings in playing at the hundred, any one whereof, if there be appearance of a better game without him and that the exchange of him for another incoming card is like to conduce more for drawing of the stake, is by good gamesters without any ceremony discarded; or as the French on the Epiphany day use their *Roy de la febve*, or king of the bean, whom, after they have honoured with drinking of his health and shouting aloud, "Le roy boit, le roy boit," they make pay for all the reckoning, not leaving him sometimes one peny, rather then that the exorbitancie of their debosh should not be satisfied to the full. They may be likewise said to use their king as the players at nine-pins do the middle kyle,[145] which they call the king, at whose fall alone they aim the sooner to obtain the gaining of their prize; or as about Christmais we do the king of Misrule, whom we invest with that title to no other end, but to countenance the bacchanalian riots and preposterous disorders of the family where he is installed.

The truth of all this appears by their demeanour to Charles the Second, whom they crowned their king at Sterlin,[146] and who, though he be for comeliness of person, valour, affability, mercy, piety, closeness of counsel, veracity, foresight, knowledge and other vertues both moral and intellectual in nothing inferiour to any of his hundred and ten predecessors, had nevertheless no more rule in effect over the Presbyterian senate of Scotland then any of the six foresaid mock-kings had above those by whom they were dignified with the splendour of royal pomp.

That it is so, I appeal to the course taken by them for assisting him whom they called their king against them whom I must confess they hate more then him; for admitting of none to have any charge in state, church, or army but such as had sworn to the eternity of the Covenant and inerrability of the Presbyterian See, lest otherwise, like Achan's wedge, they should bring a judgement upon the land,[147] some lords and many others so principled, after that by their king they had been intrusted with commissions to levie regiments of both horse and foot, together with other officers subordinate to them, did, under pretext of making the king a glorious king and the Covenant to triumph at the gates of Rome with a pseudo-sanctimonial trick of zeal – legerdemain – subtilty and performing the admirable feats of making a little weak man, unfit for military service, a tall strong and warlike champion, and that onely by the sweet charm of laying twenty rexdolars[148] upon his head and shoulders, as also by the archangelical inchantment of fifteen double angels,[149] had the skill to make an Irish hobbie[150] or Galloway nag as sufficient for the field fight as any Spanish genet or Naples courser.

In prosecution of which wonderful exploits, some of them approved themselves such exquisite alchymists that many of both the cavalry and infantry with their arms, ammunition and apparel were by them converted into pure gold and silver; by means whereof, although the army shrunk into half the proposed number in both horse, foot and dragoons and all the most necessary accommodations for either camp, leaguer,[151] or march, was chymically transformed into the aforesaid wel-beloved metal, they nevertheless put such undoubted confidence into the goodness of their cause that by vertue thereof no less miraculous acts were expected and promised by the prophecies of their Neo-Levites out of scripture [to be] atchieved by them against the malignants and sectaries then those of Gideon with his water-lappers and Jonathan with his armour-bearer against the Midianites and Philistims,[152] to so great a height did their presumption reach. And yet when it came to the push, those that had received greatest profit by the country assesments and ruined with cruellest exactions the poor yeomanry were the first that returned homewards, being loth to hazard their precious persons lest they should seem to trust to trust to the arm of flesh.

Notwithstanding this backsliding from martial prowess of the godly officers, with the epenthesis of an "l"[153] (in which number I inrol not al, but the greater part of those that were commissionated with the Scot-ecclesiastical approbation), their rancour and spleen being still more and more sharpned against the English nation, they in their tedious pharisaical prayers before supper and sesquihoral[154] graces upon a dish of skink and leg of mutton would so imbue the mindes of the poor swains, on whose charge they were, with vaticinations of help from heaven against the Sennacheribs that were about to infest Hezekiah's host[155] and the peace of their Israel that the innocent sufferers having sustained more prejudice by quartering, plundering and continual impositions of those their hypocritical countrymen then ever their predecessors had done by all the devastations of the ancient English, Saxons, Danes and Romanes, the holier they were in outward shew, their actions proving still the more diabolical, they in recompence of those aerial, or rather fiery ejaculations, recommended the avenging of their wrongs to God and heartily loaded them, and that deservedly, with as many curses and execrations as they had lost of pence; the pretty effect of a good cause and result sutable to the project of making the jure-divine Presbytery a government, which, besides its universality and eternity, should in matter of dominion be for its sublimity placed above all the potentates on the earth, preferring by that account a Scotish moderator to a Romane dictator, although they minded not that such as claimed most right to this generalissima-jurisdiction were, unknown to themselves, chained in fetters of iron as slaves to the tyrannie of two insolent masters, the concupiscible and irascible appetites.

Who doubteth, that is not blinded with the ablepsie[156] of an implicite zeal, but that by such contrivements the three foresaid dominions, together with Wales, were as fully projected to be subject to the uncontrolable commands of the Kirk as the territories of Romania, Urbino, Ferrara and Avignon to the See of Rome, though with this advantage on the Pope's side that joynt to the power wherewith he is invested by his Papality, he ruleth over those parts by the right of a secular prince, which title they cannot pretend to.

Were those kirkmen free from covetousness and ambition, whereinto that most of them are no less deeply plunged then any laick in the world, sufficient proof within these two yeers hath been given in Scotland by their laying claim to the fifth part of all the rents of the land under the notion of tythes, devesting noblemen of their rights of patronages and bringing their persons to stand before them on penitentiary pews (like so many varlets) in mendiciary and gausapinal garments,[157] not so much for any trespass they had comitted as thereby to confirm the soveraignty of their hierarchical jurisdiction, which is neither monarchical, aristocratical nor democratical, but a meer plutarchy, plutocracy, or rather plutomanie,[158] so madly they hale after money and the trash of this world – if so, I say, they were not guilty of suchlike enormities, and that according to their talk of things above their lives were answerable, or yet the result of their acts when all together in assemblies, synods, or presbyteries they are congregated into one body, then to require such matters might in some measure seem excusable, because an unfeigned zeal to the furtherance of learning, piety and good works should be seconded with power and wealth; but that for a meer aerial discourse of those whose hearts are ingulphed in the dross of worldly affections others should part from their own means and dignities to enrich the wives and children of hypocrites is a crying sin before God (contrary to Saint Paul's admonition, who accounteth men infidels that do so) and the abusing of those benefits he hath vouchsafed to allow us for the maintenance of our families and provision for posterity.

Is there any more common saying over all Scotland in the mouthes of the laicks then that the minister is the greediest man in the parish, most unwilling to bestow anything in deeds of charity? and that the richer they become (without prejudice be it spoken of some honest men amongst them) the more wretched they are? grounding that assertion on this, that by their daily practice, both severally and conjunctly, it is found that for their splendour and inrichment most of them do immire their spirits into earthly projects, not caring by what sordid means they may attain their aims, and if they make any kinde of sermocination tending in outward appearance to godliness (which seldom they do, being enjoyned by their ecclesiastical authority to preach to the times, that is, to rail against malignants and sectaries, or those whom they suppose to be their enemies) they do it but as those augurs of old, of whom Aulus Gellius speaking saith, "Aures verbis ditant alienas, suas ut auro locupletent crumenas."[159]

I know I touch here a string of a harsh sound to the Kirk, of a note dissonant from their proposed harmony and quite out of the systeme of the intended oecumenick government by them concerted. But seeing there are few will be taken with the melody of such a democratical hierarchie that have not preallably[160] been stung with the tarantula[161] of a preposterous ambition, I will insist no longer on this purpose, and that so much the rather that he whose writings I in this tractate intermix with my own tempers his Heliconian water with more hony then vinegar and prefers the epigrammatical to the satyrick straine, although I think there be hardly any in Scotland that proportionably hath suffered more prejudice by the Kirk then himself, his own ministers, to wit, those that preach in the churches whereof himself is patron, Master Gilbert Anderson, Master Robert Williamson and Master Charles Pape by name, serving the cures of Cromarty, Kirkmichel and Cullicudden, having done what lay in them for the furtherance of their owne covetous ends to his utter undoing; for the first of those three, for no other cause but that the said Sir Thomas would not authorize the standing of a certain pew (in that country called a desk) in the church of Cromarty, put in without his consent by a professed enemy to his house, who had plotted the ruine thereof, and one that had no land in the parish, did so rail against him and his family in the pulpit at several times both before his face and in his absence and with such opprobrious termes, more like a scolding tripe seller's wife then good minister, squirting the poyson of detraction and abominable falshood unfit for the chaire of verity in the eares of his tenandry, who were the onely auditors, did most ingrately and despightfully so calumniate and revile their master, his own patron and benefactor, that the scandalous and reproachful words, striving which of them should first discharge against him its steel-pointed dart, did often-times, like clusters of hemlock or wormewood dipt in vinegar, stick in his throat, he being almost ready to choak with the aconital bitterness and venom thereof, till the razor of extream passion, by cutting them into articulate sounds, and very rage it self in the highest degree by procuring a vomit had made him spue them out of his mouth into rude, indigested lumps, like so many toads and vipers that had burst their gall.

As for the other two, notwithstanding that they had been borne, and their fathers before them, vassals to his house and the predecessor of one of them had shelter in that land by reason of slaughter committed by him when there was no refuge for him anywhere else in Scotland and that the other had never been admitted to any church had it not been for the favour of his foresaid patron, who, contrary to the will of his owne friends and great reluctancy of the ministry it self, was both the nominater and chuser of him to that function and that before his admission, he did faithfully protest he should all the days of his life remain contented with that competency of portion the late imcumbent in that charge did enjoy before him, they nevertheless behaved themselves so peevishly and unthankfully towards their forenamed patron and master that by vertue of an unjust decree both procured and purchased from a promiscous knot of men like themselves, they used all their utmost endeavours, in absence of their above-recited patron, to whom and unto whose house they had been so much beholding, to outlaw him and declare him rebel by open proclamation at the marketcross of the head town of his owne shire in case he did not condescend to the grant of that augmentation of stipend which they demanded, conforme to the tenour of the above-mentioned decree; the injustice whereof will appeare, when examined by any rational judge.

Now the best is, when by some moderate gentlemen it was expostulated why against their master, patron and benefactor, they should have dealt with such severity and rigour, contrary to all reason and equity, their answer was they were inforced and necessitated so to do by the synodal and presbyterial conventions of the Kirk under paine of deprivation and expulsion from their benefices. I will not say,| κακοῦ κορακὸς κακὸν ᾠον,[162] but may safely think that a well-sanctified mother will not have a so ill-instructed brat and that *injuria humana*[163] cannot be the lawfull daughter of a *jure divino* parent.

Yet have I heard him, notwithstanding all these wrongs, several times avouch that from his heart he honoureth the ministerial function and could wish that each of them had a competency of livelihood to the end that for not lacking what is necessary for him, he might not be distracted from the seriousness of his speculative imploiments, with which above all things he would have one busied that were admitted to that charge, and to be a man of a choice integrity of life and approved literature: he alwayes esteeming philosophy in all its mathematical, natural and prudential demonstrations, rules and precepts so convenient for inbellishing the minde of him whose vocation it is to be sequestred from the toil of worldly affairs, that the reason and will of man being thereby illuminated and directed towards the objects of truth and goodness, a churchman or pretender to divinity regardless of those sciences might be justly suspected to be ignorant of God by caring so little for the knowledge of his creatures and upon a sacred text oftentimes to make an unhallowed comment.

I have heard him likewise say he would be glad that in every parish of Scotland there were a free schoole and a standing library, in the custody of the minister, with this proviso, that none of the books should be embezeled by him or any of his successors, and he impowered to perswade his parishioners in all he could to be liberal in their dotations towards the school and magnifying of the library; to the end that besides the good would thereby redound to all good spirits, it might prove a great encouragement to the stationer and printer, that being the noblest profession amongst merchants and this, amongst artificers; as also to intreat the civil magistrate by the severity of the law to curb the insolency of such notorious and scandalous sinners as should prove unpliable to the stamp of his wholesome admonitions.

As for his wife and children, if he follow the footsteps of Solomon and ask sincerely for wisdome of God before he wed, he will undoubtedly endow him with wealth sufficient for both; for whoever marieth, if he be wise, will either have a vertuous or a monyed woman to his mariage-bed; by means of either whereof, the discretion and foresight of a judicious husband will provide a dowry for her and education for her issue, which in a well-policied country is better then a patrimony.

The taking of this course will advance learning, further piety, improve all moral vertues, establish true honour in the land, make trades flourish, merchandise prosper, the yeomanry industrious, gentlemen happy and the ministers themselves richer then when their mindes were totally bent on the purchase of money; for, as patterns of godliness without morosity and literature without affectation, being men qualified as aforesaid by their sweetness of conversation and influence of doctrine, they would gaine so much ground upon the hearts of their acquaintance that countrymen would not onely gratifie them dayly and load them with variety of presents, but would also after their decease rather chuse to starve themselves then suffer the wives and children of persons so obliging to be in any want or indigence, specially if the traffick and civility of Scotland were promoved by a close union with England, not heterogeneal, as timber and stone upon ice stick sometimes together, bound by the frost of a conquering sword, but homogeneated by naturalization and the mutual enjoyment of the same priviledges and immunities.

HUGH BINNING (1627–53) became professor of philosophy at Glasgow University at the age of 20 and later was minister of Govan. He sided with the extreme or Protester party among the Covenanters. Except for his *Treatise of Christian Love* of 1651, his works, mostly sermons, were published posthumously. *The Common Principles of the Christian Religion* (1659) is a series of sermons on the catechism. Sermon 1, "God's Glory the Chief End", conveys an almost Miltonic sense of the divine energy passing through creation and making return to God. I chose Sermon XI, "God is a Spirit", pp. 125–140, because it gives lucid and vigorous expression to the Calvinist idea of true worship that lay somewhere behind Protester politics. Clearly, though, in Binning's exposition of how the soul must bear the stamp or image of God there is a much finer spirit at work than in the writings of those other Protesters, Wariston and Rutherford. Faced with a sermon so long, the reader may feel like Charles II at the Covenanters' "sesquihoral graces upon a dish of skink". But I have not tried to shorten it. It shows the seventeenth century Calvinist mind at its best, not just its high and exacting idea of the relation between God and men but its intellectual edge. It is also a good example of Binning's new method of discoursing upon "a common head" (see Introduction, pp. 14–15). Binning was probably the author of *An Useful Case of Conscience* (1693), a pamphlet stating the Protester reasons for not joining with the "Malignants" (those the Protesters thought had betrayed the Covenants) to fight for Charles II. If he was, then sadly his judgement did not equal his intellectual rigour or his gift for developing a position from first principles with clarity and force; the pamphlet is fanatical.

THE COMMON PRINCIPLES OF THE CHRISTIAN RELIGION, SERMON XI.

Joh. 4. 23. "GOD is a Spirit," etc.

There are two common notions engraven on the hearts of all men by nature, that God is and that he must be worshipped, and these two live and die together. They are clear or blotted together; according as the apprehension of God is clear and distinct and more deeply ingraven on the soul, so is this notion of man's duty of worshipping God clear and imprinted on the soul, and when ever the actions of men do prove that the conception of the worship of God is obliterate or worn out, when ever their transgressions do witnesse that a man hath not a lively notion of this duty of God's worship, that doth also prove that the very notion of a Godhead is worn out and cancelled in the soul; for how could souls conceive of God as he is indeed, but they must needs with Moses (Exod. 34) make haste to pray and worship. It is the principle of the very law of nature, which shall make the whole world inexcusable "because that when they knew God they glorified him not as God". A father must have honour and a master must have fear, and God, who is the common parent and absolute master of all, must have worship, in which reverence and fear mixed with rejoycing and affection predomines. It is supposed and put beyond all question that it must be "he that worships him must worship him in spirit and in truth". It is not simply said, God is a Spirit and must be worshipped; no, for none can doubt of it. If God be, then certainly worship is due to him, for who is so worshipfull? And because it is so beyond all question, therefore woe to the irreligious world that never puts it in practice. O what excuse can you have, who have not so much as a form of godlinesse? Do you not know that it's beyond all controversie that God must be worshiped? Why then do you deny it in your practice, which all men must confesse in their conscience? Is not he God, the Lord, a living and self-being spirit? Then must he not have worshippers? Beasts are not created for it; it is you, O sons of men, whom he made for his own praise, and it is not more sutable to your natures then it is honourable and glorious. This is the great dignity and excellency you are priviledged with beyond the brute beasts, to have spirits within you capable of knowing and acknowledgeing the God of your spirits. Why then do you both rob and spoyl God of his glory and cast away your own excellency? Why do you love to trample on your ornaments and wallow in the puddle like beasts void of religion, but so much worse then beasts, that you ought to be better and were created for a more noble design? O base spirited wretches, who hang down your souls to this earth and follows the dictates of your own sense and lust and have not so much as an external form of worshipping God, how far are you come short of the noble design of your creation and the high end of your immortall souls. If you will not worship God, know he will have worshipers; certainly he will not want it, because he hath designed so many souls to stand before him and worship him, and that number will not fail.

He might indeed have wanted worshippers, for what advantage is it to him? But in this he declares his love and respect to man, that he will not want honour and service from him. It is rather to put honour upon him and to make him blessed and happy then for any gain can amount to him by it. For this is indeed the true honour and happinesse of man, not to be worshipped and served of other fellow creatures, but to worship and serve the Creator. This is the highest advancement of a soul, to ly low before him, and to obey him and have our service accepted of his Majesty. I beseech you strive about this noble service, since he must have worshippers. O say within your souls, I must be one; if he had but one, I could not be content if I were not that one. Since, the Father is "seeking worshippers" (vers. 23.), o, let him finde thee. Offer thy self to him, saying, Lord, here am I. Should he seek you, who can have no advantage from you? Should he go about so earnest a search for true worshippers, who can have no profite by them? And why do ye not seek him, since to you all the gain and profite redounds? Shal he seek you to make you happy, and why do ye not seek him and happinesse in him? It is your own service, I may truely say, and not his so much, for in serving him thou dost rather serve thy self; for all the benefite redounds to thy self, though thou must not intend such an end, to serve him for your self, but for his name's sake; else thou shall neither honour him nor advantage thy self. I pray you let him not seek in vain, for in these afflictions, he is seeking worshippers, and if he finde you, you are found and saved indeed. Do not then forsake your own mercy to run from his who follows you with salvation.

As none can be ignorant that God is and must be worshipped, so it is unknown to the world in what manner he must be worshipped. The most part of men have some form in worshipping God and please themselves in it so well that they think God is well pleased with it, but few there are who know indeed what it is to worship him in a manner acceptable to his Majesty. Now you know it is all one not to worship him at all, as not to worship him in that way he likes to be worshipped. Therefore the most part of men are but self-worshippers, because they please none but themselves in it; it is not the worship his soul hath chosen, but their own invention; for you must take this as an undeniable ground that God must be worshipped according to his own will and pleasure and not according to your humor or invention; therefore his soul abhores will-worship devised by men out of ignorant zeal or superstition, though there might seem much devotion in it and much affection to God, as in the Israelites sacrificing their children – what more seeming self-deniall? and yet what more real self-idolatry? God owns not such a service, for it is not service and obedience to his will and pleasure, but to men's own will and humor; therefore a man must not look for a reward, but from himself. Now it is not only wil-worship when the matter and substance of the worship is not commanded of God, but also when a commanded worship is not discharged in the appointed manner. Therefore, O how few true worshippers will the Father finde! True worship must have truth for the substance and spirit for the manner of it, else it is not such a worship as the Father seeks and will be pleased with. Divine worship must have truth in it, that is plain. But what was that truth? It must be conformed to the rule and patern of worship, which is God's will and pleasure, revealed in the word of truth. True worship is the very practice of the word of truth. It carries the image and superscription of a command upon it, which is a necessary ingredient in it and constituent of it. Therefore if thy service have the image of thy own will stamped on it, it is not divine worship, but will-worship. Thus all humane ceremonies and ordinances enjoyned for service of God carry the inscription not of God, but of man, who is the author and originall of them, and so are but adulterated and false coyn, that will not passe current with God. I fear there be many rites and vain customs among ignorant people, in which they place some religion, which have no ground in the word of God, but are only old wives' fables and traditions. How many things of that nature are used upon a religious account, in which God hath placed no religion. Many have a superstitious conceit of the publick place of worship, as if there were more holinesse in it then in any other house, and so they think their prayers in the church are more acceptable then in their chamber. But Christ refutes that superstitious opinion of places and so consequently of dayes, meats and all such externall things. The Jews had a great opinion of their temple, the Samaritans of their mountain, as if these places had sanctified their services, but saith our Lord (vers. 21), "The houre cometh when ye shall neither worship in this mountain," etc. But it's any where acceptable if so be ye worship in spirit and truth. Many of you account it religion to pray and mutter words of your own in the time of publick prayer, but who hath required this at your hand? If ye would pray your selves, go apart, "shut the door behind thee," saith Christ. Private prayer should be in private and secret, but when publick prayer is, your heart should close with the petitions and offer them up joyntly to God. It is certainly a great slight of that deceitfull destroyer, the devil, to possesse your mindes with an opinion of religion in such vain bablings that he may withdraw both your ears and your hearts from the publick worship of God, for when every one is busied with his own prayers, you cannot at all joyn in the publick service of God, which is offered up in your name. The like I may say of stupid formes of prayer and tying your selves to a plate form written in a book, or to some certain words gotten by the heart. Who hath commanded this? Sure not the Lord, who hath promised his spirit to teach them to pray and help their infirmities, who know not how nor what to pray. It is a device of your own, invented by Satan to quench the spirit of supplications, which should be the very naturall breathing of a Christian. But there are some so grosely ignorant of what prayer is that they make use of the Ten Commands and Beleef as a prayer. So void are they of the knowledge and spirit of God that they cannot discern betwixt God's commands to themselves and their own requests to God, betwixt his speaking to men and their speaking to him, between their professing of him before men and praying and confessing to him. All this is but forged imaginary worship, worship falsly so called, which the Father seeks not and receives not.

But what if I should say that the most part of your worship, even that which is commanded of God, as prayer, hearing, reading, etc. hath no truth in it? I should say nothing amiss. For though you do those things that are commanded, yet not as commanded [but] without any respect to divine appoyntment and only because you have received them as traditions from your fathers and because yee are taught so by the precepts of men and are accustomed so to do, therefore the stamp of God's will and pleasure is not engraven on them, but of your own will, or of the will of men. Let me pose your consciences, many of you, what difference is there between your praying and your plowing, between your hearing and your harrowing, between your reading in the Scriptures and your reaping in the harvest, between your religious service and your common ordinary actions? I say, what difference is there in the rise of these? You do many civill things out of custome, or because of the precepts of men, and is there any other principle at the bottom of your religious performances? Do you at all consider these are divine appointments, these have a stamp of his authority on them, and from the conscience of such an immediate command of God and the desire to please him and obey him, do you go about these? I fear many cannot say it. O, I am sure all cannot, though it may be, all will say it. Therefore your religious worship can come in no other account then will-worship or man-worship. It hath not the stamp of truth on it, an expresse conformitie to the truth of God as his truth.

But we must presse this out a little more. Truth is opposed to ceremonie and shadow. The ceremonies of old were shadows, or the externall body of religion, in which the soul and spirit of godlinesse should have been enclosed, but the Lord did alwayes urge more earnestly the substance and truth then the ceremonie, the weightier matters of the Law, piety, equitie and sobrietie than these lighter externall ceremonies. Hee sets an higher account upon mercy then sacrifice and upon obedience then ceremonies. But this people turned it just contrary. They summed up all their religion in some ceremoniall performance and seperated these things God had so neerly conjoined. They would be devout men in offering sacrifices, in their washings, in their rites and yet made no conscience of heart and soule pietie towardes God and upright just dealling with men. Therefore the Lord so often quarrels them and reflects all their service as being a device and invention of their own, which never entered into his heart (Isa. I, from 10 to 16., Jer. 7. throughout, Isa. 66. to 6., Isa. 28). Now if you will examine it impartially, it is ever just so with us. There are some externall things in religion, which in comparison with the weightier things of faith and obedience are but ceremoniall; in these you place the most part, if not all your religion and think your selves good christians if you be baptized and hear the Word and partake of the Lord's Table and such like, though in the mean time you be not given to secret prayer and reading and do not inwardly judge and examine your selves that ye may flee unto a mediator, though your conversation be unjust and scandalous among men. I say unto such souls, as the Lord to the Jews, who hath required this at your hands? Who commanded you to hear the Word, to be baptized, to wait on publick ordinances? Away with all this, it is abomination to his Majesty. Though it please you never so well, the more it displeases him. If ye say, why commands he us to hear etc? I say, the Lord never commanded these externall ordinances for the summe of true religion. That was not the great thing which was in his heart, that he had most pleasure into, but the weightier matters of the Law, piety, equity and sobriety, a holy and godly conversation adorning the gospel: "What hath the Lord required of thee but this, O man? to do justly, and walk humbly with thy God?" So then thou dost not worship him in truth, but in a shadow. The truth is holinesse and righteousnesse. That external profession is but a ceremony. While you separate these externall ordinances from these weighty duties of piety and justice, they are but as a dead body without a soul. If the Lord required truth of old, much more now when he hath abolished the multitude of ceremonies that the great things of the Law may be more seen and loved.

If you would then be true worshippers, look [to] the whole mind of God and especially the chief pleasure of God's mind, that which he most delights into, and by any means do not separate what God hath conjoined; do not divide righteousnesse towards men from a profession of holinesse to God, else it is but a falshood, a counterfeit coyn. Do not please your selves so much in externall church priviledges without a holy and godly conversation adorning the gospel, but let the chief study, endeavour and delight of your souls be about that which God most delights into. Let the substantials of religion have the first place in the soul; pray more in secret; that will be the life of your souls. You ought indeed to attend publick ordinances, but above all, take heed to your conversation and walking at home and in secret. Prayer in your familie is a more substantiall worship then to sit and hear prayer in publick, and prayer in secret is more substantiall then that. The more retired and immediat a duty be, the more weighty it is. The more it crosse thy corruptions and evidence the stamp of God on thy affections, the more divine it is. And therefore to serve God in these is to serve him in truth. Practise hath more of truth in it then a profession. "When your fathers executed judgement, was not this to know me?" Duties that have more opposition from our natures against them and lesse fewell or oyl to feed the flame of our self-love and corruption have more truth in them, and if you should worship God in all other duties and not especially in those, you do not worship him in truth.

Next, let us consider the manner of divine worship. And this is as needfull to true worship as true matter. That it be commanded and done as it is commanded, that compleats true worship. Now, I know no better way or manner to worship God into then so to worship him as our worship may carry the stamp of his image upon it, as it may be a glasse wherein we may behold God's nature and properties. For such as himself is, such he would be acknowledged to be. I would think it were true worship indeed which had engraven on it the name of the true and living God, if it did speak out so much of itself, "That God is, and that he is a rewarder of them that seek him diligently." Most part of our service speaks an unknown God and carries such an inscription upon it, "To the unknown God". There is so little either reverence, or love, or fear, or knowledg in it, as if we did not worship the true God, but an idol. It is said that the fool sayes in his heart that there is no God, because his thoughts and affections and actions are so little composed to the fear and likenesse of that God, as if he did indeed plainly deny him. I fear it may be said thus of our worship: it sayes, "There is no God". It is of such a nature that none could conclude from it that it had any relation to the true God. Our prayers denies God because there is nothing of God appears in them; but this is true worship, when it renders back to God his own image and name: *unde repercussus redditur ipse sibi.*[164] As it is a pure and clean fountain in which a man may see his shadow distinctly, but a troubled fountain or myre in which he cannot behold himself, so it is pure worship which receives and reflects the pure image of God, but impure and unclean worship which cannot receive it and return it. I pray you, christians, consider this, for it is such worshippers the

Father seeks. And why seeks he such, but because in them he finds himself, so to speak, his own image and superscriptions upon them? His mercy is engraven on their faith and confidence; his majesty and power is stamped on their humility and reverence; his goodnesse is to be read on the soul's rejoycing; his greatnesse and justice, in the soul's trembling. Thus there ought to be some engravings on the soul answering the characters of his glorious name. O how little of this is amongs them that desire to know something of God! How little true worship, even among them whom the Father has sought out to make true worshippers! But alace, how are all of us acquainted with this kind of worship! We stay upon the first principles and practises of religion and goeth not on to build upon the foundation. Sometimes your worship hath a stamp of God's holinesse and justice in fear and terrour at such a majesty, which makes you to tremble before him. But where is the stamp of his mercy and grace which should be written in you faith and rejoicing? Tremble and fear indeed, but rejoice with trembling because there is mercy with him. Sometimes there is rejoicing and quietnesse in the soul, but that quickly degenerats into carnall confidence and makes the soul turn grace into wantonnesse and esteem of itself above what is right, because it is not counterpoised with the sense and apprehension of his holinesse and justice. But, O to have these joyntly written on the heart in worship, fear, reverence, confidence, humility and faith! That is a rare thing. It is a divine composition and temper of spirit that makes a divine soul. For the most part, our worship savours and smells nothing of God, neither his power nor his mercy and grace, nor his holinesse and justice, nor his majesty and glory, a secure, faint, formall way, void of reverence, of humility, of fervency and of faith. I beseech you, let us consider as before the Lord, how much pains and time we loose and please none but our selves and profite none at all. Stir up your selves, as in his sight, for it is the keeping of our souls continually as in his sight which will stamp our service with his likenesse. The fixed and constant meditation on God and his glorious properties – this will beget the resemblance between our worship and the God whom we worship, and it will imprint his image upon it, and then it should please him, and then it should profit thee, and then it should edifie others.

But more particularly, true worship must have the stamp of God's spiritual nature and be comformed to it in some measure, else it cannot please him. There must be a conformity between God and souls. This is the great end of the gospel, to repair that image of God which was once upon man and make them like God again. Now it is this way that Jesus Christ repairs this image and brings about this conformity with God by the soul's worshipping of God suitable to his nature, which as it grows more and more sutable to God's nature, it is the more and more like God and happy in that likenesse. Now, "God is a spirit," therefore saith Christ, you "must worship him in spirit and truth." The worship then of saints must be of a spirituall nature that it may be like the immortall divine spirit. It is such worshippers the Father seeks. He seeks souls to make them like himself, and this likenesse and conformity to God is the very foundation of the soul's happinesse and eternall refreshment.

This is a point of great consequence, and I fear not laid to heart. The worship must be like the worshiped. It is a spirit must worship the eternall spirit. It is not a body that can be the principle and chief agent in the businesse. What communication can God have with your bodies, while your souls are removed far from him, more then with beasts? All society and fellowship must be between these that are like one another. A man can have no comfortable company with beasts, or with stones and trees. It is men that can converse with men, and a spirit must worship the self-being spirit. Do not mistake this, as if under the dayes of the gospel we were not called to an external and bodily worship, to any service to which our outward man is instrumentall. That is one of the deep delusions of this age, into which some men "reprobat concerning the faith" have fallen, that there should be no externall ordinances, but that christians are now called to a worship all spirit, pure spirit, etc. This is one of the spirits and spirituall doctrines (that calls themselves so) which ye must not receive, for it is neither the spirit of God nor of Christ that teacheth this. Not the spirit of God the Creator, because he hath made the whole man, body and soul, and so must be worshipped of the whole man. He hath created man in such a capacity as he may offer up externall actions in a reasonable manner with the inward affections. As the Lord hath created him, so should he serve him, every member, every part in its own capacity, the soul to preceed, and the body to follow, the soul to be the chief worshipper, and the body its servant imployed in the worship. True worship hath a body and a soul, as well as a true man; and as the soul separated is not a compleat man, so neither is the soul separated a compleat worshipper without the body. The external ordinances of God is the body, the inward soul affection is the spirit, which being joyned together makes compleat worship. Neither is it the spirit of Christ which teacheth this because our Lord Jesus hath taught us to offer up our bodies and spirits both in a reasonable service (Rom. 12. 1, 2). The sacrifice of the bodily performance offered up by the spiritual affection and renewed minde "is a living sacrifice, holy, acceptable and reasonable." That spirit which dwelt in Christ above measure did not think it too base to vent itself in the way of external ordinances. He was indeed above all, above the Law, yet did willingly come under them to teach us, who have so much need and want to come under them. He prayed much, he preached, he did sing and read to teach us how to worship and how much need wee have of prayer and preaching. This was not the.spirit Christ promised to his disciples and apostles, which spirit did breath most lively in the use of the externall ordinances all their dayes. And this is not the spirit which was at that hour in which Christ spoke, "The hour is come and now is (vers. 23) in which the true worship of God" shal not be in the external Jewish ceremonies and rites, void of all life and inward sense of piety; but the true worship of God shal be made up of a soul and body, of spirit and truth, of the external appointed ordinances according to the word of truth and the spirit of truth and of the spirit and inward soul-affection and sincerity, which shall quicken and actuat that externall performance. There were no such worshippers then as had no use of ordinances. Christ was not such, his disciples were not such, therefore it is a new gospel, which if an angel would bring from Heaven ye ought not to receive it.

As it is certain then that both soul and body must be imployed in this businesse, so it is sure that the soul and spirit must be the first mover and chiefest agent in it, because it is a spiritual businesse and hath relation to the fountain-spirit, which hath the most perfect opposition to all false appearances and external shews. That part of man that cometh nearest God must draw nearest in worshipping God, and if that be removed farre away, there is no real communion with God. Men judges according to the outward appearance and can reach no further then the outward man, but God is an al-searching spirit who trieth the heart and reins, and therefore he will passe another judgement upon your worship then men can do because he observeth all the secret wanderings and escapes of the heart out of his sight. He misses the soul when you present attentive ears or eloquent tongues. There is no dalying with his Majesty; painting will not deceive him; his very nature is contrary to hypocrisie and dissimulation, and what is it but dissimulation, when you present your selves to religious exercises as his people, but within are nothing like it, nothing awaking, nothing present? O consider my beloved, what a one you have to do with! It is not men, but the Father of spirits, who will not be pleased with what pleases men or your own flesh, but must have a spirit to serve him. Alace, what are we doing with such empty names and shews in religion? Busied in the outside of worship only, as if we had none to do with but men who have eyes of flesh, all that we do in this kind is lost labour and will never be reckoned up in the account of true worship. I am sure you know and may reflect upon your selves that you make religion but a matter of outward fashion and external custome. You have never almost taken it to heart in earnest. You frequent the ordinances, you may have a form of godlines consisting in some outward performances and priviledges, and O how void and destitute of all spirit and life and power! Not to speak of the removal of affection and the imploying of the marrow of your soul upon base lusts and creatures, or the scattering of your desires abroad amongst them, for that is too palpable, but even your very thoughts and minds are removed from this busines. You have nothing present but an ear or eye, and your minds is about other businesse. Your desires, your fears, your joyes and delights, your affections did never run in the channel of religious exercises. All your passion is vented in other things, but here you are blockish and stupid, without any sensible apprehension of God, his mercy, or justice, or wrath, or of your own misery and want. You sorrow in other things but none here, none for sin; you joy for other things, but none here; you cannot rejoice at the gospel; prayer is a burthen not a delight. If your spirits were chiefly imployed in religious duties, religion would be almost your element, your pleasure and recreation, but now it is wearisome to the flesh because the spirit taketh not the chief weight upon it. Oh, be not deceived! God is not mocked. You do but mock your selves with externall shows, while you are satisfied with them. I beseech you look inwardly and be not satisfied with the outward appearance, but ask at thy soul where it is and how it is. Retire within and bring up thy spirit to this work. I am sure you may observe that any thing goes more smoothly and sweetly with you then the worship of God because your minde is more upon any thing else. I fear the most part of us who endeavour in some measure to seek God have too much drosse of outward formality and much scum of filthy hypocrisie and guile. O! pray that the present furnace may purge away this scum. It is the great ground of God's present controversie with Scotland. But alace, the bellows are like to burn, and we not to be purged. Our scum goes not from us. We satisfie our selves with some outward exercises of religion. Custome undoes us all, and it was never more undoing then when indignation and wrath is pursuing it. Oh that you would ponder what you loose by it, both the sweetnesse and advantage of godlinesse, beside the dishonour of God. You take a formall, negligent and secure way as the most easie way and the most pleasing to your flesh, and I am perswaded you find it the most difficult way because you want all the pleasant and sweet refreshment and soul-delights you might have in God by a serious and diligent minding of religion. The pleasure and sweetnesse of God tasted and found will make diligence and pains more easie then sloathfulnesse can be to the sloathfull. This oyls the wheels and makes them drive swiftly; formality makes them drive heavily. Thus you live alwayes in a complaining humor, "sighing and going backward," because you have some stirring principle or conscience within, which bears witnesse against you, and your formall, sluggish disposition on the other hand refuseth to awake and work. You are perplexed and tormented between the two when thy spirit and affections goes one way and thy body another. When thy conscience drives on the spirit and thy affections draws back, it must needs be an unpleasant businesse.

CHAPTER THREE

THE RESTORATION

With the Restoration, civil politics became distinct from church politics. Constitutional questions and power games were not entirely played out in the sort of terms the Covenant set up. The political divisions of the Covenanting period remained and the business of government was to avoid civil war. Yet the great issue was not a matter of ideology but how to manage the government of the country, whether by persecuting and coercing religious nonconformists or by indulging them outside the established Church or by accommodating them inside a broader church settlement. The settlement of the Church was first of all a matter of civil order. High Presbyterians and high Episcopalians were still bound to divine right claims for their schemes. But the high Presbyterians, in spite of their turbulence, never got to the centre of political power, and even the Episcopalians of James VII's reign never attempted a Laudian reform of the Scottish Church.

At the Restoration the Resolutioner party imagined that after their efforts on the king's behalf, they could take over the Church. The Protesters imagined they had a claim on a king who had taken the Covenants. And each party hoped to exclude the other. But by the Act Rescissory of 1661, the Scottish Parliament abrogated the Covenants along with all the legislation since 1638, and a moderate Episcopacy was restored. The rule of bishops replaced the General Assembly, but the other church courts, kirk sessions, presbyteries and synods, remained. Ministers who refused to conform were deprived. In the South West a majority were in fact deprived, though in the South East only a minority and almost none north of the Tay. This was the origin of those conventicles that took up so much of the government's attention. Especially in the South West, the nonconforming ministers drew congregations from their official ministers to illegal services. The response of the government was to use troops to exact fines from those who did not attend church and to break up conventicles. Sir James Turner, who was in charge of the operation (he gives a fascinating account of his experiences in his memoirs), fell into the hands of a small party who had decided to resist, and almost by accident the Whigs rose throughout the South West and marched on Edinburgh, only to be scattered at Rullion Green (1666). The government now turned to gentler methods. The repressive archbishop of Glasgow was deposed and Leighton put in his stead. Leighton had a scheme for accommodating the deprived ministers within the Episcopal church. He sent men who shared his views, like Gilbert Burnet and Lawrence Charteris, on a preaching tour to recommend his scheme. But neither Leighton's efforts nor his "Bishops' evangelists" were able to bring in the nonconforming Presbyterians. There was little pressure to conform anyway, for Lauderdale's government was trying what indulgence might do. The Indulgences of 1669 and 1672 provided that peaceable ministers who had been deprived might be appointed to vacancies without Episcopal collation. The moderate Presbyterians who took advantage of the Indulgences were now split from the rigid party who kept to the Covenants and stayed outside

Already during the spell of conciliation, conventicles were on the increase. In 1673 the government again turned to repression. Leighton resigned from the see of Glasgow and left for England. When other methods of suppressing conventicles failed, troops were again quartered on the South West. A second and more formidable rising broke out following the murder of Archbishop Sharpe and was crushed at Bothwell Brig (1679). Only a fanatical remnant, the Cameronians, remained in arms. In their manifestoes they declared the king a usurper and excommunicated him and his principal servants. Otherwise, James, Duke of York, as Charles's commissioner, succeeded with the dragonnades, for which Claverhouse became notorious, in terrifying the South West into quietness. In 1681 a Test was framed, which even moderates like Charteris found inconsistent with their principles, but in spite of resignations and deprivations there was no effective resistance. As king, James put his Protestant supporters, however royalist, in a difficult position by suspending the penal laws against the Catholics. Moreover, in his Declaration of Indulgence of 1687 he not only undid Episcopal policy but gave an opportunity to the Presbyterians to reappear as a force in the country. Still in Scotland developments waited on the events in England.

GILBERT BURNET (1643–1715) is remarkable partly for the men he knew. His tutor in mathematics was George Keith, later to become the associate of the Quaker, Robert Barclay, and he was a member of the circle of Leighton, Charteris and Nairne. On a visit to London in 1664, he was taken up by Sir Robert Murray, who as President, introduced him to the Royal Society, and for a time he enjoyed Lauderdale's friendship.

He was a nephew of Johnston of Wariston on his mother's side but had from his father his moderate, Erastian, Episcopal views. When Leighton was a man of influence in Scottish affairs, he took part in the schemes for conciliating the Presbyterians and in 1669 was appointed professor of divinity in Glasgow. Lauderdale, he says, consulted him on the second Indulgence of 1672. When repression began again in 1673 and Leighton left the country, Burnet found himself in trouble. The Scottish bishops were his enemies because of his part in the conciliatory policy and Lauderdale feared his influence at the English court. It seemed wise to leave the country.

He settled in London, where as chaplain to the Rolls Chapel and lecturer at St Clements, he enjoyed a considerable reputation as a preacher and scope for his spiritual and political interests. He converted the rake, Rochester, on his deathbed. He reformed Charles's mistress, Miss Roberts. He even tried to reform Charles – the king bore him no ill will for the unsuccessful attempt. He had indeed always been a great admonisher. As minister of Saltoun the twenty-three-year-old Burnet had sent a protest concerning the Scottish episcopate to all the bishops of his acquaintance, but it seems to have caused more surprise than trouble. In the later years of Charles's reign, he associated with the opposition. He was the friend of Russell and Essex, and when the Rye House Plot was discovered in 1683, he attended Russell at his execution. On James's accession, he left the country on a tour to the Continent, which ended in his joining the circle of emigrés in Holland who advised William on his course as the crisis developed in England. Burnet advised William against supporting a Presbyterian settlement for Scotland in his Declaration of 1688. William made him Bishop of Salisbury, but while he continued to exercise some political influence, he was increasingly isolated in the English church.

Burnet was a copious writer of pamphlets, sermons and histories. The first volume of his *History of the Reformation in England,* which came out in 1679 during the crisis of the Popish plot, was a best seller. His position as an author is latitudinarian, one might say Leightonian. There is one significant shift. Until the later 1680s he maintained the duty of passive obedience to the king. This is the position he explains in the *Memoirs,* which he started writing in 1683. But at some time before he went over to William he must have changed his constitutional views. So the *History of My Own Time*, which in its earlier parts is a revision of the *Memoirs*, omits the reflections on the high Presbyterian resistance to civil government below. Strictly the portraits of the Scottish politicians, which are from the *History*, are not seventeenth century prose since they were probably revised from a missing part of the *Memoirs* in 1702 and 1703 (Foxcroft, p. viii), but they were too good to leave out. For remarks on Burnet as a historian, see Introduction, pp. 5–6.

The *History of My Own Time* was published after Burnet's death, volume 1 in 1724, volume 2 in 1734. The parts of the *Memoirs* that differ substantially from the *History* were printed by H. C. Foxcroft in volume 3, *A Supplement* (1902) to Osmund Airy's edition of *Burnet's History of My Own Time*, 2 vols. (Oxford: Clarendon, 1897). The text for the *Memoirs* is based on Harleian MS. 6584 ff. 3–3v; 6v–8v; 19–22; 26–27; for the *History*, Bodleian MS. Add. D 18, ff. 52–54. I have placed the pieces from Burnet before pieces that were written earlier because they make a good introduction to the period.

Burnet's *Memoirs*: the King's Character

The king is certainly the best bred man in the world, for the queen mother observed often the great defects of the late king's breeding and the stiff roughness that was in him, by which he disobliged very many and did often prejudice his affairs very much, so she gave strict orders that the young princes should be bred to a wonderfull civility. The king is civill rather to an excess and has a softeness and gentleness with him, both in his air and expressions, that has a charm in it. The duke would also pass for an extraordinary civill and sweet tempered man if the king were not much above him in it, who is more naturally and universally civill than the duke. The king has a vast deal of witt (indeed no man has more) and a great deal of judgement when he thinks fitt to employ it. He has a strange command of himselfe. He can pass from business to pleasure and from pleasure to business in so easy a manner that all things seem alike to him. He has the greatest art of concealing himselfe of any man alive, so that those about him cannot tell when he is well or ill pleased, and in private discourse he will hear all sorts of things in such a manner that a man cannot know whether he hears them or not, or whether he is well or ill pleased at them. He is very affable not only in publick but in private, only he talks too much and runns out too long and too farr. He has a very ill opinion both of men and women and so is infinitely distrustfull. He thinks the world is governed wholly by interest, and indeed he has known so much of the baseness of mankind that no wonder if he has hard thoughts of them. But when he is satisfyed that his interests are likewise become the interests of his ministers, then he delivers himself up to them in all their humours and revenges. For excusing this he has often said that he must oblige his ministers and support their credit as necessary for his service. Yet he has often kept up differences amongst his ministers and has ballanced his favours pretty equally among them, which, considering his temper, must be uneasy to him, except it be that there is art necessary and he naturally inclines to refineings and loves an intrigue. His love of pleasure and his vast expence with his women, together with the great influence that they have had in all his affaires both at home and abroad is the chief load that will lay on him; for not only the women themselves have great power, but his court is full of pimps and bauds, and all matters in which one desires to suceed must be put in their hands. He has very mercifull inclinations when one submitts wholly to him, but is severe enough on those that oppose him, and speaks of all people with a sharpness that is not suitable to the greatness of a prince. He is apt to belive what is told him, so that the first impression goes deepest, for he thinks all apologies are lies. He has knowledge in many things, chiefly in all navall affaires. Even in the architecture of ships he judges as critically as any of the trade can do and knowes the smallest things belonging to it. He understands much naturall phylosophy and is a good chymist. He knowes many mechanicall things and the inferiour parts of the mathematicks, but not the demonstrative. He is very little conversant in books, and young and old, he could never apply himself to literature. He is very kind to those he loves, but never thinks of doeing anything for them, so that if they can find things for themselves, he will easily enough grant them, but he never setts himself to find out anything for them; and I never heard of above three or four instances of any places that he gave of his own motion, so that those who have receivd most of his bounty thinks they owe the thanks more to their instruments than to himself. He never enters upon business with any himself, but if his ministers can once draw him into business, they may hold him at it as long as they will. He loves his ease so much that the great secret of all his ministers is to find out his temper exactly and to be easy to him. He has many odd opinions about religion and morality. He thinks an implicitness in religion is necessary for the safety of government, and he looks upon all inquisitiveness into those things as mischievous to the state. He thinks all appetites are free and that God will never damne a man for allowing himself a little pleasure, and on this he has so fixed his thoughts that no disorders of any kind have ever been seen to give him any trouble when they were over, and in sickness, except in his ague in 79, he seemed to have no concern on his mind. And yet I believe he is no athiest, but that rather he has formed an odde idea of the goodness of God in his mind: he thinks to be wicked and to design mischief is the only thing that God hates and has said to me often that he was sure he was not guilty of that. I think I have gone pretty farr and scarce know how I should scape under the present chief justice if this should happen to be seised on.[1]

Burnet's *History*: [Characters of the Scottish Politicians].

Having now said as much as seems necessary to describe the state of the court and ministry at the restoration, I will next give an account of the chieffe of the Scotts and of the parties that were formed among them. The Earle of Lauderdale, afterwards made Duke, had been for many years a zealous Covenanter. But in the year 47 he turned to the king's interests and had continued a prisoner from Worcester fight, where he was taken. He was kept for some years in the Tower of London, in Portland Castle and in other prisons, till he was set at liberty by those who called home the king. So he went over to Holland. And since he continued so long and, contrary to all men's opinion, in so high a degree of favour and confidence, it may be expected that I should be a little copious in setting out his character, for I knew him very particularly. He made a very ill appearance: he was very big; his hair was red, hanging odly about him; his tongue was too big for his mouth, which made him bedew all that he talked to; and his whole manner was rough and boistrous and very unfit for a court. He was very learned, not only in Latin, in which he was a master, but in Greek and Hebrew. He had read a great deal in divinity and almost all the historians ancient and modern, so that he had great materialls. He had with these an extraordinary memory and a copious but unpolished expression. He was a man, as the Duke of Buckingham called him to me, of a blundering understanding, not allwaies clear, but often clouded, as his looks were allwaies. He was haughty and insolent beyond expression, abject to those to whom he saw he must stoop, but imperious and brutall to all others. He had a violence of passion that caried him often to fits like madnes, in which he had no temper. If he took a thing wrong, it was a vain thing to study to convince him. That would rather provoke him to swear he would never be of another mind. He was to be let alone, and then perhaps he would have forgot what he had said and come about of his own accord. He was the coldest friend and the violentest ennemy I ever knew; I felt it too much not to know it. He at first seemed to despise wealth, but he delivered himselfe up afterwards to luxury and sensuality, and by that means he run into a vast expense and stuck at nothing that was necessary to support that. In his long imprisonment he had great impressions of religion on his mind, but he wore these out so entirely that scarce any trace of them was left. His great experience in affairs, his ready compliance with every thing that he thought would please the king and his bold offering at the most desperate councells gained him such an interest in the king that no attempt against him nor complaint of him could ever shake it till a decay of strength and understanding forced him to let go his hold. He was in his principles much against Popery and arbitrary government, and yet by a fatall train of passions and interests, he made way for the former and had almost established the latter. And whereas some by a smooth deportment make the first beginnings of tyranny lesse unacceptable and discernable, he by the fury of his behaviour, heightened the severity of his ministry, which was liker the cruelty of an inquisition than the legality of justice, not to say mercy. With all this he was at first a Presbiterian and retained his aversion to king Charles the 1st and his party to his death.

The Earle of Crawford had been his fellow prisoner for ten years, and that was a good title for maintaining him in the post he had before of being lord treasurer. He was a sincere but weak man, passionate and indiscreet, and continued still a zealous Presbiterian. The Earle, afterwards Duke, of Rothes had maried his daughter and had the merit of a long imprisonment likewise to recommend him. He had a ready dexterity in the management of affairs with a soft and insinuating addresse. He had a quick apprehension with a clear judgment. He had no advantage of education, no sort of literature nor had he travelled abroad. All in him was meer nature, but it [was] nature very much depraved, for he seemed to have freed himselfe from all the impressions of vertue or religion, of honour or good nature. He delivered himselfe, without either restraint or decency, to all the pleasures of wine and women. He had but one maxime to which he adhered firmly that he was to do every thing and deny himselfe in nothing that might maintain his greatness, or gratify his appetites. He was unhappily made for drunkennes, for as he drunk all his friends dead and was able to subdue two or three sets of drunkards one after another, so it scarce ever appeared that he was disordered. And after the greatest excesses, an hour or two of sleep caried them off so entirely that no signe of them remained. He would go about busines without any uneasines, or discovering any heat either in body or mind. This had a terrible conclusion. For after he had killed all his friends, he fell at last under such a weaknes of stomack that he had perpetuall colicks, when he was not hot within and full of strong liquor, of which he was presently seised; so that he was always either sick or drunk.

The Earle of Tweedale was another of Lauderdale's friends. He was early engaged in busnes and continued in it to a great age. He understood all the interests and concerns of Scotland well. He had a great stock of knowledge, with a mild and obliging temper. He was of a blamelesse, or rather an exemplary, life in all respects. He had loose thoughts both of civill and ecclesiasticall government and seemed to think that what form soever was uppermost was to be complied with. He had been in Cromwell's Parliaments and had abjured the royall family, which lay heavy on him. But the dispute about the guardianship of the Dutchesse of Monmouth and her elder sister, to which he pretended in the right of his wife, who was their father's sister, against their mother, that was Rothes's sister, drew him into that compliance that brought a great cloud upon him, though he was in all other respects the ablest and worthiest man of the nobility; only he was too cautious and fearful.

A son of the marquis of Dowglas, made Earle of Selkirk, had maried the heiresse of the family of Hamilton, who by her father's patent was Dutchesse of Hamilton, and when the heiresse to a title in Scotland maries one not equall to her in rank, it is ordinary at her desire to give her husband the title for life; so he was made Duke Hamilton. He then past for a soft man, who minded nothing but the recovery of that family from the great debts under which it was sinking, till it was raised up again by his great manageing. After he had compassed that, he became a more considerable man. He wanted all sorts of polishing. He was rough and sullen, but candide and sincere. His temper was boisterous, neither fit to submit nor to govern. He was mutinous when out of power and imperious in it. He wrote well, but spoke ill, for his judgment when calm was better than his imagination. He made himselfe a great master in the knowledge of the lawes, of the history and of the families of Scotland and seemed allwaies to have a great regard to justice and the good of his countrey. But a narrow and selfish temper brought such an habituall meannes on him that he was not capable of designing or undertaking great things.

Another man of that side that made a good figure at that time was Bruce, afterwards Earle of Kincardin, who had maried a daughter of Mr Somelsdyck in Holland, and by that means he had got acquaintance with our princes beyond sea and had supplied them liberally in their necessities. He was both the wisest and the worthiest man that belonged to his countrey and fit for governing any affairs but his own, which he by a wrong turn, by his love of the publick, neglected to his ruine; for they consisting much in works, coals, salt and mines, required much care, and he was very capable of it, having gone farre in mathematicks and being a great master at all mechanicks. His thoughts went slow, and his words came much slower, but a deep judgment appeared in every thing he said or did. He had a noble zeal for justice, in which even friendship could never biasse him. He had solid principles of religion and vertue, which shewed themselves with great lustre on all occasions. He was a faithful friend and a merciful enemy. I may be perhaps enclined to carry his character too farre, for he was the first man that entred into friendship with me. We continued for seventeen years in so entire a friendship that there was never either reserve or mistake between us all the while till his death, and it was from him that I understood the whole secret of affairs, for he was trusted with every thing. He had a wonderfull love to the king and would never believe me when I warned him what he might look for if he did not go along with an abject compliance in every thing. He found it true in conclusion, and the love he bore the king made his disgrace sink deeper in him than became such a philosopher or so good a christian as he was.

I now turn to another set of men, of whom the Earles of Midletoune and Glencairn were the chieffe, and they were followed by the rest of the cavalier party, who were now very fierce and full of courage over their cups, though they had been very discreet managers of it in the field and in time of action. But now every one of them vaunted that he had killed his thousands, and all were full of merit and as full of high pretensions, farre beyond what all the wealth and revenue of Scotland could answer. The subtilest of all Midletoun's friends was Sir Archibald Primerose, a man of long and great practise in affairs, for he and his father had served the crown successively an hundred years, all but one, when he was turned out of imployment. He was a dextrous man in busines. He had alwaies expedients ready at every difficulty. He had an art of speaking to every man according to their sense of things and so drew out their secrets, while he concealed his own, for words went for nothing with him. He said every thing that was necessary to persuade those he spoke to that he was of their mind and did it in so genuine a way that he seemed to speak his heart. He was allwaies for soft councells and slow methods and thought that the chieffe thing that a great man ought to do was to raise his family and his kinred, who would naturally stick to him, for he had seen so much of the world that he did not depend much on friends and so took no care of making any. He allwaies advised the Earle of Midletoune to go on slowly in the king's busines, but to do his own effectually before the king should see that he had no farther occasion for him. That Earle had another friend, who had more credit with him, tho Primerose was more necessary for managing a parliament. He was Sir John Fletcher, made the king's advocate or attorney-general, for Nicolson was dead. Fletcher was a man of a generous temper, who despised wealth, except as it was necessary to support a vast expense. He was a bold and fierce man, who hated all mild proceedings, and could scarce speak with decency or patience to those of the other side, so that he was looked on by all that had been faulty in the late times as an inquisitor-general. On the other hand, Primerose took money liberally and was the intercessor for all who made such effectuall applications to him.

Burnet's *Memoirs*: [Characters of Ministers]

For the other ministers off Edinburgh,[2] I neither admired their persons nor their sermons and much less their conversation, which was all made up of news. Their sermons were subtile divisions of very ordinary matter hung full of quotations of scripture, but there was nothing in them that struck either on my fancy or reason, or that went to my heart. They were plain dull things sometimes sett off with an appearance of quickness and witt, which made them rather worse than better.

The two eminentest of them were Mr. Douglas and Mr. Hutchesone. The former was a bastard of a bastard, but it is believed his father was Mary Queen of Scotland's son, for he was born soon after she was conveyed out of the Castle of Lochleven and was educated with great care by the gentleman that helped her away, so that it was believed there were more than ordinary endearments between them and that this son was the fruit of these. It is certain Mr. Douglas was not ill-pleased to have this story passe. He had something very great in his countenance. His looks shewed both much wisdome and great thoughtfullness, but withall a vast pride. He was generally very silent. I confess I never admired anything he said. I wondred to see him express such mean complyances with some silly women of their party as I have seen him do to my own mother and sister. He went over when he was a young man chaplain to a regiment in Germany, where for want of other books, he got the scripture so by heart that he could not only repeate any part of it, but could have readily quoted chapter and verse for every passage in it. And this was his great faculty in preaching, that he laid all the scriptures relating to any point together, but it was a skeliton of bones, for he neither connected them well nor made he lively reflections on them. His chief excellence in preaching was that he would have made his matter look towards the present times with such dexterity that, tho it was visible what he meant, yet he could not be questioned upon it. He was a man of great personall courage, which he shewed often in Germany more signally than became his profession, yet he was a very mild, good-natured man, tho that did not appear much in his countenance, and he was of an unblameable conversation as to all private matters. The other has written many books, as on Job and St. John's Gospel two folios and 3 books in octavo on the 12 lesser prophets. He had a great subtility in his preaching and drew out one thing very ingeniously from another, which I thought was like wire drawing and ever dispised it. He affected great mirth and was much given to raillery, but it was neither grave nor witty, and he seemed to be a very proud man. He married my cousin germain so that I was well acquainted with him, but could never have any great value of him. Yet the Dutchesse of Hamilton and some others whom I esteem very much have told me that he was a much better man than he appeared to be upon a generall acquaintance and that the more any one knew him, they would value him the more.

Bishop Leighton's Character

But there was another Scotch clergyman then in England, who for his health had gone to the Bath, on whome, because I have known him so particularly and esteem him beyond all the churchmen I every yet knew, I will dwell a little longer. He was son to Dr. Leighton, a Scotchman that lived in England and was censured in the Star Chamber for a seditious book that he had writt against the bishops of England. He was sent by him to be educated in the Colledge of Edenburgh because he lookt on the English universities as much corrupted, so he was bred under all the prejudices to Episcopacy and the Church of England that a father of hot principles and inflamed by ill usage could infuse into him. He was a man of a most quick and piercing apprehension. He had a life in his thoughts and expressions that were inimitable, only his language was too fine, too much laboured and too full of figures and sentences. This was the effect of study in his youth and became a habit, or rather nature, in his old age. He spake Latine with a readiness and purity that I never knew in any except Sir James Langham,[3] and he was a great master of the Greek and had almost all their poets by heart. He had the Hebrew very well, so that I have mett with many curious criticisms from him which I have found never in any author. He spoke French like one born in France, tho it is now 45 yeares since he came out of it. He had read the fathers so exactly that I never happened to talk with him of any particular relating to ecclesiasticall learning, but he was as ready at it as if he had just come from studying it. And he was most conversant in the lives of all the devout men that have been of all religions, and out of them all he formed the highest idea of devotion that I every yet met with, for he had laid together with great judgement all the extraordinary passages of bishops and churchmen and had read most of the lives written in the latter ages and had pickt out of them what was most remarkeable and imitable among them and used to say that when he met with a good passage, he did not much care whether it was true or not, so that it raised in him some good thought. He was sent again by his father into Scotland in the year 38, and was at the Assembly of Glasgow. He told me he was even then disgusted at their heats and the manner of their proceedings, but these prejudices were not yet strong enough in him to overcome education. Some time after that he took Presbyterian ordination and signed the Covenant and was minister at Newbattle within four miles of Edinburgh, where the Earle of Lothian dwellt. He led so examplary a life, that it was rather like a pattern framed out of fancy than what a man could really attain to. He entered upon a course of almost perpetuall fasting, for tho he had a quick and craveing appetite, he never eat above what seemed necessary to keep him alive. He never allowed himselfe any sort of diversion, except rideing abroad. He was never merry nor familiar with any, but lived in a perpetuall reserve and silence, and every word he spok had an impression of religion on it. Those that knew him before me and I that have now lived one and twenty yeares in greater intimacy with him than he has been ever observed to live in with any person must say this of him that I never saw him angry at any thing nor ever perceved in him any concern for any thing in this world, or the lest appearance of pride or vanity. And I scarce ever heard him speak an idle word and never once found him in any other temper, but such as I would wish to be in when I were to die. He has a heart the fullest of all the melting affections and devotions in religion, and yet has nothing of enthusiasme, or of a schismaticall temper under it. He had the most universall charity for persons and things that I ever knew in man. He had such a way in preaching that I [n]ever knew any come near it. His thoughts were the most ravishing, his style the most beautifull, if not too fine, but his way of uttering them so grave and so tender together that I never heard him preach without trembling for one great part of the sermon and weeping for another. And I confess his way of preaching was so much above all others that I had ever heard, or any thing that I could ever hope to attain to, that for some time after every sermon that I heard of his, I both preached my selfe and heard all others with a sort of indignation. And yet he really seemed so to under value himself that he always chose to preach to mean auditories, and when he was tyed to a charge, he used to imploy every man he could gett to preach for him. And tho he never made any so much his own friend as he did me, yet he was a friend to a great many and was very full of tenderness and christian concern for them, and I see it still lives with him. He soon came to see the follies of the Presbyterians. He hated their Covenant and their rebellion against the king, their imposeing of oaths and their fury against all that differed from them and their rough sourness and narrowness of soul, and he openly preached up an universall charity. He would never meddle in their matters, but withdrew from them and only minded his pastoral care in his own parrish. They saw he grew to hate their wayes, but the reputation he was in was such that they durst not lett it be thought that he was against their courses, yet he openly declared himself for the Engagement in the year 48 that was made for delivering the king. And when after the defeat of that army some that were in it came to profess their repentance for it, in his church, according to the order of the General Assembly, he being to exhort them to a true repentance, told them they had been in an expedition in which he was affraid they had been guilty of much swearing, drunkenness, oppression and other sins, besides the neglect of God and religion, and charged them to repent seriously for those things, but did not say one word of the unlawfullness of the expedition. Hee likewise openly owned his esteem of all the Episcopall party, and when my father was absconding for refuseing to swear the Covenant, he visited him often. He wished that the Presbyterians would have questioned him for those things or put him again to renew the Covenant that so he might have found a fair colour for breakeing with them, but they thought it more adviseable to lett him alone. At last he grew so weary of mixing with them that he left his charge and retired into England. He would never engage in janglings so he wou'd not declare against them, but thought it was better to leave them. He likewise found that his English accent and that politeness to which he had accustomed himself made him less capable of doeing good among the commons, and so he thought he could not hold a liveing with a good conscience where he was as a stranger and almost a barbarian to the greater part. Soon after that the mastership of the Colledge of Edinburgh fell vacant, and that being in the town's gift, the offer of it was made him. It was an employment seperated from all ecclesiasticall matters, so he accepted of it. But tho the heads of the Colledge were generally considered as members of the presbytery, yet he never went to their meetings, and continued to live in great reservedness with all people. The English judges and officers then in Scotland courted him much and endeavoured often to hear him preach. Upon that he gave over all preaching in the pulpits of Edinburgh, for which the lowness of his voice furnished him with a very good excuse, but he preacht often within the Colledge and did it for the most part once a week. But finding crouds break in upon them from the town, he ordered that the gates should be shutt when he preached. Yet the judges were too great to be shutt out, so once when he came into the pulpit and saw them there, instead of preaching in English, he did it in Latine and so was delivered from their company. He went often into England in vacation time and once or twice over into Flanders. He grew a little accquainted with all the great preachers about London and the high flown men about Cromwell's court, but he often told me he could never be taken with any thing he observed among them and that all he heard from them was dry, unsavoury, bombast stuff. He was much taken with some religious men he saw in Flanders. Some of them were Jansenius's followers[4] and he thought they were men of extraordinary tempers. He did not stick to declare him self freely against the humour of magnifying and widening controversies of all hands, not excepting those with the Papists, and did often preach up a greater largeness of charity. Thus he had lived about twenty years in Scotland and was the most admired man that was in that kingdom.

[The Presbyterian Ministers]

The Presbyterian ministers were now turned out.[5] They were generally a grave and sober sort of men. They had little learning among them, but that of systems, commentaries and the Aristotelian philosophy; the reformers were the ancientest authors they read. They had much of the scripture by heart, and their sermons were full of quotations out of them, tho they were seldom criticall in the application of them. Their way of preaching was plain and intelligible but very dull. It went generally on doctrine, reason and use;[6] only those of a more exalted form ran out much into subtilities about scruples which they called cases of conscience. They prayed long and with much fervour. They preached twice on Sunday and for most part once on a week day. They catechised all their people at least once a year before their communiouns, and they used to visit the families in their parishes oft and to pray to them and exhort them in secret. They had also frequent private meetings, where those that were of a higher dispensation than the rest mett, sometimes without the minister and sometimes with him, and used to propose their cases and discourse about them and pray concerning them. And by these meanes the people, especially in the west, where those practices were frequenter, grew to that readiness, both in discoursing about sacred things and in praying, that it has astonished me oft to overhear them at these exercises; not but that they had many impertinences among them, yet it was a wonderfull thing to me, and perhaps not to be paralelled any where, that the generality of the commons should have been able to pray extempore sometimes for a whole hour together. Besides this, there was great severity in punishing some sins, such as whoredome, drunkeness, swearing and breach of Sabbath, and the church session and the pillar of repentance were great terrours. For fornication one was to make publick profession of repentance for three severall Lord's dayes, and this was executed on all with out respect of persons. The present Duke Hamilton submitted to it before his marriage. They were held in great esteem with the people. They were likewise for [the] most part men either of birth themselves, or had married with gentlemen's families, and they lived very decently in the country. By all these things they had so great an interest both with the gentry and commonalty that it was no wonder if the turning out so many all at once made great impressions on them. Their faults and defects were not so conspicuous. They were generally little men that had narrow souls and low notions. Many of them were fawning and servile, especially to the ladies that were much esteemed for piety. They were affected in their behaviour and extreamly apt to censure all that differed from them and to believe and report every thing they heard to their prejudice, and were a sowere and supercilious sort of people.

Their Opinions Concerning Civil Government

The greatest part of them had very ill principles as to civill government, of which there were two classes. The one was of these that thought the people had an unalienable right to them to assert their liberty and religion in opposition both to king and Parliament and to all the lawes that could be made. And ever after the riseing of the western counties in the year 48 against the Parliament and their committee,[7] all the high men amongst them have been forced in order to the justifying of that to assert this principle, which seemed ever to me the most distructive to the peace of mankind that could be. For if such a number of people as find them selves in a capacity to resist the government may lawfully do it, then all governments are left to an eternall danger since it is not possible to govern so, but very many will be dissatisfyed, and these will think the ends of government are broken by every ill administration. And as for religion, that is of a spiritual nature, in which wee are to expect only such rewards as are in this life internall and spirituall and that will be eternall here after. It is certain wee are to cast that care on him whose providence governs all humane affaires and are to think it enough if we are truly religious our selves and diffuse it among such as are about us. But there being such a vast difference of opinion concerning religion, it is certainly inconsistent with the peace of mankind (the preserving which must be a great part of religion) that men should raise commotions on that account. And this is yet much clearer in the christian religion, in which as we have the declaration of our Saviour that his kingdome was not of this world (for other wise his servants would have fought for him) and his practise likewise in reproveing St. Peter when he drew his sword in his defence, so it is also plain, both from St. Paul's Epistles to the Romans and St. Peter's first Epistle, that the apostles condemned all resistance; for indeed words can scarce be found out that are more express and plain than theirs are upon the subject. The nature of the christian religion proves this yet more fully than any particular text can do. It is a doctrine of faith, patience, humility, self-denial, contempt of the world and resignation to the will of God. We are called in it to bear crosses, to suffer persecution and to be ready to offer up our lives with joy for it, so that I much less wonder to find men that are very serious christians to be against all warrs whatsoever than to see them led into opinions about the lawfullness of resistance on that account.

It is also clear from the practise of all nations and from what is sett downe both in the Old and New Testament that a state of slavery is neither contrary to lawes of nature nor religion, nor to the christian doctrine; for in the New Testament masters are no where charged to manumit their servants but only to use them well, and St. Paul thought himself obliged to send Onesimus back to Philemon, for a servant haveing by a fair bargain given up his liberty was ever thereafter subject to his master; and by a greater congruity of reason, if a nation had chosen representatives, who had consented to lawes that gave away their liberty in the matter of resistance, the thing is done and can never be reversed, but by the same authority that established it. So farr I have given my sense of this very dangerous opinion that many of them held.

A Digression Concerning Government

The second opinion was that the king and the law were never to be resisted (that is the king [and] parliament, or the king governing according to law), but that lawes were the measure of subjects' submission as well as of their obedience and that the king was as much bound to his people by his coronation oath as they were bound to him by the oath of alledgiance; and therefore when he brake the one, they were absolved from the other and might defend themselves, particularly if there were any provisoes in the law that seemed to reserve this right to them. This becomes a question of law, whether the king is the head of the government, or is only trusted with it as the chief minister in it. In our case this seems to me to be out of doubt, for a king among us has his full power before he is crowned, so that whatever coronations might have been anciently, they are now only the pompous declarations of his power and not the investitures by which he receives it, and therefore his oath is only an obligation on himself to God. And since by plain and express lawes all the power of the militia is vested singly in the king with as positive exclusions of the subjects useing force against him as can be contrived in words, all this falls to the ground, and whatever power of selfe-preservation may be supposed to be in men before such lawes were made, yet these being once made, all that ceases, and the liberty of the subject is in so far given up. This has been alwayes my opinion in this matter, yet I do not deny but the thing will bear a great debate from the nature and ends of government in cases where they are visibly violated by high degrees of rage and cruelty. But all I can say in that case is that it is certain a madman ceases to be a man and naturally falls under guardians and tutors, and every man has a right to stop him if he runns about to do mischiefe. So the rage of a monstrous tyrant may be presumed to be really a phrenzy, and in that case he may be restrained, and the next heir is guardian, not so much because his people cease to be subjects as because he ceases to be a man. But this falls out so seldome that it signifies nothing to the debate as it is stated amongst us. I will go a little farther on this head because I studied it much with Mr. Nairn at this time and have since that time applied my thoughts so much to it that if I am able to search any one thing to the bottome, I have done it in this matter. And indeed my aversion to the ill conduct of affaires and somewhat of naturall heat and carelesness in my temper has given me the byass rather in favour of resistance than against it, so that nothing but the force of reason and conscience has determined me against it. I confess I could never understand what they meant who setled monarchy or the power of princes upon a divine right. Indeed under the Mosaicall dispensation, in which the Jews had the land of Canaan by an immediate grant from heaven, God did reserve the supream civill government to himselfe, and by prophets, solemnly authorised, he declared on whome he would have it fall. So it was done in the cases of Saul, David, Jereboam and Jehu. Therefore all that is in the Old Testament concerning civill government belonged only to the policy of the Jews and signifies nothing to the present matter. But in the New Testament there are no particular formes of government prescribed, only generall rules both for governours and subjects are given. The Roman government was then in one person, not only by conquest, but by the surrender the senate had made to Augustus, which gave him and his family a good title. I was for sometimes pleased with Dr. Hammond's notion[8] that the power of the sword must be from God since the people could never devolve it, for no man can give that which he has not; since then no man has a right either to kill himselfe, or to kill another, the right of killing can only come from God. This looked fine and plausable, but I thought it too fine and at last found the flaw in it. In order to the opening this, I shall give the best account I can of the beginning and nature of government. Certainly every father had an absolute power over his children, but upon his death they were all free, for primogeniture cannot be supposed by the law of nature to give the elder brother any sort of authority over his younger brethren. So upon the multiplication of mankind, their first seats growing too narrow for them, wee cannot but suppose that they hived out to the next fields and countries and the first possession gave a man as much right to any fields as he that came first could imploy or mannage, and he that came next had a right to sitt downe at a competent distance from him. Now self-preservation being a part of the law of nature, every man has it entire that is a free man, and such were all men upon the death of their father. There are two branches in self-preservation: the one is a right to beat off a violent and unjust aggressor, the other is a right to take reparation of any sudden or violent invasion, and without the second, the first cannot effect its end, which is self-preservation, and a man's whole property comes under the generall notion of himself. Every man likewise owes his neighbour assistance in the case of invasion, both as it is an act of humanity to another and as it is a mean to cover himself, for he cannot expect that another should assist him but as he is ready likewise to give him assistance when he needs it. Now government or civil society is nothing but a compromise for the use of this second branch of self-preservation, that is the takeing just revenge or reparation, in which men reserve the first part entire still of covering them selves from an unjust aggressor, for that will not admit of delayes nor stay for formes; but they resign up the other. Therefore I think with reverence to Dr. Hammond, whose memory I highly honour, that every man had a right to the sword against his neighbour that invaded him, both for self-defence and for just revenge and that government is the resigning up the second of these to be managed in such a method as shall be agreed on. Now the first occasion of these compacts seems to have risen from the loose companies of robbers who lived on spoyl and entered into combinations for the managing their designes and dividing the spoil. And as they prevailed over the weaker and more industrious part of mankind that gave them selves to agriculturre, so conquest and absolute monarchies did grow and spread it self by those troops of successfull robbers; and the combination[s] of the more industrious seem to have given the beginnings to commonwealths, which oft times or at times were eaten up by the conquerours. Another beginning of governments seems to have risen out of the industry and success of some and the lazieness and unsuccessfullness of others, who were thereby reduced to such extremities, as to sell themselves to the others, and by this means a rich man like Abraham came to have a great family, and with his 318 males he must have grown up quickly to a vast empire since we see to what a number 72 souls increased in Egypt in 400 years' time. So it is probable that those masters of numerous families took larg countries and gave their servants a great deal of their liberty again, but retained still a dominion over their properties or lives tho they did not always use it; and out of this the more regular and lasting monarches seem to have risen.

But upon the whole matter, since property and liberty are things alienable, we are not now to examine what were the first fountains or beginnings of this power, but must take things as we now find them. Those who assert a divine right had best shew where God has declared it, how it has come into such a family, how it comes to goe in some governments to the heir generall and in others only to the heir male, besides many other vast diversities that are in government; and how to derive all these from God is that which I could never concieve. But on the other hand, tho I do not derive my property to my goods from the law of God, but hold it only by the law of the land where I live, yet haveing this property once vested in me, the law of God setts a fence about it and binds up all men's consciences so that they cannot break in upon this property without sinning against God. So likewise tho I can see no divine right on which the king can found his title, there being no declaration made by God, unless it be in his supernaturall cureing the king's evill, on which I belive he would not willingly ground his title, yet he has otherwise a very good right: first, a long and immemorial possession, which is the first title to any property. This has been often confirmed in his ancestors and in himself by plain and express lawes and is more particularly bound upon the consciences of his people by the Oath of Alledgiance, all which are indeed humane titles, but they vest in him the same right to the crown and to all the prerogatives of it, and in particular to that of the militia, that any other man has in his property. And as the law of God secures every man in his property so that it is theft or robbery for another to invade it, so the same rule secures the king in his so that it is usurpation and rebellion to invade any part of it. And thus I have taken occasion to give this full and plain account of my opinion as to civill government and all rebellion against it, which I have so openly and frequently declared both in books, in sermons and in familiar discourses, that if I had not seen too much of the injustice and baseness of the world to wonder at any thing, I should wonder much to find my self aspersed as a favourer of rebellion, whereas I think there is no man living whose principles determine him more steadily against it.

JAMES KIRKTON (1620?–99) was deprived of his charge of Mertoun in Berwickshire for refusing to conform with the Restoration church establishment. Under the Second Indulgence, the authorities would have let him act as minister of Carstairs, but he rejected the offer and began to hold conventicles, for which in 1674 he was declared a rebel. In 1676 he was seized by Captain Carstairs, a government spy. Kirkton's account of the incident represents it as a violation of civil rights by a ruffian (of "feeble body"), backed up by scoundrels in power. But there are some puzzling things in his story, and the involvement of the Hamilton party in the affair was by no means disinterested. Kirkton got away to Holland but took advantage of the Indulgence of 1687 to return to Edinburgh. At the Revolution he was settled again in his old parish at Mertoun and assisted in the purge of Episcopalians from Edinburgh University. In Pitcairne's *Assembly*, he is Mr. Covenant Plaindealer and in the *Scotch Presbyterian Eloquence* "the everlasting comedian of their party" (p. 20). He was ridiculed for his popular way of preaching. But obviously the author of *The Secret and True History of the Church of Scotland* is not a fool, though he may not perhaps be very amiable. He has a dry, cool way of speaking (his writing catches a speaking voice), and he distances himself from the extravagances of his party. He has very little in common with the wild men like Peden. (See p. 171 ff. below.)

The Secret and True History was written in 1690. With Kirkton, as with Burnet, I have placed his account of affairs before pieces that were written earlier because it supplies historical background. *The Secret and True History* was published in 1817, edited by Charles Kirkpatrick Sharpe. The text below is based on an early eighteenth century copy in the National Library, Wodrow MS., Octavo 5, 2, ff. 205v–206v; 281–85; 304v–306v.

These two years in my opinion were the best two years that ever Scotland saw. For though alwayes since the Assembly at Glasgow the work of the gospell had prospered, judicatories being reformed, godly ministers entered and holy constitutions and rules daily brought into the church, yet now after Duke Hamilton's defeat[9] and in the intervall betwixt the two kings, religion advanced the greatest step it had made for many years. Now the ministry was notablie purified, the magistracy altered and the people strangely refined. It is true at this time hardly the fifth part of the lords of Scotland were admitted to sitt in Parliament, but these who did sitt were esteemed truely godly men. So were all the rest of the commissioners for Parliament elected of the most pious of every corporation. Also godly men were employed in all offices, both civill and military, and about this time the Generall Assembly, by sending abroad visitors into the countrey, made almost ane entire change upon the ministry in severall places of the nation, purgeing out the scandalous and insufficient and planting in their place a sort of godly young men, whose ministry the Lord sealed with ane eminent blessing of success, as they themselves sealed it with a seal of heavy sufferings, but so they made full proof of their ministrie. Scotland hath been, even by emulous foreignes, called Philadelphia, and now she seemed to be in her flouer. Every minister was to be tryed 5 times a year, both for his personal and ministerial behaviour; every congregation was to be visited by the presbytery that they might see how the vine flourished and how the pomegranate budded. And there was no case nor question in the meanest family in Scotland, but it might become the object of the deliberation of the Generall Assembly, for the congregational session's book was tryed by the presbyterie, the presbyterie's book by the synod and the synod's book by the Generall Assembly. Likewayes, as the bands of the Scottish Church were strong, so her beauty was bright. No error was so much as named; the people were not only sound in the faith, but innocently ignorant of unsound doctrine. No scandalous person could live, no scandall could be concealed, in all Scotland, so strict a correspondence there was betwixt ministers and congregations. The Generall Assembly seemed to be the priest with Urim and Thummim,[10] and there were not ane 100 persons in all Scotland to oppose their conclusions. All submitted, all learned, all prayed, most part were realy godly, or at lest counterfeited themselves Jews. Then was Scotland a heap of wheat set about with lillies, uniform, or a palace of silver beautifully proportioned. And this seems to me to have been Scotland's high noon. The only complaint of prophane people was that the government was so strict they had not liberty enough to sin. I confess I thought at that time the common sort of ministers strained too much at the sin which in these dayes was called malignancie, and I should not paint the moon faithfully if I marked not her spots. Otherwayes I think if church officers could polish the saints on earth as bright as they are in heaven, it were their excellency and the churches happiness. But this season lasted not long.

[The first Indulgence, 1669, and Leighton's Accommodation]

Now every body came to say it were better there should be liberty granted to dissenters in Scotland, who could not be subdued to the bishops, than that the land should be laid waste to make room for bishops. And as the countrey cryed for it, so our great men promised it and began in privat to shape the forme of it, especially the Earle of Tweddale, quho was frequently in discourse about it with Mr Robert Douglasse and Mr John Stirling. Lauderdale was ever thought to have retaind his old maxims till his unhappie second marriage and till he made Hatton, his brother, his substitute in the government.[11] Indeed, after these two he brought forth little other fruit than his serving his wife's avarice and his brother's violence. So at length Tweddale, at that time in great favor with the king and friendship with Lauderdale, made a voyage for court and brought down with him the first letter of indulgence. In it the king allowes his Councill to appoint such of the Presbyterian ministers as had been ejected by the act of Councill at Glasgow, 1662, to preach and exerce their ministry in vacant congregations and churches, with consent of the patrons, requireing these ministers to attend their respective presbytries and synods, otherwayes to have no right to the stipend, but only to the manse and gleib, and to confyne themselves to the limits of their respective paroches; requireing them also to keep fair quarter with their neighbour ministers, the conformists, and not to admitt any of any other congregation than their own to their sermons or sacraments, and that at their highest perrill. Also he allowes a pension of 400 merks to be payed yearly to such of them as are found moderat, peaceable men till vacant churches can be provided. This was the substance of the letter, and it bare date June 7, 1669. But quhen it came to the Councill table, great was the opposition the bishops made to it, so that no use was made of it till July 27; upon quhich day the Councill called before them some dozen of ministers for quhom friends had procured a speciall indulgence to so many churches. And quhen they appeared, the Councill read to them ane act containing the substance of the king's letter, commanding them all that are allowed to exerce the ministry to keep presbyteries and synods (that is, to joyn with the bishops), otherwayes confyning them within the limits of their respective

paroches, dischargeing them strictly to admitt any of their neighbors' congregations, either to sacraments or sermons, except the
congregation be vacant, and this upon their highest perrill. They
gave them also another act of a lyne or two telling them that the
patron of such a church having consented to their settlement in such
a paroch, therefore the Councill appoints such a man to exerce his
ministry at such a church, and this was all. The ministers being
informed how the Councill would proceed, conveened in private
and appointed Mr George Huchison, the most considerable of their
number, to declare in their names that whatever the Councill said or
did that might either look like, or really be Erastianisme, it was their
principle they had received their ministry from the Lord with full
prescription to direct them in the exercise thereof (that is, none else
they could acknowledge), upon quhich they were accountable to
him; and giving thanks to the king for his favour, promising also all
dutifull obedience and desyreing the same favor may be extended to
their brethren, he concluded. This was the first view the Presbyterians had of their indulgence, and truely even at the first glance
diverse deformities appeared in it. It was deryved from the king's
supremacy and so judged a bitter fruit of a bitter root. Ministers were
obtruded upon diverse congregations upon the consent of the patron
without respect to the call of the people. They were required to doe
evil, that is, to acknowledge Episcopal government. They were
made prisoners and punished in the harsh indulgence. No body
might partake of their ministry that they might keep good
neighbourhood with the curats,[12] and that was to conform their
sinfull ministry. Some ansyred that hard beginnings were good;
afterward the indulgence would be made both more clear and large.
Indeed this answer was not received, for the first view was the
fairest. The longer it continued, the more grievous it became. So that
the dispute turned upon these termes, quhether it was really a favor
done to the Presbyterians, or only a snare to wheedle them into
destruction. And certainly ane ambiguous overture it behooved to
be that was called friendship to the Presbyterians, but could never
passe at the Councill table till it was demonstrat by the chief advocats
for it, particularly my Lord Stair, that it would prove the ruine of the
Presbyterians, both because ministers were shutt up from visiting
the countrey and watering the dissatisfied party and likewise because
correspondencies among ministers were broke and no fear there was
of new ordinations, that quhich the bishops abhorred most of all.
And because it was in effect to extinguish the Presbyterians, I can
never think but the contrivers of it designed to give the bishops the
weather gage,[13] the reall advantage, and to give the Presbyterians a
false medicine to skin the ulcer before it was cleansed. However, all

the ministers named by the Councill were willing to accept, and by the consent of their brethren; also all the people of Scotland were willing to own their ministry. And indeed it was observed some of them had as great assistance in preaching the word as ever at any time before. Onely Mr John Brown, one of the exiled ministers in Holland, wrote over to Scotland (as he did frequently) and in a small treatise[14] endeavoured to prove the unlawfullness of undertaking a charge by virtue of the indulgence. Yet this hindered not the people of Scotland, especially the gentry, to procure licences for ministers, nor yet the Councill to goe on for half a year's time, dureing quhich space they past about 43 ministers, men of all sorts, and then they shutt the door. But because Mr Hutcheson's discourse, tho generall enough, had offended them, they never suffered any indulged minister to appear before them after him, but sent alwayes their act and licence to every one privately lest they should perchance have been troubled with a more clear declaration or protestation.

As soon as the ministers were once entered and settled in their churches, they begun then to understand their own case better than before. For first, the Councill took upon them to direct them in the duties of their ministry and worship, particularly dischargeing them to lecture[15] upon the scripture under the pain of losing their ministry. And shortly thereafter they sent west a committee, partly to protect and vindicat the curats, quho were disturbed by some of their people, and partly to inspect the ministeriall behaviour and censure the errors of the indulged ministers, whoes ordinary[16] they were pleased to call themselves. Then men began to perceive quhat they did not apprehend. However, these ecclesiastick visitors thought good to call before them all the indulged ministers in the west and strictly to examine their ministeriall behaviour, chiefly whether they obeyed the Councill's act discharging lectures, to quhich question few of them gave that answer that satisfied either their visitors or their party. Many of them also at that time changed their way; some of them changed their practise. Quhen as formerly they used only to read a part of a chapter, or one whole chapter at most, they begun then to read two chapters, quhich though, as they pleaded, it was near the form of the directory,[17] yet it was not approven that they should enter themselves at such a time to the schoole of ane Erastian magistrate to learn from him to worship God. Some of them read a whole chapter and without praise or prayer choised one verse for the text of their sermon, and so they thought they lectured in going through a chapter and might be said not to lecture because they made the whole chapter one text and so might please both a jealous people and ane usurping magistrate. Some of them lectured in place of the afternoon's sermon, and some of them laid it wholly aside. These courses nobody thought were either ingenuous, or constant, or wise. And quhen they were challenged quhether they observed the 29 of May or not,[18] they answered and practised the same way they lectured. When the visitors returned, Duke Hamilton related to the Councill the five ridiculous wayes they both observed and not observed that day; for some of them appointed their weekly sermon upon that day of the week quhich would fall by course to be the 29 of May for that year, some catechized that day, some baptised, some marryed and exercised on a chapter and some made evening exercise as on other nights. These practices, instead of satisfyeing both parties, offended all and were nothing for their honor. Mr John Livingstone, minister at Ancrum, then ane exile in Holland, a person of great worth and authority, in a letter he wrote to his parishoners, heavily complained upon their behavior, tho he commended the men themselves.[19] These and the like made the honest men's lives bitter and their ministry unconfortable. But beside the vexation they had from the Councill and the visitors, they were attended with a sort of rivals, quhom our governours sent west to darken their ministry by the excellency of their gifts, quhich our Councill hoped would either make the indulged ministers unsavoury and tastless in respect of their Hectors quhom they sent, or at lest would make the world say the people of the west countrey were ignorant and unreasonable if they slighted or disrelisht them. These were by the countrey people called in a mock "the bishops' evangelists".

The men were: Mr James Nairn, their paragon, a man of gifts, but much suspected as unsound; Mr Gilbert Burnet . . . , a man more disdained in the west countrey than followed at London, for tho he speaks the newest English diction, he spoke never the language of ane exercised conscience; another was Mr Laurence Charters, a silent grave man, but most unfitt to make countrey proselytes because of his very cold utterance, men wondered he should have undertaken it; then Mr James Aird, commonly called Mr Lighton's ape, because he could imitat his shrugge and grimache but never more of him; Mr Patrick Cook, so ordinary man I have nothing to say of him; and Mr Walter Patersone, a man so obscure I never heard of him. The harvest they reapt was scorn and contempt. A congregation they could never gather; they never pretended to have made a proselyte. In some places some few went to hear them for once, and that was all. In some places they baracado'd the doors upon them, in some places stole the rope, in some places the tongue from the bell. So they quickly wearyed of this foolish employment. But they would not serve the Lord for nought, for beside the stipend which belonged to the church quhair they served, every one of them hade a liberall reward from the Councill. And Gilbert Burnet gott money to buy soules, tho I never heard he either purchased one, or reckoned for the money. Moreover, at this time Bishop Leighton was placed at Glasgow to administrat that bishoprick while Burnet was laid aside.[20] He, to shew that he was not a bishop of the ordinary straine, will shew himself both pure and peaceable, forsooth, as men of heavenly minds should be. . . .

The proof the bishop gave of his peaceableness was in his famous overture for ane accommodation, quhich was nothing else but a trick to bring the Presbyterians into ane unperceived subjection to bishops. But the story was this. The commissioner Lauderdale at Leighton's request wrote to some of the most eminent indulged ministers in Leighton's diocie, Mr Hutchesone, Mr Wedderburn and Mr Baird, to be at Edinburgh, Aug. 9, 1670. Quhen they appeared, Lauderdale and Leighton propounded to them the overture for ane accommodation betwixt the 2 dissenting parties in the west, requireing them to give their judgement presently. They answered the case concerned their whole party and they had no commission, so they had a day in November following assigned, betwixt and quhich they should be clear. This happened the following year, but I put the whole purpose of the indulgence together. The substance of the overture was since presbytries were now settled through Scotland, the Presbyterian ministers should joyn in their respective presbytries and synods, quhair they should have their liberty to protest their judgement against Episcopacy; that matters should be carried by plurality of votes, and the bishop should pass from both his negative and positive vote. The ministers mett together both in the south and west and unanimously refused this accommodation as inconsistent with their principles and consciences. Their reasons were: the presbytries were not legal, being founded only upon the bishop's commission, quhich he enlarged or straitened as he pleased; they were destitute of the essential power of the keyes, both ordination and jurisdiction, quhich the bishop reserved for himself; they wanted their constituents, the ruleing elders. The bishop was still bishop in the presbytry and cloathed with episcopall power, tho he should forbear the exercise of it, so going to the presbytery should be a homologation of[21] Episcopacy. It is true the old Presbyterian ministers had kept presbytries, but these presbytries had all the essentialls of presbytries, so the case was not the same. However, Leighton insisted much upon it and gott a new meeting called, first at Pasley, where 26 ministers mett with him, and there he offered to alter his overture, but to the same purpose and to none effect. And lastly the ministers were called before the chancellor, Duke Hamilton and Tweddale at Halyrudehouse, quhair Leighton offered to dispute for Episcopacy against Presbytery, quhich Mr Hutcheson refused because against law. This made Gilbert Burnet, then present, to triumph that they would not disput for Christ's kingdom. And this made Mr Wedderburn accept the challenge, if the chancellor would desyre him, but the offer was not accepted, and so the bussiness concluded, and the project evanisht.

Moreover, this indulgence to a few was accompanied with the persecution of the body. All the Presbyterian ministers were banisht Edinburgh. Conventicles were punished with rigor and sometimes with cruelty. In June, 1670, happened the famous conventicle at Beeth-hill. The Councill catched some that had been present, and some of these they kept in irons five weeks. Charles Campbell and Robert Orre they banished upon an act of Parliament made after their crime, quhich was to refuse to betray their neighbors. Mr John Vernor they kept in irons at bread and water till his leg gangren'd, quhich cost him his life. This was thought ane ugly shaddow of ane indulgence. It was also thought ane unreasonable bargan that for a licence to 40 ministers, all the Presbyterians in Scotland should captivate their soules to the wretched curats through the countrey, and the body sell themselves for ease to a few. And tho the Presbyterians kept together, discontents and conventicles multiplied through the countrey all the time of this first indulgence.

[The "arrest" of Kirkton, June 1676]

At this time Lauderdale govern'd Scotland at his pleasure. Quhatever he desyred of the king was granted. Quhatever he required of the Councill was obeyed more readily than a hundred of our old kings. And truely quhatever the man was, he was neither judged a cruel persecutor nor ane avaritious exactor, excepting his brother and wife's solicitations, all the times of his government. So after the ministers were intercommuned,[22] things continued pretty quiet till a small spark kindled a great flame, and because much followed upon this particular and that it hath been falsly printed, I shall give it more distinctly. Mr James Kirton, one of the outed ministers, walking Edinburgh street about noon, was very civily accosted by a young gentleman, Captain Carstaires, attended by another gentleman and a lacky. Carstaires desyred to speak a word with him, to quhich he answered he would wait upon him, but because he knew not to quhom he spake, he quietly asked the other gentleman (James Scot of Tushilaw) quho this young gentleman might be, but Scot answered with silence and staring. Then Mr Kirton perceived he was prisoner among his enemies, but was very glad they carried him to a privat house and not to the prison, quhich they were very near. But they carried him to Carstair's chamber, ane ugly dark hole in Robert Alexander, messenger, his house. As soon as ever he was brought into the house, Carstaires abused him with his tongue and pusht him till he got him into his own chamber, quhich made the people in the house weep. After he had got him into his ugly chamber, he sent away Scot and Douglass his lacky, Mr Kirton supposed, to fetch his companions. But as soon as they were alone, Mr Kirton askt him quhat he meant, what he would doe with him. Carstares answered, "Sir, you owe me money". Mr Kirton askt him quhom he took him to be, denying he owed him any thing. Carstaires ansyred, "Are not you John Wardlaw?" Mr Kirton denyed, telling him quho he was indeed. Then Carstaires ansyred, if he were Mr Kirton, he had nothing to say to him. Mr Kirton askt him quho he was. He ansyred he was Scot of Erkiltone,[23] quhom indeed he did much resemble, but spoke things so inconsistent Mr Kirton knew not quhat to think, for if Carstaires had designed to make him prisoner, he might easily have done it before. But after they had stayed together about half ane hour, Mr Kirton began to think Carstaires desired money and was just beginning to make his offer of money to Carstaires quhen Jerriswood,[24] Andrew Stevensone and Patrick Johnston came to the chamber door and called in to Carstaires, asking quhat he did with a man in a dark dungeon all alone. Mr Kirton, finding his friends come, took heart. "Now", sayes Mr Kirton to Carstaires, "there be honest gentlemen at your door quho will testify quhat I am and that I am not John Wardlaw. Open the door to them". "That will I not", sayes Carstaires, and with that layes his hand on his pocket pistol, quhich Mr Kirton perceiving, thought it high time to appear for himself and so clapt Carstaires closs in his armes, so mastering both his hands and his pistoll. They struggled a while in the floor, but Carstaires being a feeble body, was born back into a corner. The gentlemen without, hearing the noyse and one crying out of murther, burst quickly the door open (for it hade neither key nor bolt) and so entered and quietly severed the struglers, tho without any violence or hurt done to Carstaires. As soon as Mr Kirton and the gentlemen had left Carstaires alone, Scot, his companion came to him, and they resolved not to let it go so, but to turn their privat violence into state service. And so to Hatton they goe with their complaint, and he upon their story calls all the lords of the Councill together, tho they were all at dinner, as if all Edinburgh had been in arms to resist lawfull authority, for so they represented it to the Councill. And he to[ld] the Councill quhen they were conveened that their publick officers had catcht a fanatick minister and that he was rescued by a numerous tumult of the people of Edinburgh. The Councill tryed quhat they could and examined all they could find and after all could discover nothing upon quhich they could fasten. Mr Kirton hade informed his friends that it was only a reall robbery designed and that indeed money would have freed him if Carstaires and he hade finished quhat he begun to offer, and the Councill could find no more in it. And so some councellors were of opinion the Councill might doe best to pass it so altogether. But Bishop Sharp told them that except Carstaires were encouraged and Jerriswood made ane example, they needed never think a man would follow the office of hunting fanaticks, and upon this all these quho resolved to follow the time and please the bishops resolved to give Sharp his will. So the nixt councill day, after much high and hot debate in the Councill, Jerriswood was fyned in 9000 merks, 3000 of it to be given to Carstaires for a present reward, Andrew Stevenson was fyned in 1500 merks and Patrick Johnston in a 1000, and all three condemned to ly in prison till Mr Kirton were brought to relieve them. This act bare date July 3, 1676, and occasioned great complaining. All the reason the Councill gave of their severe sentence is that they found Jerriswood guilty of resisting authority, by Captain Carstaires' production of his warrand before the Councill. But this did not satisfie men of reason. For, first, it was thought unaccountable that a lybell should be proven by the single testimony of ane infamous accuser against the declaration of 3 unquestionable men and all the witnesses examined. Nixt Carstaires' produceing of a warrand at the Councill table did not prove he produced any warrand to Jerris-wood, and indeed he produced none to him, because he had no warrand himself at that time. As for the warrand he produced, it was writt and subscribed by Bishop Sharp after the deed was done, tho the bishop gave it a false date long before the true day. It was well known Carstaires had a warrand from the bishop some moneths before, but it is as well known he burnt his warrand in the Earle of Kincairn's[25] house a moneth before he took Mr Kirton, so the foundation upon quhich the Councill built was a forgery. But at that time they were in such a rage that because a great number of the toun of Edinburgh went to see quhat they would doe in so odious a particular, a question was stated at the councill table whether all the people in the lobby should be imprisoned or not, and they escapt prison only by one vote. But Sharp and Hatton must have their will, and it was strange to consider quhat a flame this spark kindled. The first thing done after the vote was Hatton sent up a false information of the affair to his brother, quhairin he accused all who had spoke against the vote, as if they had agreed to subvert authority; upon quhich the Secret Council of Scotland was changed, and all who had spoke against the vote were ejected. Among these were Duke Hamilton, quho had said very much, the lord privy seall, the Earle of

Kincairn, formerly Lauderdale's great friend, the Lord Cochrane and severall others. The nixt thing they did was they intercommuned all the 16 ministers quho hade been formerly denunced rebells and were not intercommun'd, and among these Mr Kirton had the first place. But Mr Kirton in his distresse thought fitt to try his friendship at court, and therefore he took the boldness to write to the Dutchesse of Lauderdale, quho had made great professions of friendship to him some little time before. So he wrote and sent up a true information of the whole affair to her, complaining sadly of the wrong that was done him and his friends. All the kindness he had from her was after she had shewed his letter and information to the Duke, quho was indeed astonished at the information, confessing he had never in his life seen two informations differ so far as Mr Kirton's differ'd from my Lord Hatton's, she sent down his letter and information to the enraged Councill to see quhat they would make of it for ane accusation. This made Hatton foam and rage and swear, but at that time it was not in his power to doe more. The Earle of Kincairn and some others rode to court to complain and shew the king the truth in the matter and used great plainness with the king, lamenting much that Scotland was abused by Hatton's tyrrany under his brother's authority, supported alwayes by the king. But all to no purpose, for he had no more of the king but two or three fair words, and so he came away. Only he and Lauderdale of great friends became bitter enemies and so continued to the day of their death. Now their was nothing to be seen in the countrey but violence and persecution. A Presbyterian might not sett his head out at doors.

SIR GEORGE MACKENZIE of ROSEHAUGH (1636–91) was "that noble wit of Scotland" for Dryden ("A Discourse Concerning the Origin and Progress of Satire" [1692]; others thought of him as "bluidy Mackenzie". The most interesting and ambitious literary productions of the noble wit belong to his early years as a lawyer before his legal and political career absorbed his energies. *Aretina*, his romance, came out in 1660 and *Religio Stoici* in 1663. Not that he stopped writing. Other essays in the manner of *Religio Stoici* followed. He wrote *Memoirs of the Affairs of Scotland* and published vindications of his own and the government's policy and treatises on heraldry, Scots Law and legal eloquence. His literary reputation, however, rests on his early work.

As for bloodiness, that was the Covenanting party's view. He was a man of firm Royalist principles, who held office under a repressive government and discharged his duties ably and severely. After having made his mark as a lawyer and member of Parliament, he was appointed King's Advocate and Privy

Councillor in 1677. As King's Advocate, he was prosecutor of those who resisted the government's ecclesiastical policy. He helped to shape some harsh measures and has been charged with arbitrary and cruel dealings. Yet he took pains to make the rules for prosecution fair, and besides, according to his dignified *Vindication* of 1691, he felt severity was required to prevent civil war. It was a matter of civil, not religious, policy and not inconsistent with the professions of religious tolerance in the *Religio Stoici*. To the Presbyterian resistance, however, he was a persecutor, and along with Charles, James, General Dalyell and others he was excommunicated by the Cameronian preacher Cargill in 1680.

There were limits to Mackenzie's royalism, though. He opposed James's Catholic policy and was dismissed from his post as King's Advocate in 1686. He was reinstated in 1688, but the Revolution put him out again. Though the country was no longer safe for him, he attended the Convention Parliament of 1689 and almost alone voted against the act declaring that James had forfeited the crown. It then seemed wise to leave: "I punisht crimes but committed none & yet I will not return till things be setld, for others may want justice tho' I want not innocencie" ("Letter to Lord Melville", in Andrew Lang, *Sir George Mackenzie: His Life and Times* [London: Longmans, 1909], p. 303). He spent his last days in Oxford and the Bodleian.

Mackenzie along with Sir James Dalrymple of Stair, author of *The Institutions of the Law of Scotland* (1681), shows in an early form the literary culture of lawyers that was to be characteristic of the Edinburgh Enlightenment. He was the moving spirit behind the founding of the Advocates' Library. I wish I could admire the *Religio Stoici* more. Certainly Mackenzie is witty. He makes some sharp observations. He corruscates. The "Adresse to the Phanaticks" is full of the "turns" he recommended to Dryden, fuller than the succeeding chapters of *Religio Stoici*. But his way of saying things is often more remarkable than what he has to say, and his wit is always diminishing. For all the freedom of his opinions, the spirit behind his essays does not seem a liberal one, and although he gives us his opinions, he does not take us into his confidence or put us at our ease – his manner is too unrelentingly brisk for that. These are shortcomings in an essay writer. Yet in spite of an inadequate notion of urbanity, Mackenzie is remarkable among Scottish writers of the century for treating religion from the point of view of a man of culture. And obviously he shows literary gifts in the *Religio Stoici* that it is a pity the pressure of affairs did not allow him to develop.

141

"The Stoick's Friendly Adresse to the Phanaticks of All Sects and Sorts", *Religio Stoici*

The madcap zealots of this bigot age, intending to mount heaven Elias-like in zeal's fiery chariot, do, like foolish Phaeton, not only fall themselves from their flaming seat, but by their furious overdriving, invelop the world in unquenchable combustions, and when they have thus set the whole globe on a blaze, this they tearm a new light. It is remarkable in scripture that Jehu, who drove furiously and called up the prophet to see what zeal he had for the house of God, was even at that instant doing it more wrong then ever was done to it by unconcerned Gallio, who flantingly[26] cared for none of those things,[27] and that none of all the apostolick conclave desired ever fire might rain from above upon misbelievers, except the sons of Zebedee, who immediately thereafter arrived at that pitch of vanity as to desire to sit in heaven upon Christ's right and left hand, and that Peter, who was the first who did draw a sword in his master's quarrel, was likewayes the first who denied him. Firy zeal blows soon up such combustible mater as the sons of Zebedee, and that flash being spent and evaporat, a fall follows, as befell Peter. As that body is hardly cureable which entertains such ill-suited neighbours as a cold stomach and a hote liver, so the body of the visible Church may be now concluded to be in a very distempered condition when its charity waxeth cold and its zeal hot beyond what is due to either; and these feaverish fits of unnatural zeal wherewith the Church is troubled in its old and cold age betokens too much that it draws near its last period.

The inconsiderableness likewayes of our differences and inconsideratness wherewith they are persued induces me to believe that the zeal now à-la-mode is not that holy fire which is kindled by a coal from the altar, but is that *ignis fatuus,* or wild-fire, which is but a meteor[28] peec'd up of malignant vapours and is observed to frequent churchyards ofter then other places.

I am none of those who acknowledge no temples, besides these of their own heads. And I am of opinion that such as think that they have a church within their own breasts should likewayes believe that their heads are steeples and so should provide them with bells. I believe that there is a Church militant, which, like the Ark, must lodge in its bowels all such as are to be saved from the flood of condemnation, but to chalk out its bordering lines is beyond the geography of my religion. He was infallible who compared God's Spirit to "the wind which bloweth where it listeth; we hear the sound of it, but knows not whence it comes, or whether it goeth". And the name graven upon the whit-stone, none knows but he who hath it.[29] Eli concluded Hannah to be drunk when she was pouring out her soul before her Maker, and Elias believed that the Church in his dayes was stinted to his own person; and yet God told him that there were seven thousand in Israel who had not bowed their knees to Baal. Why then should any private christian determine magisterially that wherein the greatest of prophets erred?

The reed wherewith the Temple was to be measured (Rev. II. 2) was only entrusted to an angel, and yet he had not in commission "to measure the court that was without, because it was given to the gentiles". And albeit (Rev. 7.) the number of the Jews who were saved is determined, yet the number of gentiles is left indefinit and said to be numberless.

There is nothing more ordinar then for each nation to confine the Church within themselves. And in that nation again, one corner will have themselves the *sanctum sanctorum*[30] of that only temple, albeit our Saviour in his gospel assures us that men shall come from all corners of the world and sit down with Abraham, Isaac and Jacob, and John in his Revelation tells us that multitudes of all nations, kindreds and families were seen following the Lamb. Upon this same block do these likewayes stumble who put the bolt of their uncharitableness upon the gates of heaven to debar whole professions such as lawyers and physitians from entring in thereat, notwithstanding that the above cited place tells us that there were only twelve thousand of the tribe of Levi, the priest, chosen, and the like number was prickt[31] in the tribe of Judah, the law-giver. Aaron the priest did mould the golden calf and not Moses the judge, and Korah and Dathan were Levits and yet mutined against their magistrates.[32]

I say not this to disparage that holy function, for none shall wish Aaron's rod to flourish more then my self, and ordinarily these who love not to touch the Lord's anointed will likewaks be sure to do his prophets no harm, but I say it to take off an aspersion which hath stain'd too long and too injustly these of my own profession. Is not the Church our common mother, albeit, I confess, she is likewayes their nurse in a more particular way? And since there is heavenly mannah enough to aliment us all, why should christians deny to admit their brethren to an equal partage?

It grieves me sore to see my mother, the Church, tortur'd like Rebecca by carrying strugling twaines in her pained bowels.[33] And seing all christians are but pilgrims here, I admire that these pilgrims should leave off to journey and stand skirmishing and fighting with all such as will not travel their road, and albeit we acknowledge that the Spirit of God takes pains and is sufficient for leading all men in the way wherein they should walk, yet we must compell them, as if

143

either he needed our help, or we resolved to share with him the glory of their conversion. Thus God, who loves us all infinitly better then one any of us doth another, leaves us upon our own hazard a freedom in our choice, albeit we poor miscreants compell one another, denying to our fellow-creatures that freedom which he allowes all the creation. I wish we would consider how each man eats, drinks, cares for his family and performes all common duties rational enough without any compulsion, and yet in the affairs of religion, wherein doubtless man is led by a far more infallible assistance, there are many slips committed daily and grossly, notwithstanding of all the pains taken and force used by one man towards another. Thus it fairs with us as with patients whom when the physitians stints to a narrow dyet, then they loath even that food which their unreined appetite would never have rejected. And this makes me apt to believe, that if laws and law-givers did not make hereticks vain by taking too much notice of their extravagancies, the world should be no more troubled with these then they are with the chimeras of alchimists and philosophers. And it fairs with them as with taps,[34] which how long they are scourged keep foot and run pleasantly, but fall how soon they are neglected and left to themselves.

In order to which, it was wittily observed by our great King James the Sixth that the Puritans of his age strove with him and yet ceded at first in a difference between them and the shoemakers of Edinburgh, for not only pleases it their humour to contend where they may gain honour and can loss none, but likewayes by contesting with monarchs, they magnifie to the people their pious courage, assuring the world that such attempts require a particular assistance from heaven, and when their jangling hath extorted some concessions from the magistrate, as ordinarily it doth, then they press that success as an infallible mark of the jure-divinoship of their quarrel. Albeit I confess, that when these not only recede from the canonized creed of the Church, but likewayes incroach upon the laws of the state, then as of all others they are the most dangerous, so of all others they should be most severely punished.

Opinion kept within its proper bounds is an pure act of the mind, and so it would appear that to punish the body for that which is a guilt of the soul is as unjust as to punish one relation for another. And this blood-thirsty zeal which hath reigned in our age supposes our most mercifull God to be of the same temper with these pagan deities who desired to have their altars gored with blood and being devils themselves, delighted in the destruction of men; whereas the Almighty, who delights not in the death of a sinner, but rather that he should repent and live, hath left no warrand upon holy record for persecuting such as dissent from us, but even then when he commands that the prophets who tempts others to idolatry should be slain, yet speaks he nothing of punishing these who were seduced by them. And why should we shew so much violence in these things whereof we can show no certain evidence, as ordinarily we cannot in circumfundamental debates? Are we not ready to condemn to day as phanatick what yesterday was judged *Jure divino*? And do not even those who persecuted others for their opinions admire why they should be upon that score persecuted themselves? So that, victory depending upon event, we legitimat the persecutions to be used by others against our selves by the persecutions used by our selves against others. Our Saviour forbids us to pluck up the tears lest the wheat be pulled up with it; and how can the most pious persecutors know that the saints are not destroyed with the sinners?

It is remarkable that our Saviour disarmed zealous Peter, even when he was serving him in person in his greatest straits and against the most profligat of his enemies, the Jews, and that to prevent the irregular zeal even of the first and best of Christians, the blessed apostles, their divine master thought it fit to arme them not with swords, but with scrips, and to root out of their hearts all thoughts of violence, did oft inculcat in them that his kingdom was not of this world, convincing them by an excellent argument that he had no need of armes or armies, for else he could have commanded thousands of angells. Did ever God command the Jews to war against any neighbouring nation because they were pagans, a quarrel which would have lasted till all the world had been conquered? Or did our Saviour leave in legacie to his servants that they should force others to turn prosylits, which doubtlesse he had done if he had resolved to allow such a rude mean of conversion? All which makes me admire why in our late troubles men, really pious and naturally sober, could have been so transported as to destroy whom they could not convince and to perswade these who were convinced that religion obliged them to destroy others.

My heart bleeds when I consider how scaffolds were dyed with christian blood and the fields covered with the carcasses of murthered christians, and it's probable that there were more damned by unprepared deaths in the fields then were saved by peeping sermons in incendiary churches. And in this I admire the clemency of our royal master, who albeit his cause was more just then theirs, albeit he might have convinced them by obtruding to them their own practices, yet hath rather chosen to command with his scepter then his sword. But if the glory of God were the mark at which these do levell, why bestow they not their zeal rather in converting such as scarce know or acknowledge that there is a God? And why are they more enraged against these who agree with them in most things then these who dissent from them in all? Take not christians more pains to refute one another then to convince gentiles? And stand not Episcopists and Presbyterians at greater distance then either do with Turks and pagans? And to evidence that rather humour then piety occasions our differences, we may easily percieve that the meaner the subject is, the heat is always the greater.

If I had ever known so much as one whose faith had been the trophy of a debate, I should allow of debates in maters of religion, but seeing men cannot be convinced by miracles, it were ridiculous to presse conversion by arguments. All the divines in Europe could not press the best founded of their contraverted and polemick truths with so much scripture, or so many miracles as our blessed Saviour did his own divinity, which is the foundation of all truths, and yet the Jews and all the world besides slighted this infallible doctrine. And to evidence that there is a season of grace independent from arguments, did not many thousands turn prosylits at Peter's sermon, whom all our Saviour's homilies and miracles could not perswade? If one should say that the testimony of a few fishermen should not be believed in a mater of so great consequence as is the salvation of the whole world, especially when they did depone as witnesses in a matter wherein both their honour and livelyhood was concerned, might not this stagger some mean christian? And yet I believe these truths so much the more because such as these were its first asserters, for certainly it is one of the greatest of miracles that so few and so illiterate persons were able to convince the whole world. Thus we see that one may account that a miracle which another looks upon as a folly, and yet none but God's Spirit can decide the controversie; maters of religion and faith resembling some curious pictures and optick prismes which seems to change shapes and colours according to the several stances from which the aspicient views them.

The ballance of our judgments hath catched such a bruise by Adam's fall that scarce can we by them know the weight of any argument. But which is worse, there is as great a defect in our partial weighing as in the scales themselves. For when we take either the pro or con of any controversie into our patronage, we throw alwayes in arguments into that scale wherein our own opinion lyes without ever taking leisure to consider what may be alledged for the antipode proposition, and then when we receive an answer, our invention is busied, not in pondering how much conviction it hath in it, but by what slight it may be answered. And thus either passion, interest or frequent meditation, are still the weights which cast the ballance.

This firy zeal hath likewayes made another pimple flash out in the face of the phanatick Church, and that is a conceit that the saints have the only right to all God's creatures, the wicked being only usurpers and not masters of them. But I have heard this opinion, so beastly is it, confuted by Balaam's asse, who could tell it's master, "am not I thine own asse?" When Aaron and the people did covenant without Moses, then every man did bring his ear-rings to make up the golden calf. And we have lived in an age wherein we have seen our countreymen, like the Chaldeans, take the furniture both of the Temple and of the king's house and carry them away to their Babylon of confusions and in an age wherein sober men were forced to lend monies to buy for their own armes the heavy shekles of slavery: "Tantum religio potuit suadere malorum".[35]

Religion doutbless aims at two great designes. One is like the first table,[36] to perswade us to adore God Almighty. Another is to perswade us, like to the second table, to love our neighbour and to be a mean to settle all these jealousies and compesce[37] all these animosities which interest might occasion. And this appears by the Doxology jubilyed by the angels at our saviour's birth, "Glory to God, and peace and good-will towards men". And therefore as every private christian should be tollerated by his fellow subjects to worship God inwardly according to his conscience, so all should conspire in that exterior uniformity of worship which the laws of his countrey injoins. The first remark which God made of us after the creation was that it was not fit for man to be alone. There was only one Ark amongst the Jews by God's own appointment. And seing the gospel tearms the Church, Christ's spouse, it were absurd to think that he will divorce from her upon every error or escape, especially seing his blessed mouth hath told us that under the gospel it is not lawfull to divorce upon all occasions. And if he will not for these deny her to be his spouse, much less should we deny her to be our mother. May not one who is convinced in his judgment that monarchy is the best of governments live happily in Venice or Holland? And that traveller were absurd who would rather squable with these amongst whom he sojourns then observe these rites and solemnities which are required by the laws of the places where he lives. What is once statuted by a law, we all consent to in choosing commissioners to represent us in these Parliaments where the laws are made. And so if they ordain us to be decimated, or to leave the nation if we conform not, we cannot say when that law is put to execution, that we are opprest, no more then we could complain if one did remove us legally from these lands which he purchas'd from our trustee whom we had impowered to sell it.

As David said to Saul (I Sam. 26. 20), why went the king out to catch a flea? so may I say to our great divines, why contravert they about shadows? Is it fit that christians, who find it too great a task to govern their private souls, should be so much concerned how the

Church is governed by others? Wherefore, seing many have been saved who were most inexpert in these questions and that foolish zeal, passion and too much curiositie therein hath damned many, I may conclude that to pry in these is neither necessary because of the first nor expedient because of the last.

Since discretion opened my eyes, I have always judg'd it necessar for a christian to look oftner to his practice of piety then to his confession of faith and to fear more the crookedness of his will then the blindness of his judgment, delighting more to walk on from grace to grace, working out the work of his own salvation with fear and trembling then to stand still with the Galileans[38] curiously gazing up to heaven. True religion and undefiled is to visit the widow and the fatherless, and the dittay[39] drawn up against the damned spirits shall be that when our Saviour's poor ones were hungry, they did not feed them, when they were naked, they did not cloath them, without mentioning any thing of their unbelief in maters of controversie or government. And therefore I hope that these to whom I address my self in this discourse will rather believe me to be their friend because of their piety then their enemy because of their errors.

ROBERT LEIGHTON (1611–84) bent his life by an intellectual and moral effort of self-discipline toward an ideal of Christian simplicity and disinterestedness. Such a character may involve self-contradiction, but the misunderstanding and distrust he met with in Scotland arose rather from the bitter divisions of the country than from genuine doubts about the man. It is unfortunate that Gilbert Burnet's naively self-serving portrait of him (pp. 121–24) should be the kind of unmeasured eulogy that sinks its subject.

The main points about Leighton's career have already come up in Burnet's portrait and the headnote to this chapter. He was born in London, the son of a Scottish doctor, who was plundered, mulcted, whipped, mutilated, pilloried and imprisoned by order of the Star Chamber for his pamphlet, *Sion's Plea against Prelacie*. He was sent to Edinburgh University, where there was less danger, even under the bishops, of his being infected with prelatical ideas than at Oxford and Cambridge. With that sort of background, his openness on the subject of church government is remarkable. He lived in France for some time, however, and was impressed by Catholic pietism. On his return to Scotland, he became minister of Newbattle. He took the Covenants, but his uneasiness with the measures forced on him by Covenanting politics led him to resign his charge in 1652.

He was made Principal of Edinburgh University in 1653. At the Restoration he went along with the Episcopal settlement of the church and accepted the bishopric of Dunkeld. But his objections to the policy of religious coercion were so strong that he would have resigned if he had not been given a chance, as Archbishop of Glasgow, to put his plan for accommodation into practice. When that failed, he did resign and left for England. Toward the end of his life he was again involved in plans to conciliate the Presbyterians after the Battle of Bothwell Brig.

Men of party, Presbyterian or Episcopal, distrusted Leighton for his indifference to forms of church government, and the moral and intellectual authority that drew men like Nairne, Charteris and Burnet round him sharpened their feelings. Kirkton for instance sneers at Leighton's saintly ways and heavenly mindedness (p. 136). Leighton has a distinguished place among seventeenth century divines. He read more widely and thought more disinterestedly than those he had to deal with, and so his ideas were freer and clearer. But it is not easy to think how he imagined his accommodation would work. A similar plan, put forward by Archbishop Usher and Richard Baxter in England, had failed. It is not possible to be tolerant of intolerance. But it must be added that Leighton was asking the Presbyterians to renounce not just a narrow belief in the divine right of Presbytery, but their fundamental principle of the separation of the powers of church and state. For Leighton's broad view that differences between forms of church government were insignificant as far as religion was concerned meant that there was no good reason for not accepting the form of church government the civil power set up, and that was Erastianism. Besides, *The Rule of Conscience* shows that he held the duty of passive obedience categorically and shows also in its asperities an impatience with those whose principles he thought muddled and obstinate. His belief in the wisdom of the authorities does not seem well founded after we have read Burnet's portraits of them.

Though *The Rule of Conscience* is organized as an encyclopaedic Aristotelian treatise, it comes to life as a polemic against Presbyterian rebelliousness, a polemic that avoids a standard controversial pitched battle against the system of Presbyterian thought on church and state, but goes instead for its moral centre, the conscience. His method, which is to clear up the proper use of the term and to expose false and mystifying ones, belongs to the critical movement of the time. So does his easy and lucid expository style. Some of that is lost in selection, for

149

part of Leighton's lucidity lies in his orderly unfolding of the subject.

The Rule of Conscience is not a typical work. Leighton is one of the finest of the seventeenth century christian moralists. To appreciate how impressive he is in that character, the best course is to go to Coleridge's *Aids to Reflection*, an arrangement of aphorisms, chiefly drawn from Leighton's works. He is more penetrating and mature than Binning or Henry Scougal, and the equal probably of any British divine. But his excellence as a moralist comes out more in the maxims about how to live well scattered throughout his sermons and commentaries than in his attempt to develop his ideas systematically in *The Rule of Conscience* and more in his observations on the moral psychology of the individual than in his ideas about the regulation of human life in society. Again the style of *The Rule of Conscience* is untypical. It is true that Leighton's commentaries and sermons have the same clear and level sort of exposition. And Leighton, with Binning, was one of those who introduced a more simple way of preaching (see Introduction, p. 14). But with Leighton's sermons, unlike Binning's, one can see what Baillie's sour remark about a "high romancing style" might be getting at. Others have admired a style that conveys "his sublime view . . . of religion and morality as the means of reforming the human soul in the divine image", as Coleridge has it, and his overriding concern with a lively and heartfelt piety.

Leighton published none of his work. Collections of his sermons and his commentaries appeared in the 1690s. *The Rule of Conscience* is incomplete and the manuscript is missing. It was first published as *The Four Causes of Things* in *The Whole Works of Robert Leighton*, ed. George Jerment, vol. 5 (London: Ogle, 1808). This is the text I have used (pp. 181–84; 189–99; 201–202; 205–206), though I have taken the title and some emendations from William West's edition of *The Remains of Archbishop Leighton* (London: Longman, 1875). West suggests the piece was written between 1671 and 1675. Other treatments of conscience can be found in Rutherford's *A Free Disputation against Pretended Liberty of Conscience* (1649) and Barclay's *Apology* (1678).

The Rule of Conscience

Conscience is that light which God hath set up in every intelligent and rational creature to direct them, admonish and censure them: it exercises the office of a lawgiver in directing them, of a monitor and witness to advertise or testify for or against them, of a judge to sentence them.

Conscience is the clearest beam of divine light and of the image of God in the soul of man. It is the purest fountain of morality and that which most hardly admits of a wrong bias. When men are most corrupt in their judgments, vitious in their wills and affections, debauched in their profane practices, yet their conscience will still check and challenge them.

Conscience is a light which God hath set up in man to be witness. The malice of devils and men cannot totally extinguish it, but of necessity they must believe there is a God to judge and punish them, notwithstanding all their endeavours to extinguish this light and of their desires to believe that there is not a God. They may sear, cauterize and stupify their conscience, yet as a drunken man, it awaketh out of sleep, though it speak not distinctly and efficaciously. So much, however, shall they know by the voice and smatterings of it that it is alive. Conscience is either the best friend, or the worst enemy a man hath.

Conscience is of high esteem amongst all. It is our perpetual companion and most useful in all our actions. It is much spoken of, but little known, much professed, but little practised. Some mistake the very nature of conscience so far that they take other things for it, and that which is will, humour and interest in them they call their conscience. The reason of this seems to be conscience is a thing tender and sacred and not to be violated, and they flee to it as a sanctuary. If you ask them a reason for what they do, instead hereof they will tell you it is their conscience. If you ask them a reason why they will not do such things, which either the law of God or human authority commands, they tell you it is for their conscience sake they cannot do it. You must stop and go no further; this is a sufficient salve for all things, this is the strong buckler under which men may do all things or nothing, according as their will, humour, or interest inclines them. It is ready upon all occasions. Ye can no sooner draw the sword of the sharpest wit and strongest reason nor bring forth the most express precepts of the word of God nor any law or ordinance of man, enforced by the strength of supreme authority, but the buckler of conscience is ready at hand to repel all that can be said. The exercise of this piece of armour is so easily learned that the dullest blockhead can take it up at the first reading.

Others there are who very unhappily mistake the measures, authority and limits of conscience, allowing it more than is due to it, extending its legislative power beyond whatever God assigned it. Hence arise errors of very dangerous consequence. It is most fit that in a matter of so much importance, we make some enquiry after the nature, power and office of conscience.

Conscience, as to the signification of the name, imports a

knowing together with another. There is a science presupposed and a conscience. This may relate either to God, or to ourselves. God knows a thing, and together with God, we know it. Or it may relate to ourselves: we know speculatively by the word of God and by sure reason that such a thing is good, and yet by a reflex knowledge, we know also that we have neglected and not done that good. The direct act of our knowledge is science; the reflex act, whereby we consider our ways and doings, is that which more precisely is conscience. Knowledge directs conscience, and conscience presupposes knowledge . . . .

But if it shall be inquired to which of the faculties conscience is to be reduced and in which of them doth it specially reside, we hesitate not to say that is is radically in the understanding, this being the principal faculty of the soul. Conscience is the clearest beam and the most eminent ray of knowledge in the understanding, the most divine thing in man, the very eminence, cream and flower of the soul. . . .

There are two extremes in the matter of conscience very dangerous, on which many do rush to their own great hurt. The one is that many make little or no account of keeping a good conscience; they make shipwreck of it. There are some, of whom it is said that their conscience is defiled and that their conscience is seared with a hot iron (Tit. 1, 15; Tim. 4, 2). They disregard the voice of God and their own conscience. There are another sort who run to the opposite extreme, who magnify their own conscience above all that is called God, yea, the most express laws of Jesus Christ they contemn, slight and prefer to them the dictates of their own erroneous conscience. They make their conscience their Bible, their lord and their lawgiver. They think themselves sufficiently warranted to do what they please, or leave undone what they list, if so be their conscience (as they pretend) allow them. They plead for such immunities upon the account of their consciences and suppose themselves to be set above the reach of all check from any power upon earth.

We shall take notice of something on which they build the monarchy and sovereignty of conscience.

One argument by which they try to prove the sovereignty of conscience is that conscience is God's deputy and vicegerent in man. The voice of conscience is supposed to be the voice of God, and whatever any power on earth says to the contrary, the voice of God in the conscience is to be preferred.

To this grand objection or argument we return these considerations for clearing the case. 1st. We grant that God hath placed in every man a conscience to be as a light to direct him, to warn and check him, a judge to acquit and condemn him. This is the office of the conscience according to God's intention and primary institution, and for this end is conscience called God's deputy and vicegerent in man, and the voice of it is supposed to be the voice of God. But upon the other part, it is as true that as his fall did crush, deface, disorder and debilitate all the other faculties of his soul, so also that of the conscience; by reason whereof it is not now able rightly to exercise the function first committed to it. Neither is it true that every man's conscience is to be supposed to be the voice of God, but oftentimes it is the voice of Satan. There is an evil conscience, an ignorant conscience, an erroneous conscience, a cauterized conscience, and no man can suppose these consciences to be the voice of God. If man had stood in his primitive integrity, much more could be said in favour of conscience than can rationally be pretended now in its lapsed condition. And to descend to particulars, on examining the offices of conscience and its abilities to perform them, it will easily appear that no such confidence is to be put in the infallibility of some men's consciences as they vainly pretend to. The office and exercise of the conscience may be comprised in these three acts: 1st. it directs us by its light and knowledge; 2dly. by a reflex act it examines and compares our actions with the rules of religion and right reason, whether they be conformed to these or not; 3dly. it pronounces sentence for or against us. Now if conscience fail in all or any of these, it is clear that it is not any such safe guide to be trusted and followed without all doubt or hesitation. How fallible it is in all of these may easily appear. 1st. If we consider what darkness, blunders, ignorance and error are upon the understandings and minds of men, even of the best, and that the light of our conscience is nothing else but that light which is in our minds and intellects, we have not reason to be too confident that this light will prove an unerring and infallible guide. 2dly. If we consider the second act of conscience, which is to compare our actions with the rule, how apt are we to mistake the true measures and proportions of the rule and how often do ignorance, interest, prejudice and self-love bias us in thinking that we are walking exactly according to the rule when it is not so. "All the ways of a man are clean in his own sight, but the Lord weigheth the spirits (Prov. 16, 2)." 3dly. Consider the third act of conscience, which is to give sentence upon a man's actions, and how often doth the conscience err in this! Oftentimes the erroneous conscience justifies man in those things wherein they are truly condemnable and condemns that which is justifiable. But if it be replied that although a mere natural conscience instructed by the mere light of nature be a defective guide, yet a sanctified and renewed conscience, instructed by the scripture and illuminated by the Spirit of God, is a very safe and sure guide and by no means to be declined, we would not let pass without notice the versatility of some such persons in shifting from one thing to another.

First, they pretend conscience itself and then shift the state of the question and fly to scripture and divine illumination. Why will they not say that scripture and divine illumination is that which we ought to follow and obey absolutely and implicitly? For scripture is not that which we properly call conscience, but it is the rule of conscience, neither is conscience properly that which we call scripture or supernatural illumination. But it seems they would have conscience and scripture synonymous words, signifying one and the same thing, so that to walk by scripture is to walk by their conscience, and to walk according to their conscience is all one as to walk according to scripture. But these are very different, for many times men walk according to conscience when they are walking quite contrary to scripture.

2dly. But [as for] what they say of their conscience conducted by scripture and illuminated, I pray how many ignorant, self-conceited persons of these times do miserably misinterpret and wrest scripture to their own perdition? And yet their conscience thinks they are walking according to scripture, and when they are walking after their own blind and brainsick fancies, they think they are walking after the illuminations of the Spirit. Hence it is that the private conscience of every man is not a fit interpreter of the scripture nor a fit discerner to distinguish between divine illuminations and satanical illusions, and therefore such consciences can be no sure nor warrantable guide nor be justly presumed to be the word of God.
. . .

2dly. But for a second answer, we say if every private man will affirm that his own conscience is God's deputy, vicegerent and voice, let him consider that his conscience is but a private deputy to order him in his own private actions, wherein he may determine himself, and in things that are not determined by the laws of God and his superiors.

But, moreover, let him consider that God hath also greater and superior deputies, whose jurisdiction is higher and more extensive than any private person or his conscience. God hath supreme civil powers upon earth, whom we are commanded to obey. He hath also ecclesiastical officers in his house to be the guides of our souls, whose lips should prescribe wisdom and teach understanding and at whose mouth we are to receive the law. Seeing that such persons as these are also God's deputies in a more public authoritative way than any private man's own conscience, why are we not to hear them and to presume that their consciences, as the voice of God, is to be followed and not disobeyed? Have we any scripture that speaks so expressly and clearly of the power of our own private consciences as it doth of their power? Are we any where in scripture tied and so strictly commanded to follow and obey the dictates of our own consciences as we are commanded to be subject to them and not resist them?

But it may be objected that both civil and ecclesiastical rulers may err.

That they may err and often do err is no question. But may not private men's consciences err also? And is it not to be presumed that private men, who walk by their own private notices, are much more likely to err than persons whom God hath placed in public authority, assisted with more public and eminent aids than private persons, and have the advantages of the public and private counsels of the best, wisest and most learned of the land to consult about laws and governments? These in all probability are more likely to prescribe better what is fit for the public good of church and state than any private persons can possibly do, who are remote and altogether unacquainted with the mysteries of government . . . .

A second argument men bring from the immunities and powers of conscience and that conscience is not subject to man nor can it be sisted[40] at any human tribunal. It belongs to God's judgement-seat; it is God that gives laws to the conscience; he is lord over it, and not man; therefore, we are not answerable to man for our consciences, nor to be punished by men for their dictates.

We grant, indeed, that God himself is lord and lawgiver to the conscience, and it is not at man's tribunal, but at God's, it must answer. But upon the other part, it is true that the superior powers on earth have dominion over our bodies and estates, over our lives and fortunes. They have power to make laws and enact penal statutes. They have power to call us to an account for our external actions and to punish our persons if we violate the laws of the commonwealth and disturb the peace of the church. They are not concerned with our conscience, but with our external obedience or disobedience; that is all they look after. And we must not pretend that we have made insurrection, sedition and rebellion, being moved thereto by our conscience, and therefore ought not to be punished because we did it according to our conscience. The magistrate is not bound to take notice of the conscience of the criminal (but refers that to God's judgement-seat, to which it belongs), but to take notice of the crime itself, and for it, to punish the person according as the law of God and of the land requires.

For this cause we must distinguish betwixt the immanent, elicit acts of the conscience and its transient and imperate[41] acts. The immanent, elicit acts of the conscience are internal in the soul, remote from the knowledge of men, not liable to his laws. They are only subject to God and his spiritual law. Though a man's private conscience judge it lawful to murder kings, overturn governments, use fire and sword against all good subjects, yet so long as this act, however bloody, remains hidden in the heart, the person is not punishable by man. But if the man vent the wickedness of his heart by words or deeds, then the acts of his conscience are transient. These acts are the imperate acts of the conscience, and so a man becomes criminal and punishable. So that a man is not properly punished for his conscience, but for the evil, external acts of a wicked conscience.

2dly. We say that magistrates have not a direct, immediate power over man's conscience, obliging them in their conscience to think that good and lawful, true and just which they determine by the laws to be so, whilst may be it is otherways. The understanding cannot be compelled to judge that to be a truth which it clearly knows to be an error, nor can the will inwardly be forced to chuse that for good which evidently it perceives to be evil, nor that to be a conscientious thing which the conscience is sufficiently and rightly instructed to be against conscience. This is not what human powers lawfully claim. Yet we say that magistrates have an indirect power from God, who hath direct power over the conscience, to make good and whole-some laws for the commonwealth, which the subject is bound to obey not only by external evidence, but even for conscience sake (Rom. 13). If he makes not conscience to obey, he sins against God.
. . .

But it may be asked when an erroneous conscience is principled with a strong persuasion, contrary to divine truth or precept, what shall a person do in that case? He cannot be bound to believe that to be truth which they are persuaded to be an error, for this were to believe not only without faith, but even contrary to the faith and persuasion of his own conscience, which thinks the contrary. Nor can he in faith act in obeying a precept which he thinks unjust; if he does, he sins, and no man can be bound to sin.

God neither doth nor can bind any man to sin or commit evil. But as to the case, when divine authority lays on a bond, the contrary persuasion of an erroneous conscience cannot take off the bond. This were to make man stronger than God. And therefore let the conscience err as wide as it will and be as confident to the contrary as it can be, yet still the yoke of divine authority lieth on. That which God requireth of a man in such a case is not that he give obedience with a doubting contradicting conscience, but that he lay aside his error and contradiction and obey in faith and in truth; otherways he is still guilty. And for this cause a man is with all humility and sincerity to use all the means that God hath appointed for finding out the truth by prayer and supplication, by searching the scripture, by going to the law and to the testimony, by taking the advice of good and wise men and the direction of those whom God hath appointed to be our spiritual guides.

But [though] divine authority must not be opposed by man's doubting and erroneous conscience, because he is supreme lord and lawgiver both over men's actions and consciences, yet the case will not hold in reference to human authorities, whose power is infinitely below the power of God, and they have not power over men's consciences, but only over their persons and actions in things civil and external; and therefore if they cannot obey them without sin, to punish men for not doing that which they cannot do without sinning seems most unjust. There is nothing endears the hearts and affections of a people so much to their prince as mercy and clemency, and therefore it would argue much goodness to shew favour and indulgence to men of tender consciences. And it would argue great prudence in a prince to bring down and accommodate his laws to the people's humour when they cannot be got screwed up to the laws. It would prevent tumults and insurrections, which are of dangerous consequence.

This query, or doubt, composes the most substantial heads and nervous[42] arguments used by some restless malcontents in this age, and because several things are here bundled up, we will take them apart and consider them distinctly . . . .

If the powers on earth command any thing contrary to the express command of God, we are no ways to give alike obedience, for it is better to obey God than man. But we must give passive obedience and suffer, for it is better to suffer than sin, and if we suffer for righteousness' sake, happy are we (1 Pet. 3, 14). But in noways are we to resist. Resistance is absolutely forbidden, and that upon pain of condemnation, and thus even when the powers were tyrannical in passing many oppressive acts, yea, when they were heathenish and idolatrous, commanding many ungodly and profane things, yea, when they were anti-christian, giving out many severe edicts, persecuting christians and all who called upon the name of Jesus; this was Paul's gospel (Rom. 13, 12). Such who now teach that christian magistrates may be resisted, let them consider whether they be not preaching another gospel than Paul taught and what is the doom of such.

The second thing to be considered is that God only is lord and master over the conscience; men have not power over the conscience, but over man in civil matters.

To this we say that God is supreme lord over men's bodies, actions and consciences, yet God, who hath incorporated men in a public, political body or commonwealth, hath for the government of that great body set over it some public supreme power as his deputy and vice-gerent upon earth. The supreme power is authorized of God to rule the body, and laws are surely the best and fittest mean of government. They have power not only to make laws, but to enact sanctions and penalties by death, confiscation of goods, by mutilation or banishment, according to the nature of the guilt, the sanction of the law, or pleasure of the prince. This public body and every member of it must be ruled by law in reference to their public politic actions. Whatever a man may do as a private man in his own affairs, wherein the public is not concerned, yet as a member of the commonwealth, he is not at his own disposal and in reference to the public, must not be ruled by his own humour and private spirit, or by his own conscience; for this which is called his conscience, what else is it but the sentiment and dictate of his own private reason, apprehension, judgment and practical understanding?

And which is much to be noticed, men would fain juggle in this matter. They will not in plain terms say that they are wiser than the public counsels of the land, that they are more intelligent and rational, that their understandings and reason is preferable to the understanding of many wise and learned men, but for all this they will prefer their own private conscience to all these. And what is that which they call their conscience? Is it any thing else but their own reason, practical judgment, sentiment and persuasion of things? If it be any thing else, let them name it. They place a great mystery in the word "conscience", so that the same very material and individual thing, when it passeth under the name of reason, understanding and judgment, they will grant that in this they are far short and below other men. But the same thing receiving another designation and let it be called conscience, then, forsooth, it must be above all the powers on earth . . . .

It is to be regretted that many now-a-days do needlessly and curiously interest and involve their consciences in opposition and wranglings and in matters not concerning them. And as Satan, the prince of darkness, undoes one part of mankind with atheism, profanity and the work of the flesh and of darkness and unconsionableness, so he can transform himself into an angel of light and undo others by heresies, errors, by dubious and scrupulous consciences, such as by ignorance, imprudence, pride, willfulness, scrupulosities and hypocrisies and by mistaking the office and limits of their conscience.

Ignorance is a great cause of the doubts and scrupulosities of some men's consciences. Were they more intelligent and rational, they would not make half the noise they do. A thing may be very clear in itself and intelligible to a man of understanding of which the ignorant make a mountain and raise a cloud of needless, nonsensical scruples. Folly and imprudence involve them to be meddling in matters not concerning them. Thus every pedlar and mechanic whose calling leads them to be meddling with their calling, chop and handy labour,[43] they, forsooth, must be handling the helm of government and canvassing all the affairs of church and state. And if things be not modelled and managed according to their foolish, ridiculous fancies, presently those in authority are quite wrong, and they cannot in conscience obey them. He who cannot well manage his own plough and cottage must canvass and censure both church and state, and can a greater folly readily possess the head of a Bedlamite?

Pride blindeth the science of some, which being done, conscience cannot but err. Some have taken up an opinion upon trust from some person of whose piety and learning they had a great veneration, as if they were men who could not readily err, or they have espoused some opinions and been the zealous asserters of them. The pride of their heart and the opinion they have of their own wits doth so inebriate them that they are ashamed to pass from their espoused principles and practices. That they will not be reputed changeable, they set all their wits and fancies to work to find out defence, which at length so steals into their minds and humours that at last they make it a matter of conscience to defend both their principles and their practices. Thus it is with many who call that conscience, which is nothing else but the shadow of an empty name and reputation.

LAWRENCE CHARTERIS (1625–1700) shared Leighton's principles. Like Leighton, he accepted the Episcopal settlement of the Restoration, but unlike him declined the offer of a bishopric. He took part in Leighton's attempt at accommodation as one of the Bishops' Evangelists in the South West (see Kirkton, p. 135). In 1675 he left his parish of Yester to take up a chair of divinity in Edinburgh but resigned over the Test of 1681. When the Test was dispensed with in 1688, he went to Dirleton as minister and at the Revolution accepted the Presbyterian settlement but tried to moderate the measures now taken against the Episcopalian clergy.

The Corruption of this Age was published posthumously in 1704. Like Leighton's *Rule of Conscience*, it is a polemic against the non-conforming Presbyterians. It takes the form of letters to a friend not a disputation, and instead of engaging with the arguments of the high Presbyterians, it makes a moral criticism of their enthusiastic temper and holds up against it what they would have thought a dry, moral sort of Christianity, in which the stress is on self-examination, self-mortification and an even tenor of religious life. It is not certain when *The Corruption of this Age* was written but it seems reasonable to place it with Leighton's *Rule of Conscience* since it must have come out of the same experience of the intransigent party.

The Corruption of this Age, pp. 20-25

It is too evident that the idea of form'd christian perfection and of an eminent measure of grace which too many have in this age in their minds is partly false and partly defective. They seem quite to mistake what true Christianity is and wherein it consists. They have not in their minds a true and compleat character of the christian spirit and temper. Neither do they sufficiently know how we should carry and behave in the world. You may observe that not a few take such persons as are careful in attending on the publick ordinances, who pray in secret and in their families and read the holy scriptures for very good christians if they do with all express a great zeal and concernedness for their peculiar notions and opinions, which they look upon, since they are opposed and controverted, as the truths for which they are obliged to contend, and if they have a great aversion from those who are not of their opinion, way and party. They look on those persons as eminent christians who besides the former character, have a great gift of prayer and great freedom in speaking to God and pouring out their hearts before him, and who can speak and talk promptly and fluently of divine things, especially if they have some singular and sublime notions which are beyond the reach of the vulgar and are much weighted as they speak and change the tone of their voice when they express their thoughts of divine things. These seem to them to be excellent christians who can give a particular account of the steps of their conversion, of the work of the Law upon them, of the effects of the spirit of bondage which they have felt and of the many sore and great exercises under which they have been, and who can tell how they closed with Christ and how many and great doubts they have had about their interest in Christ and what assurance they now have thereanent. These appear to them to be very eminent christians who can talk of their communion with God, of the extraordinary visits and special favours they have received from him and of the singular manifestations and communications of the divine goodness with which they have been favoured. You have, it's like, observed that most of the better sort of people among us seem to place almost the whole of Christianity in covenanting with God, in closing with Christ and relying on him.

They seem to think when that is done, all is done which is required of us. It is true that all good christians do joyn themselves to the Lord and give up themselves to Jesus to be ruled and saved by him and expect life and blessedness on his account, but if this their deed be not introductory to a holy and religious course of life, it signifies nothing. Unless our mental transactions with God be attended with a due care to do his will and obey his laws and to live righteously, soberly and godly in this present world, and unless we be stedfast in his covenant, we may be sure that our hearts are not right with him, in whatsoever manner we have transacted with him. It may seem strange, since it is so plainly told us in the holy scriptures what manner of persons we should be, that so many who read the scriptures are so much mistaken in a matter of so great importance and that they do so tenaciously adhere to their mistakes.

This seems not so much to be imputed to the weakness of their understanding as to the neglect of impartial and due consideration of what they read therein and to the prejudices by which their minds are not a little perverted, but chiefly to the secret but powerful influence of their lusts and passions and of their corrupt inclinations, tho' they are not aware of it and perceive it not. While finding that such a lame and false character of true Christianity and religion is consistent with the ways which they have chosen for prosecuting their carnal and worldly projects and designs, they are unwilling to quite it; they hold it fast and maintain it. It is to be feared that some pastors contribute not a little to the diffusing and supporting such wrong notions of religion among people, while they insist so much in representing to them the necessity of diligent attendance on the ordinances and of a due care for avoiding errours and unsound opinions in matters of religion, of zeal for the truth and of mental transactions, covenanting and closing with Christ, but do not so much represent to them the necessity of obedience to the laws of Jesus, of righteousness and honesty in all our dealing, of an awful regard for God, of a due care to keep his commandments and an intire submission to his will and compliance with it, of charity, mercy, purity, patience, meekness, peaceableness, humility and such other graces and virtues, which Jesus hath specially recommended to us by his precepts and example, and which were so conspicuous in the primitive christians.

These mistakes about true Christianity, its true form and nature, keep them still very low and defective christians. It is therefore necessary, if we would grow in grace and advance in virtue, that we bestow due care to have deeply sunk and impressed on our minds a great sense of what we should be and that we endeavour to fix therein a clear and exact knowledge of true Christianity and a just form and copy of a perfect man in Christ Jesus. This copy is not to be taken from that which appears from the temper and lives of even the most eminent professors and pretenders to piety in the age in which we live, but we are to take it from the laws and precepts of God, which are prescribed to us for this effect, that the image of God, which is so much defaced in us, may be repaired, from the discovery which is made to us by the holy Evangelists of these excellent virtues, which shines forth so brightly in the most holy life and death of our blessed Saviour, and from the characters of godly and religious men contained in the scriptures. From these we may fully learn what manner of persons we ought to be. There we may find a full description of the truly christian spirit, temper and life.

The North East was a generally conservative region, unreceptive to the ideas of the Covenant. The University of Aberdeen stood out as a centre of learning with the Aberdeen Doctors and Henry Scougal among its divines. Urquhart, Mackenzie and Burnet studied there and the mathematicians, the Gregorys. If one had to describe the intellectual cast of the region at that time, one would perhaps call it quietist. Towards the end of the century a mystical pietism, an unusual thing in Scotland, appeared there, and it was there earlier in the century that Quakerism made most headway.

In becoming a Quaker, ROBERT BARCLAY (1648–90) followed his father, David Barclay of Urie, who had been converted by a fellow prisoner while he was in prison in 1665 for collaborating with the Cromwellian administration. In those days Quakers seemed as dreadful to Protestants as Anabaptists had earlier. Their claim to immediate revelation threatened all conventional forms of religious authority and every clerical party wanted to persecute them. Charles and James were friendly towards the sect and Mackenzie praised their freedom from received opinions, but the enthusiastic behaviour of the early Quakers generally alarmed respectable men. In the face of such hostility Barclay and his friend George Keith took it upon themselves to defend Quakerism in a number of controversial tracts. Even Barclay's greatest work, in which he gave shape to Quaker belief, is called *An Apology for the True Christian Divinity, As the same is held forth and preached by the people called in scorn, Quakers* and is a defence of propositions originally put forward in a disputation in Aberdeen in 1675. He also shared in the demonstrations and sufferings of the movement. In 1672 he walked through the streets of Aberdeen in sackcloth as a warning to the citizens that they should repent. While travelling on the Continent, preaching and enlisting the sympathy of princes, Barclay heard that his father was imprisoned with other Quakers in the Tolbooth in Aberdeen. He returned to do what he could to have them set free and was himself imprisoned. Whatever the attitude of the local authorities, however, James as governor and later king of Scotland was well disposed to so unrebellious a sect. In 1679 Barclay secured a charter of free barony for Urie, possibly to help the Quakers, and in 1682 was made non-resident governor of William Penn's colony of East New Jersey, which was to be a sanctuary from religious persecution.

The *Apology* (1678) first appeared in Holland in a Latin version in 1676. The passage below on the authority of the spirit shows how Barclay uses his learning not just to support an argument but to open up critical thought about the partisan forms of religion. He is able to place the narrow and intense controversies of seventeenth century Britain in the context of European movements and to bring out the partiality of other sources of authority than the one he looks to. Barclay's exposition of Quaker belief retains something of the syllogistic method he was trained in, but unknotted and pared down. He keeps what is useful of the old dialectical agility and discipline and combines it with the eloquence of a man who has been moved by what he has understood and wants to move others.

"Of Immediate Revelation", *An Apology for the True Christian Divinity*, pp. 30–38

I . . . now come to the second part of the proposition,[44] where the objections usually formed against it are answered.

XIII. The most usuall is that these revelations are uncertain.

But this bespeaketh much ignorance in the opposers, for we distinguish betwixt the thesis and the hypothesis, that is, betwixt the proposition and supposition. For it is one thing to affirme that the true and undoubted revelation of God's Spirit is certain and infallible, and another thing to affirme that this or that particular person or people is led infallibly by this revelation in what they speak or write because they affirme themselves to be so led by the inward and immediate revelation of the Spirit. The first is onely by us asserted; the latter may be called in question. The question is not, who are, or are not, so led, but whether all ought not, or may not, be so led.

Seing then we have already proved that Christ hath promised his Spirit to lead his children and that every one of them both ought and may be led by it, if any depart from this certain guide in deeds and yet in words pretend to be led by it into things that are not good, it will not from thence follow that the true guidance of the Spirit is uncertain, or ought not to be followed, no more than it will follow that the sun sheweth not light because a blind man, or one who wilfully shuts his eyes, falls into a ditch at noon-day for want of light, or that no words are spoken because a deaf man hears them not, or that a garden full of fragrant flowers has no sweet smell because he that has lost his smelling doth not savour it; the fault then is in the organ and not in the object.

All these mistakes therefore are to be ascribed to the weakness or wickedness of men and not to that Holy Spirit. Such as bend themselves most against this certain and infallible testimony of the Spirit use commonly to alledge the example of the old Gnosticks and the late monstrous and mischievous actings of the Anabaptists of Munster,[45] all which toucheth us nothing at all neither weakens a whit our most true doctrine. Wherefore as a most sure bulwark against such kind of assaults, was subjoyned that other part of our proposition thus: Moreover these divine and inward revelations, which we establish as absolutely necessary for the founding of the true faith, as they do not, so neither can they at any time, contradict the scriptures' testimony or sound reason.

Besides the intrinsick and undoubted truth of this assertion, we can boldly affirme it from our certain and blessed experience. For this Spirit never deceived us, never acted nor moved us to any thing that was amiss, but is clear and manifest in its revelations, which are evidently discerned of us as we wait in that pure and undefiled light of God (that proper and fit organ) in which they are received. Therefore if any reason after this manner:

That because some wicked, ungodly, devilish men have committed wicked actions and have yet more wickedly asserted that they were led into these things by the Spirit of God:

Therefore no man ought to lean to the spirit of God, or seek to be led by it.

I utterly deny the consequence of this proposition, which, were it to be received as true, then would all faith in God and hope of salvation become uncertain and the christian religion be turned into meer scepticism. For after the same manner, I might reason thus:

Because Eva was deceived by the lying of the Serpent:

Therefore she ought not to have trusted to the promise of God.

Because the old world was deluded by evil spirits:

Therefore ought neither Noah nor Abraham nor Moses to have trusted the Spirit of the Lord.

Because a lying spirit spake through the four hundred prophets, that persuaded Achab to go up and fight at Ramoth Gilead:

Therefore the testimony of the true Spirit in Micajah was uncertain and dangerous to be followed.[46]

Because there were seduceing spirits crept into the Church of old:

Therefore it was not good, or uncertain, to follow the Anoynting,[47] which taught all things and is truth and no lye.

Who dare say that this is a necessary consequence? Moreover, not onely the faith of the saints and Church of God of old is hereby rendered uncertain, but also the faith of all sorts of christians now is liable to the like hazard, even of those who seek a foundation for their faith elsewhere than from the Spirit. For I shall prove by an inevitable argument *ab incommodo*, i.e. from the inconveniency of it, that if the Spirit be not to be followed upon that account and that men may not depend upon it as their guide because some, while pretending thereunto committ great evils, that then nor tradition nor the scriptures nor reason, which the Papists, Protestants and Socinians do respectively make the rule of their faith, are any whit more certain. The Romanists reckon it an errour to celebrate Easter any other wayes than that Church doth. This can onely be decided by tradition. And yet the Greek Church, which equally layeth claim to tradition with her self, doth it otherwise. Yea, so little effectual is tradition to decide the case that Polycarpus, the disciple of John, and Anicetus, the Bishop of Rome, who immediately succeeded them, according to whose example both sides concluded the question ought to be decided, could not agree.[48] Here of necessity one behoved to err, and that following tradition. Would the Papists now judg we dealt fairly by them if we should thence averr that tradition is not to be regarded? Besides, in a matter of farr greater importance, the same difficulty will occurr, to wit, in the primacy of the Bishop of Rome, for many do affirme, and that by tradition, that in the first six hundred years the Roman prelats never assumed the title of universal shepheard nor were acknowledged as such. And as that which altogether overturneth this presidency, there are that alledg, and that from tradition also, that Peter never saw Rome, and that therefore the Bishop of Rome can not be his successor. Would ye Romanists think this sound reasoning, to say, as ye do,

Many have been deceived and erred grievously in trusting to tradition:

Therefore we ought to reject all traditions, yea even those by which we affirme the contrary and, as we think, prove the truth?

Lastly, in the Council of Florence the chief doctors of the Romish and Greek Churches did debate whole sessions long concerning the interpretation of one sentence of the Council of Ephesus and of Epiphanius and Basilius, neither could they ever agree about it.[49]

Secondly, as to the scriptur, the same difficulty occurreth. The Lutherans affirme they believe consubstantiation by the scriptur, which the Calvinists deny as that which they say according to the same scriptur is a gross errour. The Calvinists again affirme absolute reprobation, which the Arminians deny, affirming the contrary, wherein both affirme themselves to be ruled by the scriptur and reason in the matter. Should I argue thus then to the Calvinists?

Here the Lutherans and Arminians grossly err by following the scriptur:

Therefore the scriptur is not a good nor certain rule, and *e contra.*[50]

Would either of them accept of this reasoning as good and sound? What shall I say of the Episcopalians, Presbyterians, Independents and Anabaptists of Great Britain, who are continually buffeting one another with the scriptur, to whom the same argument might be alledged, though they do all unanimously acknowledg it to be the rule?

And thirdly, as to reason, I shall not need to say much, for whence come all the controversys, contentions and debates in the world, but because every man thinks he followes right reason? Hence of old came the jangles betwixt the Stoicks, Platonists, Peripatetiks, Pythagorians and Cyniks, as of late betwixt the Aristotelians, Cartesians and other naturalists.[51] Can it be thence inferred, or will the Socinians,[52] those great reasoners, allow us to conclude because many, and that very wise men, have erred by following (as they supposed) their reason, and that with what diligence, care and industry they could, to find out the truth, that therefore no man ought to make use of it at all nor be positive in what he knowes certainly to be rational. And thus farr as to opinion, the same uncertainty is no less incident unto those other principles.

XIV. But if we come to practices, though I confess I do with my whole heart abhorr and detest those wild practices, which are written concerning the Anabaptists of Munster, I am bold to say as bad, if not worse, things have been committed by those that lean to tradition, scriptur and reason, wherein also they have averred themselves to have been authorised by these rules. I need but mention all the tumults, seditions and horrible bloodshed wherewith Europe hath been afflicted these divers ages, in which Papists against Papists, Calvinists against Calvinists, Lutherans against Lutherans and Papists assisted by Protestants against other Protestants assisted by Papists have miserably shed one another's blood, hiring and forceing men to kill one another, who were ignorant of the quarrel and strangers to one another; all meanwhile pretending reason for so doing and pleading the lawfulness of it from scriptur.

For what have the Papists pretended for their many massacres, acted as wel in France as elsewhere, but tradition, scriptur and reason? Did they not say that reason perswaded them, tradition allowed them and scriptur commanded them to persecut, destroy and burn heretiks such as denyed this plain Scriptur, "Hoc est corpus meum: This is my body?" And are not the Protestants assenting to this blood-shed, who assert the same thing and encourage them by burning and bannishing, while their brethren are so treated for the same cause? Are not the islands of Great Britain and Ireland, yea, and all the christian world, a lively example hereof, which were divers years together as a theatre of blood, where many lost their lives and numbers of familys were utterly destroyed and ruined? For all which, no other cause was principally given than the precepts of the scriptur. If we then compare these actings with those of Munster, we shall not find great difference, for both affirmed and pretended they were called and that it was lawfull to kill, burn and destroy the wicked. We must kill all the wicked, said those Anabaptists, that we, that are the saints, may possess the earth. We must burn obstinate heretiks, say the Papists, that the holy Church of Rome may be purged of rotten members and may live in peace. We must cut off seduceing Separatists, say the Prelatick Protestants, who trouble the peace of the Church and refuse the divine hierarchy and religious ceremonys thereof. We must kill, say the Calvinistick Presbyterians, the profane malignants who accuse the holy consistorial and Presbyterian government and seek to defend the Popish and Prelatick hierarchy, as also those other sectarys that trouble the peace of our Church. What difference, I pray thee, impartial reader, seest thou betwixt these?

If it be said, "The Anabaptists went without and against the authority of the magistrate, so did not the other:"

I might easily refute it by alledging the mutual testimonys of these sects against one another. The behaviour of the Papists towards Henry the third and fourth of France, their designs upon James the Sixth in the gun-powder treason, as also their principle of the Pope's power to depose kings for the cause of heresy and to absolve their subjects from their oath and give them to others proves it against them.

And as to the Protestants, how much their actions differ from those other above mentioned may be seen by the many conspiracys and tumults which they have been active in, both in Scotland and England, and which they have acted within these hundred years in divers towns and provinces of the Netherlands. Have they not oftentimes sought, not onely from the Popish magistrats, but even from those that had begun to reform, or that had given them some liberty of exercising their religion, that they might onely be permitted without trouble or hinderance to exercise their religion, promising they would not hinder or molest the Papists in the exercise of theirs? And yet did they not on the contrary, so soon as they had power, trouble and abuse these fellow-citizens and turn them out of the city and, which is worse, even such who together with them had forsaken the Popish religion? Did they not these things in many places against the mind of the magistrats? Have they not publickly with contumelious speeches assaulted their magistrats, from whom they had but just before sought and obtained the free exercise of their religion, representing them, so soon as they opposed themselves to their hierarchy, as if they had regarded neither God nor religion? Have they not by violent hands possessed themselves of the Popish Churches, so called, or by force against the magistrat's mind taken them away? Have they not turned out of their office and authority whole councils of magistrats under pretence that they were addicted to Popery? which Popish magistrats nevertheless they did but a little before acknowledg to be ordained by God, affirming themselves obliged to yeeld them obedience and subjection, not onely for fear, but for conscience sake, to whom moreover the very preachers and overseers of the reformed Church had willingly sworn fidelity; and yet afterwards have they not said that the people is bound to force a wicked prince to the observation of God's word? There are many other instances of this kind to be found in their histories, not to mention many worse things, which we know to have been acted in our time and which for brevity's sake I pass by.

I might say much of the Lutherans, whose tumultuous actions against their magistrats not professing the Lutheran profession are testifyed of by several historians worthy of credit. Among others I shall propose onely one example to the reader's consideration, which fell out at Berline, in the year 1615. "Where the seditious multitud of the Lutheran citizens being stirred up by the daily clamours of their preachers did not onely violently take up the houses of the reformed teachers,[53] overturn their librarys and spoil their furnitur, but also with reproachfull words, yea and with stones, assaulted the Marquess of Brandeburgh, the Elector's brother while he sought by smooth words to quiet the fury of the multitude; they killed ten of his guard, scarcely sparing himself, who at last by flight escaped out of their hands".

All which sufficiently declares that the concurrence of the magistrat doth not alter their principles, but onely their method of procedure. So that for my own part, I see no difference betwixt the actings of those of Munster and these others, whereof the one pretended to be led by the Spirit, the other by tradition, scriptur and reason, save this, that the former were rash, heady and foolish in their proceedings and therefore were the sooner brought to nothing and so into contempt and derision, but the other, being more politick and wise in their generation, held it out longer and so have authorized their wickedness more with seeming authority of law and reason. But both their actings being equally evil, the difference appears to me to be onely like that which is betwixt a simple silly thief that is easily catched and hanged without any more ado and a company of resolute, bold robbers, who being better guarded, though their offence be nothing less, yet by violence, do, to evite the danger, force their masters to give them good terms.

From all which then it evidently follows that they argue very ill that despise and reject any principle because men pretending to be led by it doe evil in case it be not the natural and consequential tendency of that principle to lead unto those things that are evil.

Again, it doth follow from what is above asserted that if the Spirit be to be rejected upon this account, all these other principles ought on the same account to be rejected. And for my part, as I have never a whit the lower esteem of the blessed testimony of the holy scripturs nor do the less respect any solid tradition that is answerable and according to truth neither at all despise reason, that noble and excellent faculty of the mind, because wicked men have abused the name of them to cover their wickedness and deceive the simple, so would I not have any reject or diffide[54] the certainty of that unerring Spirit, which God hath given his children as that which can alone guide them into all truth, because some have falsly pretended to it.

XV. And because the Spirit of God is the fountain of all truth and sound reason, therefore we have wel said that it cannot contradict neither the testimony of the scriptur nor right reason. Yet as the proposition itself concludeth, to whose last part I now come, it will not from thence follow that these divine revelations are to be subjected to the examination either of the outward testimony of scriptur, or of the humane or natural reason of man, as to a more noble and certain rule and touch-stone; for the divine revelation and inward illumination is that which is evident by it self, forceing the wel-disposed understanding and irresistibly moving it to assent by its own evidence and clearness, even as the common principls of natural truths do bow the mind to a natural assent.

He that denys this part of the proposition must needs affirme that the Spirit of God neither can nor ever hath manifested it self to man without the scriptur or a distinct discursion of reason, or that the efficacy of this supernaturall principle working upon the souls of men is less evident then natural principles in their common operations, both which are false.

For first, through all the scriptures we may observe that the manifestation and revelation of God by his Spirit to the patriarchs, prophets and apostles was immediate and objective, as is above proved, which they did not examin by any other principle but their own evidence and clearness.

Secondly, to say that the Spirit of God has less evidence upon the mind of man then natural principles have is to have too mean and low thoughts of it. How comes David to invite us to "tast and see that God is good" if this cannot be felt and tasted? This were enough to overturn the faith and assurance of all the saints, both now and of old. How came Paul to be perswaded that nothing could seperate him from the love of God, but by that evidence and clearness which the Spirit of God gave him? The apostle John, who knew wel wherein the certainty of faith consisted, judged it no wayes absurd without further argument to ascribe his knowledge and assurance and that of all the saints hereunto in these words, "Hereby know we that we dwell in him, and he in us because he hath given us of his Spirit" (1 Joh. 4: 13.), and again (5: 6.) it's "the Spirit that beareth witness, because the Spirit is truth."

Observe the reason brought by him, "because the Spirit is truth", of whose certainty and infallibility I have heretofore spoken. We then trust to and confide in this Spirit because we know and certainly believe that it can only lead us aright and never mislead us, and from this certain confidence it is that we affirme that no revelation coming from it can ever contradict the scriptur's testimony nor right reason; not as making this a more certain rule to ourselves, but as condescending to such who, not discerning the revelations of the Spirit as they proceed purely from God, will try them by these mediums. Yet those that have the spiritual sences and can savour the things of the Spirit, as it were in *prima instantia*, i.e. at the first blush, can discern them without or before they apply them either to scriptur or reason. Just as a good astronomer can calculate an eclipse infallibly, by which he can conclude, if the order of natur continue and some strange and unnatural revolution interveen not, there will be an eclipse of the sun or moon such a day and such an hour, yet can he not perswade an ignorant rustick of this untill he visibly see it. So also a mathematician can infallibly know by the rules of art that the three sides of a right triangle are equal to two right angles, yea can know them more certainly than any man by measur. And some geometrical demonstrations are by all acknowledged to be infallible, which can be scarcely discerned or proved by the senses, yet if a geometer be at the pains to certify some ignorant man concerning the certainty of his art by condescending to measur it and make it obvious to his senses, it will not thence follow that that measuring is so certain as the demonstration it self, or that the demonstration would be uncertain without it.

ALEXANDER PEDEN (1626–86) was one of the field preachers of the South West, who according to folk tradition had shamanistic powers of prophecy and cursing. He was deprived in 1663 of his parish of New Luce for refusing to conform and was soon wanted by the authorities for holding conventicles. After the Pentland Rising he took refuge in Ireland, but venturing back to Scotland, he was captured in 1673 and imprisoned on the Bass Rock. He refused the terms offered for his release and was sentenced to transportation. He was set free in London, however, for the captain of the ship supposed to take him to Virginia would not carry religious offenders. Between 1678 and his death Peden wandered between Scotland and Ireland. For a time he hid out in a cave by the River Ayr, but managed to die peacefully in his brother's house at Sorn.

The Lord's Trumpet consists of two sermons preached in 1682 in Glenluce during the persecution. They were published first about 1722 probably from notes taken by someone at the conventicle. Perhaps they were less rambling and repetitive as Peden delivered them. Edwin Muir talks of "Hoodicrow Peden", but that is ungenerous. The Lord's Trumpet shows how the conventicles gave ordinary people a chance to be heroic. It also shows how the persecuted party saw themselves as the suffering remnant of a once covenanted nation and read the signs of the times in an apocalyptic spirit. Peden is not free from religious vengefulness, and there is nothing solid in what he says. And still his sermons, like Rutherford's letters, are examples of enthusiastic discourse touched with imaginative power. Besides, along with his visionary strain, Peden has the knack of making his points with homely imagery and the sort of folk wit Scott made comic in Mause Headrigg in Old Mortality.

The Lord's Trumpet: The Second Sermon

Luke 24, 21. But we trusted that it had been he which should have redeemed Israel.

Where is the Kirk of God in Scotland the day? It is not among the great clergie folk. Sirs, I'lle tell you where the Kirk of God is, wherever there is a praying lass or lad at a dyke-side in Scotland. A praying partie will ruine them yet, Sirs, and a praying partie shall go throw the storm. But manie of you in this countryside, ye ken not these things. The weight of the broken Kirk of God in Scotland never troubles you. The loss of a cow, or two-three of your beasts, or an ill market day goes nearer your hearts nor all the troubles of the Kirk of God in Scotland. Well then, thou poor bodie that will resolve to follow him, pray fast. If there were but one of you, he will be the second; if there were but two of you, our Lord will be the third. Ye need not fear that ye shall want company; our Lord will be your company himself. He will condescend as low as ye like to you that will resolve to follow him in this stormie blast that is blowing upon his poor Kirk in Scotland the day.

But there is some of you that is come here the day, the next day when ye cannot get a meeting of this kind, ye will run away to your hirelings again. Take heed, Sirs, do not mock God. These Indulgence will lead you away from Christ as well as the curats.[55] O the base drag[56] the Kirk is getting from manie of the ministers in Scotland in our day. About thirtie six years ago our Lord had a great thick back of ministers and professors[57] in Scotland. But one blast blew six hundred of our ministers from him at once, and they never came back to him again. Yea, manie lords and lairds and ladies followed him then, but the wind of the storm blew the ladies' gallantries in their eyes and their ears both, which put them both blind and deaff, that they never saw to follow Christ since nor to hear his pleasant voice. The lords and lairds and ladies were all blown over the braee. Alace! for the apostacie of nobles, gentles, ministers and professors in Scotland. Scotland err long shall run in streams of blood. Yea manie of the saints' blood shall yet be shed err long. But yet the blood of the saints shall be the seed of a glorious Church in Scotland. O sirs, what are ye doing in this countryside? Christ's followers in throw in Clydsdale yonder, they have ventured fair for God and hath given a great testimonie. They have burnt the Test and the acts of the cursed Parliament.[58] There was a poor widow in that countryside as I came throw, that was worth manie of you, and when she was asked how she did in this ill time, "I do verie well", says she. "I get more good in one verse of the Bible now nor I did in it all lang syne. He hath casten me the keys of the pantrie door and bids me take my fill". Was not that a christian indeed? O sirs, I would have you taking heed what ye are doing now when the blood of the saints is running so fast.

Now Sirs, the observation that I would have you to take home with you is this, it is ay poor bodie that God hath done a good turn for that will follow him in a storm. And now people of God, ye ken this, Mary Magdalene that is here spoken of in this chapter, he cast a legion of devils out of her in a morning. I trow she never forgat that till she wan to glory. Think ye not but it was a sore heart that morning when she missed him and got a toom[59] tomb, and an emptie grave? O what would ye have thought to have seen this poor woman running through the bonds of soldiers? But that was not the thing that troubled her neither the Roman guard that was about the grave nor the heavie stone that was upon the grave's mouth nor the charge under the pain of death that they should not touch the grave. Na, na, Sirs, love to God goes beyond all that. He was their Lord and they dought[60] not want him. The note that I would have taken with you is this, and ye have gotten good of Jesus Christ, ye would go through hell at the nearest to be at him. O Sirs, them that hath suffered for Christ in Scotland, they ken this best the day. They got a stormie rough sea indeed, but a choise pleasant shore and the captain of their salvation to welcome them heartily home. O Sirs, Christ had a whein[61] noble worthies in Scotland not long ago, that set the trumpet to their mouth and gave fair warning in his name. He had a Welsh, a Cameron, a Cargill and a Wallwood,[62] a noble party of them proclaiming his name in Scotland. O Sirs, if ye could be admitted to see and speak to them, they would tell you that it is nothing to suffer for Christ. They are all glancing in glorie now. They would flee you out of your wits to behold them with these white robes and glorious crowns and palms in their hands. Follow fast if he call you to suffer for his name. But what shall I say? The most part of you knows nothing of this. Ye that are lying in black nature, ye dought not bide in heaven if ye were in it. Ye would give a thousand worlds, if ye had them, to be out of it again.

Well Sirs, I'lle tell you news. Happy they that's win cleanly through the storm since the year sixtie. Happy they, I say, that wan throw at Pentland, Bothwel and Airdsmoss.[63] Happy they that died on scaffolds, gibbets, or on the seas. O the blood of the saints will be the seed of the Church in after ages in Scotland. And I'lle tell you more, Sirs. Take heed what thought ye have of the sufferers. Look that ye have not the thought that they suffered wrong. Intertain not jealousies or hard thoughts of the people of God's case in their hard sufferings. For them that hath won through the storm and is win through Jordan hath gotten Jordan's ebbwater and is well win throw. But the ministers and professors in Scotland that are yet to go throw the storm, as well as the prophane party, shall get a stormy sea and shall find Jordan's growing water and shall find hard winning throw.

But to come to the words, I trow our Lord was blyth to hear this discourse between these two poor men.[64] There is manie a man spears[65] the gate they ken full well. Think ye that our Lord was ignorant of this discourse before he came to them? But he spears to try their zeal. I trow misbelief was verie strong in them, as it is with

173

manie professors in Scotland the day. We thought, said they, that it was he that should have restored the kingdom to Israel. I trow manie in Scotland is beginning to question the work of reformation and the Covenant which we swore with uplifted hands to God, whether it was the work of God, yea or no.

The next thing that ye will question is whether the work of God be real or no in your own bosom. Take heed to your atheism, people of God. I'lle tell you your atheism and your misbelief will do you an ill turn. It will put you to question the work of God in your own bosom, and that will not be good companie in a storm that ye are likelie to meet with err it be long in thir lands. Well Sirs, there is manie a plough plowing in our Lord's ackers the day in Scotland, but err long he will loose some of them and cut their cords and lay them by a while. Now Sirs, what is it that hath carried throw the sufferers for Christ these 22 years in Scotland? It is in the Phil. 3. 10. It is the filling up of Christ's sufferings in Scotland, together with the antient decrees of heaven. For my part, I seek no more if he bid me go. He bad so manie from the 60 year to Pentland go to scaffolds and gibbets for him. They sought no more but his commission and went, and he carried them well throw. Then in the 66 at Pentland, he bad so manie go to the fields and die for him and so manie to scaffolds and lay down their lives for him. They sought no more but his commission and went, and he carried them well throw. And then in the 79 at Bothwell, he bad so manie go to the fields and scaffolds and die for him. They sought no more but his commission and went. He bad so manie go to the seas and be meat to the fishes for him. They sought no more but his commission and went. And then in the year 80, at Airdsmoss, he bad so manie go to the fields and scaffolds for him. They sought no more but his commission and went. This cup of suffering hath come all the way down from Abel to the 82 year in Scotland. Our Lord hath held this cup to all the sufferers' heads whenever he had a Kirk in the world, and all the martyrs hath tasted of this cup, and it will go to all the martyrs' lips that will suffer for Christ, even to the last trumpet sounding. But yet, people of God, it is but the brime that the saints tastes of. But be ye patient in believing, for God shall make the wicked, his enemies and your persecutors in Scotland, wring out the bitter dregs of this cup to all eternitie and to spew and fall and rise no more. Believe it, our master will set by this cup and close and swallow up time in endless eternitie and blow that great trumpet, and then heaven and earth shall all go to a red low[66] at once. O long for that noble day, believers, for it will put an end to all your sad days and suffering days . . . .

Now people of God in Scotland, there is another thing that I have to tell you, and that is this, I would have you to get preservatives, for ye walk in a pestellentious air and are nearer unto hazard nor ye are aware of. If any of you were going throw a citie where the plague were hot, ye would seek something to be a preservative to put in your mouths and noses to keep you from being infected with the smell. There will be need of this in Scotland err long, Sirs. I know ye think me but a fool for saying these things, but I man[67] tell you this in the name of the Lord, who sent me this day to tell you these things, that err it be long the living shall not be able to bury the dead in thee, O Scotland, and manie a myle shall ye go and ride and shall not see a fire house, but ruinous wastes for the quarrel of a broken Covenant and wrongs done to the Son of God in Scotland. And then the testimonie of a good conscience will be a good feast in that day . . . .

There is manie a little ferry boat going through Scotland. Take heed, people of God that ye go not aboard in them, for they will sink you. There is likewise manie cross winds to blow you off Christ's shore. But if ye would wait patiently, persecuted people of God, the Lord is about to raise a northern blast on these blades[68] that shall raise them off their cricks[69] and louse their plough that is plowing deep in our Lord's ackers in Scotland.

Now these ministers that is fallen silent at this sinfull blast of the sinfull command of these sinfull magistrates, tell them, people of God, that they have consented fullie to take Christ's crown off his head and set it upon the head of a prophane man. Put them to it either to own their ministry, or to renounce it, now when it is come to this push in Scotland. And now, Sirs, if any of you would bide by Jesus Christ in this storm, try how ye have covenanted with him and how ye have closed the bargain with him and upon what terms. But I trow there is manie of you in this age that is like young daft folk that runs fast together and marries, but never lays their account how they will keep house, but presentlie they fall to beggarie and povertie. I trow it falls out to be so with manie of you that is the professors in this generation. Ye take up your religion, and ye wot not how and ye cannot give an account how ye came by it. I'lle tell you, Sirs, ye will bide by Christ's back no longer than a storm blow, then ye will quat[70] his back and denie his cause. Ye had need to take heed to this; it will ruine your souls in the end of the day. But I will tell you more, Sirs. The right way in covenanting with God is when Christ and the believer first meets, our Lord gives him his laws and his statutes, and he charges him not to quat a hoof, no, and ye should be torn in a thousand pieces, and the right Covenanter says Amen. O but you people of God, like fools, would have your stock in your own hand, but and ye had it, ye would soon debush[71] it as your old father Adam did. Adam got once his stock in his own hand, but he soon played it at the capiehole[72] one morning with the devil at two or three throws of the game. He lost you all, that is his posteritie. But now our blessed second Adam hath our stock in guiding, and he tutors it better. He will give you but as ye have need of it, people of God, in groats, sixpences and shillings. But and he fetch anie of you to the gallows for him, he will give you dollars in your hands. Ye shall not need to fear: he will bear your charges to the full.

CHAPTER FOUR

THE WHIG REVOLUTION

The settlement of the Church was changed for the third time in fifty years by the Whig Revolution. The Claim of Right of 1689 declared that "Prelacy ... hath been a great and insupportable grievance and trouble to this Nation, and contrary to the inclinations of the generality of the people ... and therefore ought to be abolished". William would perhaps have preferred a church ruled by bishops, but the Scottish bishops were too Jacobite to see their way to acknowledging him as king. And still though William accepted the Act Abolishing Prelacy (1689), he hesitated over setting up Presbyterianism.

While matters were still unfixed, both parties were active. James had withdrawn troops from Scotland to meet William's forces, and so the harried Presbyterian party had a chance to harry in their turn. Throughout the South West clergy were rabbled and driven out of their charges. In other parts of the country the clergy were purged for not reading the appointed prayers for William and Mary. These illegal and legal deprivations of Episcopal clergy outnumbered the deprivations of the Presbyterians at the Restoration. The Episcopal party, realizing after the death of Claverhouse at Killiekrankie that their hope of redress lay with English public opinion, opened a pamphleteering campaign in London.

In 1690 Presbyterian church government was at length established. The Act of Supremacy of 1669 was repealed, but the Covenants were not renewed and there was no suggestion of a divine right of Presbytery. The problem was now how to deal with those who would not accept the settlement. The Presbyterian ministers deprived under the Episcopacy had settled themselves into vacant parishes and new men were at hand for planting others. Though moderation was the cant of the time, the commissions set up by the General Assembly of 1690 went about the work of purging the church and universities with vigour and rigour. William was eager that Episcopalian clergy willing to conform to the Presbyterian establishment should be accommodated. But the General Assembly of 1692, fearing what an influx of men of Episcopalian views might do in the church, stalled and was dissolved. Parliament, however, passed an act accommodating those who took the Oaths of Allegiance and Assurance and who accepted the Westminster Confession and Presbyterian form of church government. Some came in, but more, like the Presbyterians in Leighton's time, preferred to take advantage of an indulgence, the act of 1696, which allowed those who took the Oaths of Allegiance and Assurance to remain in their parishes. Nothing was done for those who had been deprived, and they and those whose Jacobite loyalties prevented them from taking the oaths remained outside the established church.

There is no really interesting defence of the Presbyterian establishment. It was a compromise, too Erastian for many Cameronians, but it is hard to be sure what adjustments of principle were involved. Moderation was all the rage, but none of the writing suggests a fine tempering of the mind to actuality. The political discussion is also disappointing. The Covenanters had talked of the right to depose and elect kings and the king's swearing to Covenants perhaps involved a sort of contract between king and people – constitutional ideas with some likeness to those actuating the Revolution. But the Glorious Revolution, whatever its grass roots, was a Whig Revolution not a Whiggamore one. It is true the Scottish resistance to Charles and James had included politicians as well as church-men. But there is little serious secular political discussion. The constitutional ideas behind the Claim of Right were taken from the English Bill of Rights. They may have been what the Scots needed, but they were hardly what they had arrived at. In the general scene of jobbing and cobbling together, only the polemical writing of the intransigent Episcopalians rises to the occasion.

JOHN SAGE (1652–1711) was a minister in Glasgow and was nominated for the chair of divinity at St. Andrews. But the Revolution of 1688 put an end to that, and Sage along with other Episcopalian clergy was driven out of Glasgow by the insurgent Presbyterians. For a time he was in Edinburgh, where he joined with men like Alexander Monro, the extruded principal of Edinburgh University, in pamphlet warfare against the new establishment. He would not take the Oath of Allegiance yet continued to hold services, and so in 1693 he was banished from Edinburgh. He found shelter in various upper class households, though for a time when there was a warrant for his arrest, he had to take to the hills of Angus, passing himself off as a gentleman in need of a course of goat's milk. The non-juring Episcopalians made him a bishop without diocese in 1705.

Most of Sage's literary activity, even scholarly works like *The Principles of the Cyprianick Age*, was polemic against the Presbyterians. The more substantial pieces have been collected in *The Works of . . . John Sage*, ed. Charles Farquhar Shand et al. (Edinburgh: Spottiswoode Society, 1846), 3 vols. Even his work as editor of Ruddiman's edition of Drummond's *Works* (1711) is stamped with his Jacobite convictions. *An Account of the Present Persecution of the Church in Scotland* (1690) consists of four letters, the first by Thomas Morer, the second and third by Sage and the fourth by Alexander Monro. The DNB article on Sage mentions "Letters concerning the persecution of the Episcopal Clergy" (1689) (Wing L 1777), which is possibly an earlier edition of the same work, but the Wing location being erroneous, I have been unable to trace a copy. For other remarks on Sage, see Introduction, pp. 10–12.

"The Second Letter," *An Account of the Present Persecution of the Church in Scotland in Several Letters*

SIR,

I received yours of the date, etc., wherein as you express a mighty concern for the distress'd Episcopal clergy within this kingdom, so you prescribe me a task which will not be so easily perform'd as ye imagine. You tell me strange representations are made of them by their enemies and disseminated through the whole kingdom of England. You therefore require me to give you a just and true account of their present state and persecutions, assuring me it is not so much to satisfie your curiosity as to enable you for their vindication. This, I say, is a very hard task. For to digest an account of that nature to purpose, in my opinion, would require the diligence of a great head, the expence of much time and a considerable volume, for 'tis hardly possible to set their circumstances in their due light without deducing their affairs from the very Reformation and dipping in matters of state all alongst, as well as of ecclesiastical concern, so closely have the two interests been still linked together in this kingdom. Without that, strangers will never understand sufficiently either our constitution, or the grounds on which the clergy have been obliged to go in many transactions; neither will they be able to perceive how unjust and calumnious the representations be, which are made by their adversaries nor how partial they are in their accounts nor how carefully they take all things by the wrong handle, industriously presenting the dark side of things to the world, where there is any intricacy, and many times blackening even that which is truly fair and beautiful, when it makes for their purpose.

Such a work as that, I am hopeful, ye may see ere long, for I have good reason to believe some abler pen than mine will be employed that way by and by[1]; and therefore I was once inclined to have referred you intirely to it. But calling to mind again what earnestness ye express to have if it were but some overly[2] notice of our case and withal considering that herein you may be gratified without prejudice to that more full and large account and likewise that perhaps a present account, though never so short and rude, may have its proper usefulness, I have prevailed with my self to cast together what follows. I will use as few words as I can, and perhaps I shall not be careful to observe exact order and method, but I hope your goodness will pardon that, upon my promising to tell you nothing but what can be made appear to be true beyond all contradiction.

I take my rise from the death of that great prince, King Charles the Second. He left this Church of Scotland in more peaceful condition than it had been of a long time before. It was united to a very desirable degree. Generally all Scotchmen were of one communion, for those of the Popish persuasion were scarcely one to five hundred. The Quakers were not one to a thousand. The Presbyterians a good time before were divided into two sects: one (but by far the smaller) was against all indulgences given by the king; the other had taken the liberty which he had several times granted, but was then retracted. This party had for the most part returned to the churches unity. Their preachers were generally become our hearers, attended duely our publick assemblies, and many participated of the same sacraments with us. There were no separate meetings kept (at least publickly), but very rarely and only by that other party, now commonly known by the name of Cameronians from one Mr. Richard Cameron, who being sometimes schoolmaster at Falkland and turn'd out of that employment for insufficiency, betook himself to the trade of field preaching, became wonderfully admired of the giddy multitude, was killed at last in open rebellion at Airdsmoss and so commenced martyr anno 1680.

This is that party with whom these sharp methods were taken, which are complain'd of in the Prince of Orange his Declaration for the Kingdom of Scotland and hugely aggravated by the paper called the *Scotch Inquisition*.[3] But had his Highness known their practices, how they by their manifestos rejected King Charles as their sovereign, made many declarations of war against him, excommunicated him and when they had opportunity murthered those who in their stations according to their duty any ways supported his government, especially bishops, ministers and soldiers, pretending it was done in a just war and they had commission from King Jesus for it, etc., I doubt he would never have made the treatment they met with a grievance. And if the world knew it, as perhaps it may sooner or later, certainly it would have but a very mean opinion of the author of that most scurrilous pamphlet. I only said their practices, for all Presbyterians, at least in Scotland, as will appear in the sequel, have really the same principles. The only substantial difference is the Cameronians are the more ingenuous party, the rest the more subtle. These own their principles when they think it seasonable; those, like the honester men, upon all occasions. By these Cameronians, I say, conventicles were only then kept, and they were condemned for it by the rest of the Presbyterians, who at that time, in pretence at least, had fallen in love with moderation.

When King James came to the throne, Monmouth in England and Argyle in Scotland, you know, raised a formidable rebellion. Argyle gave out his manifestos and made many specious pretences, etc. It appeared he was earnest to have had the Presbyterians joyn with him, but his conditions did not please the Cameronians, and the rest continued still as formerly in the king's and churches peace. This made us all hopeful they had once resolved seriously never to divide any more and weaken the Protestant interest by rending the church in pieces. But it seems they went then on other principles. They found Argyle's attempt desperate and their party weak, and they had smarted lately for enterprises of that nature; therefore they found it convenient to wait a fitter opportunity.

When that rebellion was quash'd, King James, being a Roman Catholick, turn'd serious to have some ease granted to those of his own persuasion; so the business of the penal statutes came to be manag'd. For this end, it was resolved the Parliament should meet, and before it sate, several persons of greatest note within the kingdom were called up to London, the Duke of Hamilton, Sir George Lockart, the greatest lawyer in the kingdom, then President of the Session, etc. Their errand was to concert matters and make way for the king's inclinations in that particular; amongst the rest, the Archbishop of St. Andrews and the then Bishop of Edinburgh, now Archbishop of Glasgow. They made a condescension too, which afterwards was very much talked of. But I can assure you, Sir, it was nothing so odious in it self as it was represented to be. I have seen it and considered it. It did not go the length by far of Pensionary Fagel's letter.[4] And to tell the truth freely, so far as I can comprehend things, they had great reason to go so far as they went, and I doubt not it shall be sometimes published to the world and fully vindicated. But I go on.

The Parliament met; all the members were qualified according to law; they took the Test, etc. But the court designs prevailed not. The penal statutes were still kept on foot by that Episcopal Parliament (pardon the phrase, 'tis ordinary in this kingdom), and some of the bishops too were active in the matter. This, to let you see whether the Episcopal party in this kingdom can be said to be inclin'd for Popery.

This disappointment irritated his Majesty; wherefore the next great step was the suspending, stopping and disabling all the laws against Dissenters and granting a toleration to christians of all persuasions. This was done by publick proclamation: the first edition was dated Feb. 12. 1686/7. The Presbyterians, as much as any men, stood amaz'd at the dispensing power at first and seem'd to see clearly the ill consequences of a breach in that juncture. This themselves frankly confess'd at the beginning, and I know it was therefore once very near to a general resolution amongst them never to take the benefit of it. This all know, that for some months after the publication of it, no considerable breach was made: they still continued in the same communion with us.

Ye will easily believe, I think, this grated the Popish party, for they saw evidently if the unity of our church was not broken, their interests would advance but very slowly; so pains were taken with the Presbyterians to make them separate. And because perhaps they might scruple at the oath contained in the first edition of the toleration, a second edition without that oath was obtained and published. Whether the arguments which were made use of to engage them prevailed with them, or by that time the second edition came out, which was June 28, 1687, they had considered the strength of their party and found they would be able to make a figure, or they had then got secret instructions from Holland to comply with the dispensing power in subserviency to the ensuing revolution, for which I know there be very strong presumptions, I shall not readily determine. This is certain, they closed presently with the second edition.

'Tis true they pretended the terms in the first were too grievous and that considerable mitigations were made in the second, so they could not any longer be disobedient to the divine providence (you cannot quarrel the expression when ye know that according to their divinity providential occurrences make a considerable part of the rule of faith and manners) nor neglect so blest an opportunity, although 'tis evident to any who compared the two proclamations that there are no material alterations. 'Tis certain the second was design'd to carry on the same interest with the first, and it had altogether as much of the dispensing power in it. Both alike required that whoever would have the benefit of the toleration should own the king's absolute dispensing power, by which it was granted; only the oath contained in the first was left out in the second. But even in the first it was not absolutely required, for the proclamation says no more but that instead of all former oaths required by law, that only should be taken and sworn by all his Majesties subjects, or such of them as he or his Privy Council should require so to do. And moreover, it was entirely dispensed with by the king's letter to his Council, dated March 31, anno 1687. So that it can never be pretended as a reason why they did not separate for three months hereafter.

Thus the great schism began amongst us. The toleration was its parent, and that was the child of the dispensing power. But before I proceed to shew how it was carried on, let me remark one thing: it is, whatever now they may pretend, it was no ways any principle of conscience which made them separate from us on that occasion. My reasons are these. They had lived in communion with us for some years before the first edition of the toleration. They continued so, even for some months after that edition, viz. till they got the second; at least, very few broke off in that interim. While they lived in communion with us, they acknowledged their consciences allowed them. Indeed, what sort of christians had they been if it had not been so? Many (I can find their names if I be put to it) thanked God that they were reconciled to us and frequently protested all the world should never again engage them in the schism. Nay, some of the ablest of their preachers within a very few weeks before they embraced the toleration said to some of the regular clergy they should never do it; they were resolved never to preach more in their life time. Further yet, some of them, even after the second edition, continued for a long time resolved never to engage in it, and it cost their brethren much pains before they could overcome that resolution. Yea, they tell us to this very day if they were deprived of their liberty, they could return to us again. Can there be clearer evidences for any thing than these are that it was not conscience but some other interest that involved them in such a general apostacy from one of the greatest concerns of Christianity, the unity of the church? Indeed, how could ever conscience be pretended in the matter? We had not the least sinful condition in our communion. We still maintain'd what themselves, the same articles of faith. We worshipped God after the same manner. There is no imaginable difference between them and us in the administration of sacraments. If the orders of the Church of England be valid, so are ours. All that was ever controverted amongst us was the point of church government. Tis true, we use the Lord's Prayer and the Doxology, and commonly require the Creed in baptism, which they do not. If these can justifie a separation, we are guilty. But if they can, let the world judge. And now these things being so, I would further ask any man this question, whether, when they make such clamors now concerning their by-past sufferings, it can be said that ever they suffered for conscience sake? This by the way.

So was the schism circumstantiate,[5] as I have said. And being once begun, it was wonderful to see how soon it came to a considerable height. Within a few weeks, meeting houses were erected in many places, especially in the western shires, the great nests of fanaticism, and the churches were drain'd. Altar was set up against altar and the pretended presbyter against the bishop. All arts were used to increase their party and render the regular incumbents contemptible. People were not left to their own choice to joyn or not joyn with them, but all methods of compulsion, except downright force, were taken to engage them. If any man went to church, whither all had gone very lately, he was forthwith out of favour with the whole gang. If he was an husbandman, his hap was good if his neighbors' cattel were not fed amongst his corns in the nighttime. If he was a tradesman, no employment for him, if a gentleman of an estate, a laird as we call them, his own tenants would abuse him to his face and threaten him twenty violences. In short, nothing was left untryed that had the least probability of weakning our hands or strengthening their own.

On the other hand, never a more thankful people to his Majesty. Addresses, you know were then much in fashion, and none more forward than they, witness that famous one, entituled "To the King's Most Excellent Majesty, The Humble Address of the Presbyterian Ministers in His Majesties Kingdom of Scotland", and at the foot "Subscribed in our names, and in the names of the rest of the brethren of our persuasion at their desire"; in which address,

> They his Majesties most loyal subjects, from the deep sense they have of his Majesties gracious and surprizing favour in not only putting a stop to their long sad sufferings for nonconformity, but granting them the liberty of the publick and peaceable exercise of their ministerial function, as they bless the great God, who put it in his royal heart, so they do withal find themselves bound in duty to offer their most humble and hearty thanks to his majesty. (Then they make vast protestations in behalf of their loyalty). His Majesty is but just to them when he believes them loyal; and by the help of God they will so demean themselves, as his

Majesty may find cause rather to enlarge than diminish his favors towards them; and they humbly beseech that all who promote any disloyal principles or practices (as they do disown them) may be looked upon as none of theirs, whatsoever name they may assume to themselves.

And indeed for a good time, even till they had made a good party and the Prince of Orange was coming, they continued moderate and thankful to a miracle. For tho by vertue of that same toleration, swarms of Popish priests were let loose through the whole kingdom, infinitely active to gain converts, compassing sea and land to make one proselyte, yet seldom so much as one word against Popery in any meeting house, whether it was that they thought it indiscreet to fall on their brethren, who stood upon the same bottom with themselves, or they had receiv'd it amongst their injunctions from the court party not to meddle with these of the Roman Church, or they did not understand the controversies, which seems the most probable, and so found themselves obliged in prudence to let them alone, I am not concerned to determine. 'Tis certain it was so *de facto* (for once to make use here of that term),[6] and I have twenty times heard it confess'd by their constant auditors. Nay, to this very day, though now they may make bold with Popery without the hazard of giving the present court a displeasure and it might be expected they should do it for very obvious reasons, they very rarely meddle with it. Their great work is to batter down antichristian Prelacy and Malignancy. Prelacy has been the cause of all the calamities this nation has groaned under, God knows for how many years; King Jesus has been banished; the gospel has not been preached in this land these seven and twenty years by-past.

Upon my word, I am sure, Sir, there is nothing more ordinary in their sermons than such cant, and though their texts be commonly taken from the Old Testament, yet they are all pat and home to the purpose. I could easily give you a great many good notes of their prayers, as well as their sermons and condescend upon the particular persons, etc., but perhaps you may see that sometimes done by it self.[7]

While in these conventicles Popery was so kindly forborn, in our churches these controversies were our most frequent subjects, especially in these places where priests were setting up. This is well known all over the kingdom. Some suffered, and many were terribly threatned for it. I could give you part of their names and histories if it were needful.

Such was the broken state of our church from July, 1687, till October, 1688, when the late great revolution began to cast up and

185

his Highness the Prince of Orange was said to be coming to Britain to deliver us from Popery and slavery and restore our religion, laws and liberties. You know that was an extraordinary enterprise. Britain had not been invaded by any foreign prince for an hundred years before, therefore it was expedient his Highness should forecast for as kindly a reception as was possible. To this end he gave out his Declarations for both kingdoms. It seems that either his Highness has been diffident of the regular clergy in Scotland and dreaded they would not so readily embark with him as the Presbyterians were likely to do, or he has had none, or very few of the Scotch nation then about him, but such as were of that persuasion, for the Declaration for the kingdom of Scotland we found to be purely Presbyterian. I am confident Dr. Burnet did not pen it, otherwise the Act of Glasgow had not been put into it as a grievance.[8] He knows very well upon what reasons it was made, and if he pleases, can easily justifie it. Neither had the clergy of the West, for they must be the men, been so generally pronounced scandalous and ignorant; he was better acquainted with many of them than so. I had rather think the doctor had never seen that Declaration until it was published. But what though he had and for reasons of state thought fit to let it go as it was, 'tis no great matter. As I said, it was downright Presbyterian and presaged no good to us. But God be thanked, it found us generally in good preparation for suffering persecution, for we had cast up our accounts before and foreseen that possibly we might be exposed to trials, though we had not much reflected that it was to be by the hands of Protestants.

We were confirmed further yet in our suspicions when we found that those who were engaged in the Presbyterian interests were flocking up to London and making the most numerous as well as active appearances about his Highness's court, that they only had his ear and seemed to be the chief persons who upon his Majesty's retirement transferred the government of this kingdom upon him.

By these steps we began to see further too into the politicks of our brethren and upon what designs they had carried on the schism so vigorously the year before. Yet we never dreaded that such horrid barbarities would be our lot as afterwards were put in execution.

And so I am introduced to the main part of my work, which is to give you a brief account, a taste as it were, of our present sufferings; which, were they represented fully and in all their proper colours, perhaps they would not obtain belief among strangers. Nor will I make it my work at present to do it, both for that I intend brevity and am unwilling to give to the world such a disgust at my native country as the barbarities we met with fully laid open must needs produce in all those who have any sense either of Christianity or humanity. In short then.

It pleased Almighty God, to whose providence it becomes us humbly to submit in all conditions, to permit that we should have a trial of the cross, whereof God forbid we should ever be ashamed, and for that end, to give us up to the malice of our enemies that they might thrust us into the furnace; for carrying on which glorious work, this was their opportunity. When the certain accounts came of the Prince of Orange's resolutions to come into England, all our standing forces were called thither, so that this kingdom was left destitute of such means as were necessary to secure the peace if any disturbance should happen to arise amongst us. When that prince landed, King James, being deserted by his army and soon after disowned by his subjects, was put upon the necessity of leaving Britain. And here in Scotland, his Council very soon dissolved of its own accord, so that in effect, the nation was in a manner without government, by whose fault I am not now to enquire.

Upon this his majesty's sudden abdication and voluntary dissolution of his Council, our brethren found it seasonable for them to turn serious with us. But it was expedient to project how their game might be successful before they began to play it. Therefore a stratagem was contrived: a general massacre of Protestants was pretended and alledged to be intended by the Papists. But how to be effectual, seeing their numbers were so very few, especially on the south side of the Forth, which was to be the chief scene of the tragedy? For that, this salvo[9] was at hand: so many thousands of Irishmen were landed in Galloway, had already burnt the towns of Kirkhudbright all to ashes and put all to the edge of the sword, young and old, male and female. Only three or four persons like Job's nuncioes, had escaped and these savages were posting hard to be over the whole kingdom, etc.

This story flew at the rate of a miracle, for within twenty four hours or so it was spread every where through the greater half of the kingdom. No body doubts now but people were appointed at several posts to transmit it every where at the same time, for it run like lightning. And wherever it went, it was so confidently asserted to be true that he was forthwith a Papist and upon the plot who disbelieved it. At first we all wondred what it might mean, but it was not long before we learn'd by the effects what was the politick; for immediately in the western shires, where the fiction was first propagated, tumultuary rabbles knotted and went about searching for arms everybody's house whom they suspected as disaffected to their interests. The pretext was that the country might be in a posture of defence against the Irish, but the real purpose was that all might be made naked who were inclinable to retard them in the prosecution of their designs upon the clergy. Especially they were sure no minister should have sword or pistol, as indeed few had any, or any other weapon that might be useful for his defence if any attempt should be made on him. When they had thus made their preparations for the work, and you would wonder to hear how speedily and yet how dexterously it was done, they fell frankly to it.

It was on Christmas Day, that day, which once brought good tidings of great joy to all people, that day, which once was celebrated by the court of heaven it self and whereon they sung, "Glory to God in the highest, on earth, peace, good will towards men", that day which the whole christian church ever since has solemnized for the greatest mercy that ever was shewn to sinful mortals, that day, I say, it was, to the eternal honour of all, especially Scotch Presbyterians, on which they began the tragedy. For so were matters concerted amongst them that upon that same very day different parties started out of different places and fell upon the ministers. . . .

[Sage runs through some Presbyterian atrocities.]

Do not think I am imposing on you. What I have affirmed can be so attested that greater moral evidence can be had for nothing.

When ye have read thus far, and when your surprise and first horrours are over, and as your temper is, you fall a pondering what I have told you, I am apt to apprehend a great man things may offer themselves to your consideration. Such is your humanity that I know you will be casting about for topicks and apologies to alleviate this heavy charge I am giving in against our persecutors. What! so may you think, certainly no applications have been made to those in power. For what person in the world, bearing the name of a magistrate, would not have found himself obliged in credit and honour, as well as duty, to fall on speedy remedies for stopping such an impetuous current of barefaced wickedness? Or, at most, they have been but pure rabble, the scum and refuse of the people, who acted these barbarities, and they have been so numerous, so fierce and uncontrolable at that time that authority has been too weak for them. For it is not possible that any of the nobility and gentry, and much less that any of the Presbyterian preachers, could allow of or have an hand in such villanies. Or if these in power were acquainted with such things and yet gave no protection, and if the rabble had encouragement from any persons of better quality, you can hardly miss to conclude that these clergymen who were so treated have been the most profligate rogues in the world, wretches who deserve to be swept from off the face of the earth without pity and with all the solemnities of disgrace and contempt. For what else can be imagined to justifie such proceedings? Thus, I say, perhaps, Sir, you may reason with your self when you are making your reflections on what I have already told you. Be pleased therefore to have a little patience, and consider what I am to tell you further.

No sooner did these outrages begin than such applications were made as you your self, I am sure, will judge sufficient. Such of the peers of the kingdom as were Privy Counsellors and had not gone for London were addressed, but they could bring us no relief. Our next work therefore was to send up private accounts to London as we had interest or acquaintaince with those of our nobility and gentry who were there. But our enemies had well foreseen all that and had their instruments ready to run down all private letters as the blackest lies and forgeries, and we were called all the infamous things that could be. Our design was to work mischief and breed disturbances. We were Popishly affected, and the politick of such reports was to hinder the settlement of the peace and establishment of the government. In a word, we were mortal enemies to the Prince of Orange and all his glorious designs for securing the Protestant religion, etc. They received letters to the quite contrary. Sure they were their correspondents were men well acquainted with whatever passed, and besides they were men of conscience and undoubted integrity. They would not conceal the truth, far less would they write lies and falshoods, yet their accounts bore daily that there were no such persecutions of ministers, no tumults, no rabbles, etc. The kingdom was in a most profound peace, and every man had all imaginable security, especially the clergy. With such bold affirmations as these, they perswaded his Highness, on whom was transferred the government of this kingdom, that all our accounts were most false and villanous and he ought not to believe them; only by them he might judge what a pack we were, etc. . . . .

[Sage enumerates the legal injustices perpetrated on the Episcopal clergy and turns to vindicating them from some of the charges that seemed to justify the persecution].

The Church of Scotland, since the Reformation, was never generally so well provided with pastors as at the beginning of the present persecution. 'Tis true, she has sometimes had some sons, such as Doctor Forbes, Doctor Baron, etc.,[10] more eminent for learning than perhaps any of the present generation will pretend to. But what church is there in the world, wherein every day extraordinary lights are to be found? It cannot be denied neither that there are amongst us some of but ordinary parts, but in what church was it ever otherwise? It would be an odd thing, if the poor cold climate of Scotland could still afford a thousand Augustines or Aquinas[e]s. Perhaps too there may be some who are not so careful to adorn their sacred office with a suitable conversation as they ought to be. But what wonder when our Saviour himself had one a'devil of twelve in his retinue? What country is it where all the clergymen are saints? And therefore, I say it over again, the Church of Scotland was never so well planted generally since the Reformation as it was a year ago. This is a proposition which, I confess, cannot be demonstrated so by a private man sitting in his chamber as to convince the obstinate, or give full satisfaction to strangers. But so far as things of that nature can be made appear plausible and at a distance, I think this may be done very briefly in answering the charges commonly given in against them.

The first is ignorance. But what's the standard to judge by whether men have such a competency of knowledge as may, *caeteris paribus*, qualifie them for the ministery? Till that be condescended on, I might very well bid them put up their objection in their pocket till they can make palpable sense of it. At least, till that be done, this pretended ignorance cannot be sustain'd as a sufficient argument for justifying the present persecution. But how can the Scottish clergy be so very ignorant? No man since I remember was ever admitted to the ministery till he had first pass'd his course at some university and commenc'd master of arts. And generally none are admitted to tryal for being probationers till after that commencement they have been four or five years students in divinity. The method of that tryal is commonly this: the candidate gets first a text prescrib'd him, on which he makes a homily before some presbytery. Then he has an exegesis in Latin on some common head (ordinarily some Popish controversie) and sustains disputes upon it. After this he is tryed as to his skill in the languages and chronology. He is likewise obliged to answer *ex tempore* any question in divinity that shall be proposed to him by any member of the presbytery. This is called the questionary tryal. Then he has that which we call the exercise and addition, that is as it is in most presbyteries, one day he must analize and comment upon a text for half an hour or so to shew his skill in textual, critical and casuistick theology,[11] and another day for another half hour, he discourses again by drawing practical inferences, etc., to shew his abilities that way too. And then lastly, he must make a popular sermon. I believe you have scarcely so severe tryals in England. All this done, the presbytery considers whether it be fit to recommend him to the bishop for a licence to preach, and many have I known remitted to their studies. If they find him qualified and recommend him, he gets his licence, he commences probationer for the ministery and commonly continues such for two, three, four, or more years thereafter till he is presented to some benefice. Then he passes over again through all the foresaid steps of tryal and more accurately, before he is ordained. What greater scrutiny would you desire as to point of knowledge?

But besides that, I have something more to tell you: it is that generally since the restitution of Episcopacy, our divines have had better education, etc., been put on better methods of study than ever they were before. They have learned to lay aside prejudices and trace truth ingenuously and embrace it where they find it. With our predecessors, especially in the times of Presbytery, the Dutch divinity was only in vogue. Their commonplace men[12] were the great standards and are so still to that party, and whoever step'd aside one hair's breadth from their positions was forthwith an heretick. But the present generation, after the way of England, take the scriptures for their rule and the ancients and right reason for guides for finding the genuine sense of that rule; by which method, in my opinion, they are come to have their principles and thoughts far better digested. For evidence of this, be pleased to know, Sir, that upon the restitution of Episcopacy, anno 1662, there were six hundred good, who kept their stations and conformed. These were not only generally of Presbyterian education, but likewise for the most part the ablest men who were then in office. There are many of these men yet alive. Now if this experiment were made, if these men, who had that Presbyterian education were examined upon their skill and principles in divinity, and if again those who have had the posterior education were likewise tryed, I could lay an even wager (if I were much provok'd, I would venture three to one) all ingenuous and impartial judges should determine in favor of the latter sort and confess that they have clearer and more distinct ideas of things and understand the christian philosophy better. In a word I'll affirm it confidently that philosophy was never understood better nor never preached better in Scotland than it has been these twenty years by-gone.

I must confess it was never less practised. But for that we may thank the Presbyterians. Do not think this a slander, for if they, during their twenty four years usurpation, i.e. from Thirty Eight till Sixty Two inclusive, had not made many things such as rebellion and Presbytery *jure divino*, if they had not baffled people's credulity by making all the extravagances of the late times God's own work and the cause of Christ, etc., and if they had not made it their chief work ever since to create and cherish divisions and schisms among us and keep up a party for themselves by all means possible, I doubt not the gospel, with God's blessing, would have had more desirable success than it has had in this kingdom. What a pernicious thing is it needlessly to break the unity and disturb the peace of a church! I have often thought on that saying of Irenaeus, *Liber 4 adversus haereses*, cap. 62, "Nulla ab iis (schismaticis) tanta fieri potest correptio, quanta est schismatis pernicies",[13] and the more I think on it, I find still the more of important truth in it. And believe it, Sir, if ever there was a sect since Christ came into the world to whom that father's words in that same chapter were applicable, they are, only one thing excepted, to our Scotch Presbyterians:

> Suam utilitatem potius considerantes, quam unitatem ecclesiae; propter modicas et quaslibet causas, magnum et gloriosum corpus Christi conscindunt et dividunt, et quantum in ipsis est interficiunt; pacem loquentes (here it only fails) et bellum operantes; vere liquantes culicem, et camelum transglutientes.[14]

By their divisions, they have still kept up such rancors and animosities amongst us that the meek, calm, gentle, peaceable spirit of Christianity could get no footing. And how can the religion flourish without that? And by their bold entituling all their unaccountable freaks in the late times, as I said, to God's authority and abusing his holy word to justifie them, they lost all the credit of the ministery. For so soon as people's eyes opened and they began to see what legerdemain had been plaid in the pulpits, especially under such high pretensions to godliness, they look'd upon the sacred office of the minstery and continue to do so ever since as a mere imposture; so that though we are at never so much pains to persuade and convince, yet our labors are not regarded, and if they be not that, how can they be successful? I know you'll think this a digression. Be it so, I could not help it. I have such strong impressions of the truth of the thing, that I could not forbear to tell it you.

> [Sage turns to other charges against the Episcoplain clergy, immorality, negligence, error, persecuting, and then concludes.]

Thus, Sir, you have a brief prospect of the present state of the Scottish clergy, fuller by much than I at first intended, perhaps than you are pleased with, and ye may think it tedious. But I acknowledge I have that weakness; I have not the faculty of dispatching things so smoothly and so shortly as possibly your palate would require. But my apology is ready. I have omitted an hundred things proper to have been inserted. If I am tedious, it is in telling truth, and if the length of this weary you, you shall not be so troubled again. For these reasons expecting your pardon, I am, etc.

ARCHIBALD PITCAIRNE (1652-1713) was one of the early figures in the Edinburgh tradition of medicine. He went to France for his medical training and was one of the founding members of the Royal College of Physicians of Edinburgh. The celebrity of his treatise on Harvey's circulation of the blood, *Solutio problematis de historicis: seu inventoribus dissertatio*, 1688, led to his appointment in 1692 to a chair of medicine at Leyden. But he returned to Edinburgh next year, where he threw himself into bitter medical controversies. He was a proponent of mechanical theories and a Baconian. It must be said that some of his remedies, like some of Bacon's experiments, are more empirical than scientific. His medical dissertations came out in Rotterdam in 1701 and in an enlarged edition in Edinburgh in 1713. Besides contributing to medical learning, he was an active and charitable doctor among the paupers of Edinburgh. By arrangement with the town council, he treated them free, and their bodies were his when they were dead.

Pitcairne was an accomplished writer of Latin verse. His epitaph on Claverhouse was translated by Dryden, "O last and best of Scots". His flamboyant mockery of established religion got him the name of atheist or at least deist. But what he mocks in *The Assembly* and his broadside verses, *Babel* (1692), is churchmen and Presbyterian humbug. Many of the butts and jokes of *The Assembly* turn up in *The Scotch Presbyterian Eloquence* (1692). A note in the Pitcairne collection in the National Library says that Pitcairne had the help of four other Jacobite wits, and these may have collaborated on *The Scotch Presbyterian Eloquence* as well. *The Assembly* is a crude play, a travesty of Restoration comedy, but it brings the Edinburgh scene to life. Its construction is very loose, though the preface of 1752 defends that. It consists of farcical scenes satirizing the General Assemblies of 1690 and 1692 and ends as they did in the bathos of dissolution. The romantic subplot associates sexual honesty with political honesty (Jacobitism) and sexual hypocrisy with political hypocrisy (Presbyterianism). Pitcairne did not publish his play, and I have not found that it was ever performed. It came out first in 1722, and that is my text. The later editions of 1752, 1766 and 1817 have a preface, which explains who the characters represent. There is a recent edition of the play by Terence Tobin (Lafayette, Indiana: Purdue University Studies, 1972), from which the text below differs chiefly in matters of punctuation.

Lord Whigridden	Earl of Crawford, President of the Convention Parliament of 1688 and one of the Presbyterian commissoners for settling the government of the Church.
Lord Huffy	Lord Leven, "a madcap Presbyterian peer," raised a force to protect the Convention Parliament against Claverhouse.
Moderator	Hugh Kennedy, moderator of the General Assemblies of 1690 and 1692.
Salathiel Little-sense	Gilbert Rule, Principal of Edinburgh University succeeding Alexander Monro, whom, as one of the commissioners, he had helped to purge.
Turbulent	James Fraser of Brea, Covenanting minister and diarist, imprisoned for nonconformity.
Solomon	David Williamson, covenanting minister.
Cherrie-trees	One of the commissioners of the Assembly sent to congratulate William on his accession to the throne. See below, p. 212, n. 27.
Covenant Plain-dealer	James Kirkton, see above, p. 30.

THE ASSEMBLY: OR SCOTCH REFORMATION

A Comedy
by a Scots Gentleman

ACT I SCENE III

A Church
The Committee debating: Moderator, Mr Salathiel, Mr Turbulent, Mr Solomon, Mr Covenant, Lord Whigridden, Ruling Elder, Webster, Lord Huffy with a whip in his hand.

| Moderator. | I see many malignant spies here to day. They're come for ill and nae good. I have seen the day when a malignant eye got not leave to look on the work of the Lord. The greatest nobles of the nation thought it their greatest honour to stand at the door of the house of God with drawn swords to keep out the malignants, whom they knew by the first glisk of their face. |
| Turbulent. | "It's better to be a doorkeeper in the house of God than to dwell in the tents of wicked men."[15] I think |

194

it's both their honour and duty, and we should command the nobles of our time to do the like.

[*Lord Huffy starts and clacks his whip*]

Huffy.   Since I am not thought worthy to be a member of this godly and learned Assembly, I offer my self with my whip to be one of your noble guards at the door, and begs you to believe that there is no title with which I am dignified I wou'd be prouder of than in being one of the scourges of the Lord.

[*Clacks his whip again*]

Moderator.   My Lord, I cannot but commend your zeal, for I am sure among all our nobles there's none fitter to scourge the malignants out of the house of God – But to our work brethren. There is two sorts of people who have taken their hands from the work of the Lord. First, the Tories, who never put their hand to it. Secondly, the court party. So we poor men man[16] e'en put our shoulders to it and take a good lift of the cause of Christ, for I assure you it will never break one of our backs.

Covenant.   It's your own cause and your own interest, ay forsooth is't.

Moderator.   I wad fain ken what ye wad do.

Turbulent.   Why, Moderator, I think fit we have a thanks for the defeat of the Duke of Savoy.[17]

Salathiel.   Rather a fast, for he was on the confederate side.

Moderator.   I think rather Brother Turbulent has the right end of the string, for he was but a burthen to the confederates, and God's judgments came upon him for persecuting the poor Protestants.

Covenant.   Indeed Moderator, he's as good a Presbyterian as King William.

Moderator.   Out's, Brother Turbulent, had[18] your tongue o'that. We must not be too severe. We must not rip up old sores.

[*All the committee speak together, some for a fast and some a thanks.*]

Moderator.   Let's pray drown the noise and quiet our spirits.

Covenant.   What needs a' this fool praying?

Moderator.   [*Prays*] Our minds are disordered, and we do not know what we are doing or saying. Lord gi' us grace, or thou shall not get glory, and see wha will win o' that. – Now since by his providence the dinn's done, I wou'd propose a dilemma, I mean an alternative, whether ye will plant the Kirk of Scotland or the Kirk of England first.

Covenant.   Truly, Moderator, I think charity shou'd begin at hame.

Salathiel.   Of a truth, Moderator, I think ye shou'd first plant the Kirk of England, for there's no minister there, and we have a call to preach the gospel throughout the whole world. That place is all o'regrown with briars and thorns, and they'll o'rgang Scotland too, except we send able men to tread them out. You know I wrote a book proving that kingdom guilty of scandal, errors, ignorance, superstition and will-worship,[19] besides many of them have a spiritual sibness and pastoral relation to some of us.

Moderator.   Will the folk call you, or will you go back again?

Covenant.   What needs a' this pother about Mr. Salathiel's going back. They've got a good enough loan of him already. I know, likewise, he dare not go back, for there's an order for a justice of peace to apprehend him, if they can catch him.[20]

Solomon.   [From a corner] Tho' I'm not a member of this meeting of Christ's Kirk, yet I am a privy member. I am concern'd for the Kirk of Scotland, that pure virgin. Her lips are like threeds of scarlet; her speech is comely; her putting[21] breasts are like two young roes that are twins and feed among the lillies; her navel is like a round gobblet and wanteth no liquor; her belly is as a heap of wheat set about with lillies. She has been defloured these twenty eight years by the curates.[22] I intreat you then, brethren, for the mercies of Christ, get able men with soul-refreshing and inbearing gifts to do duty to her, to dress her seasonably and abundantly, ay, ay, forsooth.

Turbulent.   Moderator!

Salathiel.   Moderator!

Solomon.   Fortification!

Covenant.   Fornication with the virgin! That's as ill as the curates hobbling on the Whore of Babylon and begetting the fourteen black birds.[23] No more about that.

Ruling Elder.	Cleense out the keerats[24] that the gospel may be preech'd. Let that be first deen, it's the wark o' the Lord.
	[*One knocks at the door. Officer opens. Enter a webster.*]
Webster.	My Lord Moderator.
Moderator.	Away with these proud Prelatick titles. Call me Brother Moderator in the Lord Jesus.
Webster.	Well then my Lord Brother Moderator in the Lord Jesus, I have brought a covenant from our own people in St. Andrews to make the worthy earl a ruling elder.
Moderator.	You shou'd call that paper a commission.
Webster.	Covenant or commission, that's all one. But I think the word "covenant" sounds better. E'en ca' it what ye please, for ye'r book-lear'd.
Moderator.	My Lord, by his providence, we've got a commission from the zealous websters, suters[25] and godly women in St. Andrews for your Lordship to represent them in this judicatory. It's grivaminous[26] for you to have wanted it so long. E'en give us your opinion about what we were speaking.
Whigridden.	I have done as good service to this honourable judicatory as any man living by ruining and rabbling the curates. I have managed the whole civil interest with much wisdom. Yet as Nehemiah says, it requires me to be an office-bearer in the house of God. Therefore I desire ye pray for me six months without ceasing that I may be fit for this great work.
Moderator.	'Tis not dishonourable. E'en we seek God's blessing, and he never gave a burden, but he fitted the back for the bearing it.
Whigridden.	Tho' I be conscious to my self of my own imbecility, yet I shall offer three things about planting ye were speaking of. 1st, It's the only time to delve in order to plant. 2dly, It's the fittest month now for planting. 3dly, It's the fittest time of the foresaid month now to plant.
Moderator.	My Lord, we know not what ye would be at. We were speaking about planting o' kirks, and ye speak of planting of trees and hedges.
Whigridden.	The matter is the same, for it's the fittest time to delve out the curates by the spade of the spirit.
Moderator.	Let's adjourn now till afternoon and speak about

these things then at more length at that time when
we meet again.

ACT III SCENE II

Changeth to the Old Lady's House.
Old Lady, Mr. Solomon Cherrie-trees, etc.[27]

Old Lady.	Mr Solomon have ye not convinced my niece, my stubborn, obstinate niece, that there should be union and communion betwixt the members of the said Kirk, and that for the better performance of this, there should be a par[i]ty betwixt the members?
Solomon.	Indeed there should be betwixt ministers, but not betwixt two lay elders.
Old Lady.	But as to the fittest posture in time of exercise?
Solomon.	Indeed I can never get her convinced that standing is be far the most convenient.
Old Lady.	But remains still obstinate as to her perseverance?
Solomon.	I can hardly persuade her that a fallen member will ever rise again. But as for these things, nothing but experience, Madam. Wait but a while till she feel the inbearing work about her own heart. I resolve to visit and deal with her. She is in her chamber, I hope.

[*Solomon rushes forward into her chamber*].

Maid.	Pray you stay a little, Sir. She is quite now dressing herself.

[*Laura retires in disorder. He catcheth hold on her*].

Solomon.	No matter, I must be instant in season and out of season.
Maid.	I think you are in a prick haste in faith.
Solomon	[*aside*]. I'm resolved to be impudent for once.

Madam, tho' you should be never so obstinate,
these two fair breast of yours evidently prove parity
in the church members. Look you, do one of these
tyrannize and insult over the other? Thus and thus
they [live] in brotherly love and concord together.
Do not imagine that the natural body there is thus
orderly and that the wife[28] should suffer such a
blemish in the mystical.

[*Handling her breasts*].

198

Laura	[*retiring*]. Good Mr. Parson, ye must fetch your similies elsewhere. I'll assure you I'll be neither parable nor metaphor to your kirk government.
Solomon.	Dear Madam, forbear that antichristian name of parson. That cursed Prelacy runs still in your head. But this leads me to discourse of bare breasts and gaudy apparrel. What a hideous thing is it for a christian Protestant woman for her breasts to be strutting out thus. Yea, some will discover them this length to their eternal shame.
Laura.	Men of such mettal as you cannot endure it. But however, methinks you are too familiar. I'm sure ye never use to handle the text so closely.
Solomon.	It may be. But ye will never know the difference till you find me in the pulpit.
Laura.	I say once more, good Mr. Parson, if that will fright you, forbear. You have not these things that can attain to a body's retirement so airly, I mean youth and gallantry.

[*He looks in the glass*].

Solomon.	Nay, Madam, I think soul concerns – yet I am not so old either, but Madam, [the concerns] I have for your body, your mind, I mean – and it were a pity such a fair piece of the creation shou'd perish and these bright eyes which shine like the stars in the sanctuary. Put you confidence in me, Madam, trust in my conduct. I'll cure all your fleshly appetites that [war] again the soul. I'll carry you to a bed of roses, where you shall taste the sweets of love. O the length, breadth and deep of a true active love!
Laura.	Bold Sir, Gad I would not trust my spaniel bitch in your bed of roses among your perfumes and things. Mark, messenger, you scent strong of tobacco and such, I'll warn you. No more of your scent. I'll pardon what is past, but in time coming, if I hear one word of beds, bear breasts and sweets of love and such like gibrish, that becomes your mouth as little as that fair wig becomes your monkie face, I will reveal all, spoil your trade and make you appear, instead of a mortified Saul,[29] a preacher of the gospel of Christ, a most profane, pander, hissful, impudent old villain.

[*Exit Laura*].

Solomon. I'll get me gone and I'll tell her aunt she is a good proficient in the lesson of grace. If I irritate her, she'll mar all and betray me to the old matron. She has my thumb under her belt for once. I wish my whole hand were really so. I think for as old as I am, I should –

[*Exit*].

REFERENCES AND NOTES

REFERENCES AND NOTES TO INTRODUCTION

1. Preface, *The Fundamental Charter of Presbytery* (London: Browne, 1695), n.p.
2. *History of Scottish Literature* (London: Robert Hale, 1977), p. 128.
3. Their model here is probably Knox's *History*, first published in 1644 but probably known to both historians in ms.
4. This is a summary account. In Scotland as in England there was writing in plain and natural styles of some distinction long before the new prose of the Restoration. Knox's *History* is the outstanding Scottish example of speech based prose (in spite of its anglicized forms). In the early seventeenth century there are styles with a more literary base tending to plainness. Neatness and clarity may be found in Bishop Cowper's sermons for example, and Hume of Godscroft's version of the Senecan style is eminently natural.
5. *Winstanley: The Law of Freedom and Other Writings* (Harmondsworth: Penguin, 1973), pp. 60–61.
6. Robert McWard, *The Poor Man's Cup of Cold Water* (no place, 1678) p. 35; rackel = raucle, impetuous.
7. See Ronald D. S. Jack, *Scottish Prose, 1550–1700* (London: Calder and Boyars, 1971), pp. 23–24.
8. i.e. the sort of wit Marvell displays in *The Rehearsal Transprosed.*
9. Melville's Latin ode on the rejection of the Millennary Petition by Oxford and Cambridge Universities (1603).
10. e.g. Sir James Stewart and James Stirling, *Naphtali* (no place, 1667), p. 21.
11. Ed. Thomas Thomson (Edinburgh, 1821), p. 4.
12. Hugh Binning, *Treatise on Christian Love* (Edin.: Fleming, 1743), p. 38 (1651 not extant).
13. Robert Baillie, *Letters and Journals*, ed. D. Laing, vol. 3 (Edinburgh: Bannatyne Club, 1842), p. 258.
14. *An Account of the Present Persecution of the Church in Scotland* (London: Cook, 1690), pp. 44–46.

REFERENCES AND NOTES TO CHAPTER ONE

1. i.e. 49 years.
2. In 1561 the Convention of Estates accepted the *First Book of Discipline*, a plan for a reformed church polity; Melville's *True Narration* was written in 1610.

3. The General Assembly of Dundee (see headnote).
4. One of the Presbyterian ministers
5. cleared
6. through, i.e. sharp with
7. held
8. coming before
9. willing
10. concerning
11. Melville's letter urged the Synod of Fife to reject the articles relating to the king's supremacy in the church proposed in 1606
12. raving
13. promptly
14. John Buckeridge, Prebendary of Colwell, Bishop of Rochester, 1611
15. Thomas Bilson Bp. of Winchester, *True Difference between Christian Subjection and Unchristian Rebellion* (1585)
16. scrofula
17. into the presence (of the king)
18. Richard Bancroft
19. in doors
20. charges
21. *in thesi*: concerning the point at issue, the lawfulness of the General Assembly; *in hypothesi*: concerning subsidiary points, which he goes on to treat.
22. delegation
23. submit
24. stepped up
25. The General Assembly at Linlithgow (1606) where measures bringing presbyteries under Episcopal influence were carried.
26. inveighed
27. Possibly John Spottiswoode, Archb. of Glasgow. The king has noticed an allusion to Rev. 13, 7.
28. Lancelot Andrewes, Bp. of Chichester.
29. "directly against his text, whilk sayes that the sones of Aaron should blow the trumpets" (Wodrow MS.)
30. François, Comte de Vaudemont, Venetian General
31. I never saw such a ritual. Indeed nothing of high mass is lacking here but the adoring of the transubstantiated bread.
32. with the pride of this generation
33. John King, Dean of Christ Church, Bp. of London, 1611. The four sermons by Barlow, Buckeridge, Andrewes and King were published separately in 1606.
34. confining
35. received
36. presumably James Melville
37. Richard Bancroft, *Dangerous Positions and Proceedings*, 1593.
38. William Barlow, Bp. of Rochester, brought out *The Summe and Substance of the Conference at Hampton Court* in 1604.
39. Sir Thomas Egerton

40. William James, Bp. of Durham, had been President of University College, Oxford.
41. guest
42. lodger
43. acrimony
44. adding
45. parsons
46. possession
47. formal academic disputation
48. surety
49. i.e. his nephew, James Melville
50. Ovid, *Tristia*, 2, ll. 13–14 and 15–16: "If I were wise, I would have learnt with justice to hate the muses, powers destructive to their worshipper." "But now such madness accompanies my disease, I return demented to these rocks."
51. If
52. under his arm
53. settle debts
54. report
55. descended
56. scattering
57. Patrick Galloway, minister of St. Giles, Edinburgh, a moderate, and by no means a consistent supporter of James's ecclesiastical policy.
58. shied away from
59. Andrew Ramsay, also a moderate, who later refused to read the Prayer Book of 1637 and joined the Covenanters.
60. Here abusively, a religious sectary.
61. Thomas Sydserff, minister of St. Giles; under Charles I, Dean of Edinburgh and Bishop of Galloway.
62. trouble
63. William Struthers, minister of St. Giles.
64. aggravate

REFERENCES AND NOTES TO CHAPTER TWO

1. David Dickson, minister of Irvine
2. stiff
3. wide open
4. facing me
5. roll, scroll
6. knitted
7. nooks
8. see
9. sea
10. i.e. his own. He speaks of himself in what follows in the second person.

11. Ratho
12. i.e. communion table
13. Thomas Craig of Riccarton
14. instantaneous
15. Bishops sat on the Council and were active in Charles's government.
16. matters indifferent, e.g. in the view of some, the precise form of church government or worship
17. Rutherford is urging Loudoun to petition for a free General Assembly.
18. incubate
19. No other heads are numbered.
20. exchange
21. i.e. the Covenant is not a bargain by which men pay for the kingdom of heaven
22. choice
23. professing christians
24. Baillie is talking about the Treaty of Berwick concluding the First Bishops' War.
25. the high church party favouring the reforms of Laud, Archbishop of Canterbury
26. the King of Spain
27. growth
28. the last empire of the world (Daniel 2, 44) supposed the millennial reign of Christ
29. straws
30. Laing, p. 186, suggests the "Latine storie" was perhaps *Rerum nuper in Regno Scotiae gestarum Historia* (Danzig, 1641) by William Spang himself.
31. clock
32. clock hand
33. The supplication of 20th Dec., 1638, asked the king to agree to the ratification of the liberties of the church.
34. Charles's commissioner in Scotland
35. showed
36. *A Short Relation of the State of the Kirk . . . for the information . . . to our Brethren in the Kirk of England,* July 1638 and *An Information to all Good Christians in the Kingdome of England* (1639).
37. Sir Alexander Gibson of Durie, senior
38. Declaration, 27th Feb. 1639.
39. *The Remonstrance of the Nobility, Barones, Burgesses, Ministers and Commons . . .* (1639).
40. John Cameron (1579–1625) theologian, Principal of Glasgow University when Baillie was a student, who supported James's policies. Bilson, see above, p. 21; Grotius (1583–1645), Dutch humanist, jurist, statesman of Arminian views; André Rivet (1512–1651), Huguenot, professor of divinity in Leyden; Aberdeen Doctors, seventeenth century circle of divines, who resisted the signing of the Covenant from an Arminian and royalist standpoint.

<table>
<tbody>
<tr><td>42.</td><td>George Gillespie published A Dispute against the English Popish Ceremonies in 1637 and Reason for which the Service Book Urged upon Scotland Ought to be Refused in 1638. Neither deals directly with defensive arms but both urge the illegality of imposing ceremonies on the Scottish Church.</td></tr>
<tr><td>43.</td><td>i.e. somewhat against his inclinations, Henderson drew up Instructions for Defensive Arms.</td></tr>
<tr><td>44.</td><td>Notice that he declined the jurisdiction of the General Assembly.</td></tr>
<tr><td>45.</td><td>Dumbarton</td></tr>
<tr><td>46.</td><td>Under the authority of Strafford, Lord Deputy of Ireland, Corbet published The Ungirding of the Scottish Armour (1639). See pp. 64ff.</td></tr>
<tr><td>47.</td><td>brought before a tribunal</td></tr>
<tr><td>48.</td><td>Alexander Leslie (1580–1661), a Swedish marshal in the Thirty Years' War, made general of the Covenanting army.</td></tr>
<tr><td>49.</td><td>surrender</td></tr>
<tr><td>50.</td><td>petard, device for blowing up gates</td></tr>
<tr><td>51.</td><td>General Leslie and Colonel Hamilton</td></tr>
<tr><td>52.</td><td>Sir John Hamilton of Orbiston, lord justice-clerk</td></tr>
<tr><td>53.</td><td>Sir James Carmichael, treasurer depute</td></tr>
<tr><td>54.</td><td>pikes</td></tr>
<tr><td>55.</td><td>colonels</td></tr>
<tr><td>56.</td><td>canvas</td></tr>
<tr><td>57.</td><td>straw</td></tr>
<tr><td>58.</td><td>Erskine</td></tr>
<tr><td>59.</td><td>Dalhousie</td></tr>
<tr><td>60.</td><td>Baillie treats Montrose's campaign against the Royalists of the North East later.</td></tr>
<tr><td>61.</td><td>intend</td></tr>
<tr><td>62.</td><td>his unpredictable men in trews (highlanders) should take it into their heads to harry in their rear</td></tr>
<tr><td>63.</td><td>need</td></tr>
<tr><td>64.</td><td>quivers</td></tr>
<tr><td>65.</td><td>motto</td></tr>
<tr><td>66.</td><td>Durie (Alexander Gibson, junior) and Hope were leading lawyers</td></tr>
<tr><td>67.</td><td>James Livingston, Lord Almond</td></tr>
<tr><td>68.</td><td>cheerful</td></tr>
<tr><td>69.</td><td>lack</td></tr>
<tr><td>70.</td><td>Merse and Teviotdale</td></tr>
<tr><td>71.</td><td>failzie? penalty, forfeit</td></tr>
<tr><td>72.</td><td>the Turkish sultan</td></tr>
<tr><td>73.</td><td>suitors</td></tr>
<tr><td>74.</td><td>the English general</td></tr>
<tr><td>75.</td><td>colonel</td></tr>
<tr><td>76.</td><td>Athanasius, Archbishop of Alexandria, the fearless champion of the orthodox view of the trinity against the Arian heresy, suffered persecution under Constantius, the Eastern Emperor. Corbet is unaware that Athanasius enlisted the help of the orthodox Constans, Constantius's brother and Western Emperor, and thinks of him as a</td></tr>
</tbody>
</table>

pattern of Christian passive obedience. He pretends that a Jesuit or Covenanter would find Athanasius' course pusilanimous.

77. [*Instructions for Defensive Arms*, 4.]
78. [David Dickson], leading Covenanting minister
79. John Davenant, Bp. of Salisbury [*Determinations quaestionum*, 4] (1634).
80. The Glasgow Assembly (1638) declared the six Assemblies held since 1606 null because they were not "free".
81. [Evagrius Scholasticus], *Ecclesiastical History*, [lib 3, cap. 44]. In 513 the mob of Constantinople rose in protest against Anastasius' Monophysite reform of the liturgy of Haghia Sophia.
82. Robert [Bellarmine], Jesuit theologian, who had entered controversies concerning the oath of allegiance exacted by James as king of England. Corbet gives no more specific reference.
83. Thomas Stapleton, a moderate papalist and catholic controversialist in Elizabeth's reign.
84. The royal *Proclamation* of Nov. 1638 was met by a reading of the Covenanters' *Protestation* of July 1638.
85. [*De clericis*], *Secunda controversia generalis, De membris ecclesia militantis*, [cap. 28].
86. Walter Travers, puritan divine, whose *Ecclesiasticae disciplinae . . . explicatio* (1576) became the handbook of English presbyterianism and was translated by Thomas Cartwright.
87. Elizabethan puritan divine. The camp royal is presumably the camp of Christ, whose kingship of the Church was an important article of Presbyterian doctrine.
88. [Bellarmine] *Tractatus de potestate summi pontificis . . .* [*contra Barklaium*].
89. Joannes [Azor, *Institutionum moralium . . . tomi* 3, pt. 2, lib. 10, cap. 9].
90. George [Buchanan, *De jure regni apud Scotos*, p. 70], a work celebrated for recommending the deposing of tyrants. I cannot trace Corbet's edition. What he translates may be found in the edition of 1579 (Edin. John Ross), pp. 101–102.
91. [Franciscus Suarez, *De censuris in communi*, Disputatio 15, sect. 6].
92. [*De jure regni*, pp. 50, 56, 57]. 1579 ed., pp. 76, 78–79.
93. [*De romani pontificis ecclesiastica hierarchica, libri tres*, cap. 7].
94. deadly, probably a pun on Greek *basilikos*, royal
95. [*Instructions for Defensive Arms*, 2].
96. [Maphaeus, *In vita Ignatii*, lib. 1, cap. 2].
97. [Ribadeneira, *De vita Ignatii*, lib. 1, cap. 7]
98. [Becanus]
99. [Ribadeneira, lib. 4, cap. 18]
100. It is not known to whom the letter was addressed.
101. princes of the nobility or leaders in war
102. exclusively
103. The essential points of sovereignty cannot belong to a single body such as the General Assembly, representative of only one interest of the realm, nor to a composite body such as Parliament, made up of

three estates, nor to various bodies each in charge of a separate function of government, say legislative, executive, judicial.

104. Mark Napier's suggestion
105. respectful
106. may you will and command what is auspicious and favourable to you and the Roman people
107. let it be, let them be
108. propose a law; command a law
109. heralds who declared war, demanded redress etc
110. appealed to the people
111. Canton of Graubünden, not at that time part of Swiss Confederation
112. in the Greater Council
113. Senators; Council of Ten; the Doge
114. they can endure neither complete liberty nor complete slavery
115. Protestant resistance in Bohemia against the Emperor Ferdinand precipitated the Thirty Years War.
116. lest in the commotion it should show violence to his majesty
117. the Peace of Berwick (1641) concluding the Second Bishops' War
118. Since Charles had ratified legislation against the dissolving of Parliament without its own consent, the Long Parliament was not technically "pretended", even though at war with the king.
119. immoderate power does not remain long within just limits
120. Puzzling: The Council of Constantinople (381) actually endorsed the creed of the Council of Nicaea (325), and the canons of these councils neither contradict each other nor those of other General Councils. Drummond's note on General Councils reasserts that they may err and should only have authority where their acts are in conformity with scripture.
121. Brownists, followers of Robert Browne, were an early sort of English Separatist, who wished to withdraw from the established church into congregations of the regenerate. They were the original Independents and Congregationalists.
122. What custom has established over a long period is usually less troublesome, even if worse, than what is unaccustomed.
123. Sage's version
124. aristocracy
125. those who profess themselves (Protestants)
126. in the making
127. alchemical operation
128. truly great because good
129. There is no evil in the state that God does not bring about.
130. The Battle of Pinkie (1547) had more to do with the rivalry of England and France in Scotland than with clerical schemes. Still Cardinal Beaton had been in charge of affairs. He was murdered by a party of pro-English Protestants. The countermoves of the pro-French Catholic side brought an English army into Scotland and the Scots were heavily defeated.
131. the papal party and the aristocratic party of medieval Italy

132. Ravaillac, Catholic fanatic assassin of Henry IV; papelard, a bigot.
133. When justice is removed what else are kingdoms but bands of thieves?
134. Henry VII, Holy Roman Emperor, supposedly poisoned by a friar through the sacramental wine (1313).
135. dance tunes
136. sound than matter
137. frantic wisdom
138. holy cheats
139. Not to be is the same as not to be operant; non existent things have no influence; when the basis is removed everything that is built on top of it is destroyed.
140. Presbyterian
141. George Gordon, Marquis of Huntly, Royalist magnate of the North East, beheaded 1650.
142. A learned joke: *Basilikon Doron* (the royal gift) was James VI's treatise on monarchy; *Ikon Basilike* (the royal image) was supposedly the testament of Charles I; "Basilikos Adynastes" means "royal unking" and is not the title of a book.
143. Compare word play with Corbet's (p. 68). The sight of the basilisk was deadly.
144. doll kings
145. skittle
146. Charles was crowned at Scone, January 1651
147. See Joshua, Ch. 7; Urquhart is speaking of the levy of the army that was defeated at Worcester.
148. rixdollars, silver coins
149. gold coins
150. pony
151. siege
152. See 1 Samuel 14 and Judges 7.
153. addition of a letter, hence "goldly"
154. lasting an hour and a half
155. See 2 Kings, 18 to 19.
156. blindness
157. beggarly and coarse woollen garments
158. sovereignty, rule and madness of wealth
159. They enrich the ears of others with words so that they may fill up their own purses with gold (*Noctes Atticae*, XIV, 1, 34).
160. previously
161. the bite of the tarantula supposedly caused madness
162. a bad egg of a bad crow
163. human injustice
164. Reflected there, he is given back to himself.

REFERENCES AND NOTES TO CHAPTER THREE

1. Perhaps the notorious Judge Jeffreys
2. Burnet has just been speaking of Nairne and Charteris
3. "A very weak man, famed only for his readiness of speaking florid Latin", *History of My Own Time*, ed. Airy, 1, 483.
4. Catholic pietists, followers of the theologian, Cornelius Jansen
5. By the deprivations of 1662–63
6. i.e. the explication of the doctrine to be found in the text, confirmation and defence of the doctrine and application of it to life, a threefold division standard in sermons of the earlier seventeenth century. Cf. Sage on examining of Episcopal ministers, p. 190.
7. The Whiggamore Raid of 1648, in which the radicals of the South West drove out the Engager government.
8. Henry Hammond (1605–60), Royalist divine, author of *Of Resisting the Lawfull Magistrate under Colour of Religion* (1644).
9. i.e. at Preston, 1648
10. part of the mystical garment of the high priest, Exodus, 28.30
11. Charles Maitland, Lord Haltoun, treasurer-depute
12. Episcopalian clergy put in place of the deprived Presbyterians
13. the windward side, i.e. the advantage
14. *The History of the Indulgence* (1678)
15. to give a discourse in the form of a commentary on a chapter of the Bible
16. ecclesiastical overseer
17. i.e. the directive of the Council
18. anniversary of Charles's coronation
19. *A Letter Written . . . unto his Parishioners at Ancrum* (1671)
20. Alexander Burnet, Archbishop of Glasgow, not Gilbert Burnet
21. agreement to
22. outlawed
23. Arkleton
24. Robert Baillie of Jerviswood, Kirkton's brother-in-law, later charged with involvement in the Rye House Plot and executed
25. Kincardine, see Burnet's portrait of him above.
26. flauntingly
27. 2 Kings 9 and 10; Acts 18
28. luminous body in the sky
29. Revelation 2, 17.
30. holy of holies
31. chosen
32. Numbers, 16
33. Gen. 25.3
34. tops
35. to such wickedness could religion persuade men
36. set of commandments written on the first of Moses' two stone tablets
37. restrain

38. Acts 1, 9–11
39. indictment
40. summoned
41. commanded (by the conscience)
42. muscular, forceful
43. whose religious call distracts them from their vocation, barter or manual labour
44. The second proposition as a whole concerns immediate revelation. The substance of its second part may be gathered from Barclay's defence of it. I retain his section numbers.
45. In 1534 the Anabaptists, led as they claimed by the Holy Spirit, took over Münster and set up a rule of the Saints which involved polygamy. The ancient Gnostics were accused of similar spiritual licence.
46. 1 Kings, 22
47. 1 John, 2, 27
48. See Eusebius, *Historia ecclesiastica*, lib. 5, cap. 26 (Barclay)
49. Concilium Florentiae, Sess. 5 decreto quodam; Concilium Ephesi, Act 6, Sess. 11 and 12; Concilium Florentiae, Sess. 18:20; Sess. 21, p. 480 et sqq. (Barclay). The Council of Florence considered proposals for the union of Greek and Latin churches.
50. vice versa, substituting Lutherans and Arminians for Calvinists.
51. those whose philosophy is based on the study of nature rather than revelation
52. The Socinians denied the divinity of Christ and hoped to ground theology in reason.
53. i.e. Calvinist teachers
54. distrust
55. Episcopalian clergy who replaced the deprived Presbyterians
56. hindrance
57. professing christians
58. Perhaps alluding to James Renwick's Lanark Declaration of Jan. 1682.
59. empty
60. could
61. a few
62. All field preachers
63. Battles in which the covenanting party were defeated
64. See Luke, 24, 14, ff.
65. asks
66. glow
67. must
68. fellows
69. hinges
70. quit
71. lose (a term from nine-pins)
72. game of marbles

1. Perhaps *An Apology for the Clergy of Scotland* by Alexander Monro (1693).
2. superficial
3. *The Declaration of the Prince of Orange,* 1688; *The Scottish Inquisition* (1689), author unknown.
4. Fagel, Grand Pensionary of Holland, wrote a letter to England in 1687 explaining the Prince of Orange's views on James's dispensing of the penal laws and giving reassurances to Catholics as well as Dissenters.
5. circumstanced
6. No doubt a sarcastic reference to the fact that the Presbyterians were established *de facto* but not *de jure* at the time and the use they made of the term.
7. In *The Scotch Presbyterian Eloquence,* presumably
8. Although the Act of Council at Glasgow, 1662, expelling those who would not accept Episcopal collation from their charges, belongs to Charles's reign, William's *Declaration* seems to refer to it (p. 6) as contributing to the distress of the kingdom. Sage's point is presumably that Burnet, now a Whig, had earlier defended the Episcopal severities, e.g. in *A Modest and Free Conference Between a Conformist and a Nonconformist* (1669), pp. 9–10.
9. explanation
10. two of the Aberdeen doctors
11. Critical theology, the forerunner of nineteenth century Higher Criticism, treated wider issues of biblical philology than the explicatory concerns of textual theology. Casuistic theology dealt with the application of doctrine to moral cases.
12. Those who treated theology under *loci communes* or common topics, the standard method among Dutch and German Theologians in the seventeenth century.
13. No charge made by the schismatics is as grave as the evil of schism.
14. Considering what serves their ends more important than the unity of the church, for no very great reason or indeed any reason whatever, they rend and divide the great and glorious body of Christ and destroy whatever part they have of it themselves. They speak of peace and make war, indeed they strain a gnat and swallow a camel.
15. Psalms, 84, 10
16. must
17. Savoy joined the League of Augsburg against Louis XIV and was overrun. William's aim in forming the League was defence against the designs of the leading Catholic power but obviously his Catholic allies such as Savoy were not fighting for the Protestant cause.
18. hold
19. Gilbert Rule had been ejected in 1662 from his charge of Alnwick, Northumberland for Nonconformity.
20. possibly Gilbert Rule's *A Rational Defence of Non-conformity* (1689)
21. pouting

22. the Episcopalian clergy that replaced the nonconforming Presbyterians
23. i.e. the bishops
24. curates
25. cobblers
26. distressing
27. The background to the innuendo in this scene is the story told in *The Scotch Presbyterian Eloquence* of how David Williamson (Solomon Cherrie-trees) was dressed as a lady's maid and hidden from the dragoons in her daughter's bed by Lady Cherrie-trees. He made the daughter pregnant and so he was married to her.
28. i.e. the Church, the spouse of Christ
29. i.e. the man who was originally Saul chastened into the christian saint, Paul.

INDEX

conscience, see Leighton's *Rule of Conscience* 149–59; also 168, 183.

Constans I, Roman Emperor, 65.

Constantius II, Byzantine Emperor, 65.

constitutional conservatives, 12, 38–39, 69–71, 79–80; see Napier's *Letter about the Soveraigne Power*, 71–78, and Drummond's *ΣΚΙΑΜΑΧΙΑ* 80–89.

conventicles, 111–112, 137, 171ff., 181, 185.

Cook, Patrick, "Bishops' Evangelist", 135.

Corbet, John, 52; career, 64–65; *Epistle Congratulatorie*, 10, 65–69; *Ungirding of the Scottish Armour*, 58, 64.

controversy, the Lord's c. with the land, 5, 108.

Corsby, London apothecary, 31.

Covenanters, controversialists 3–4, 9–10, 13, 32, 57, 58; National Covenant, 37–38, 39, 43–44, 45–52, 111; Solemn League and Covenant, 38, 39, 79–80, 111; Covenants, Montrose and, 69–71; Drummond and, 79; Urquart and, 89, 91–94; Mackenzie and, 140; Leighton and 148–49; Peden and, 171, Whig settlement and, 177; see also Bishops' Wars.

Cowper, William, Bp. of Galloway, 8, n.4..

Craig, Thomas, of Riccarton, 43.

Crashaw, Richard, 45.

Crawford, Earls of, see Lindsay.

Crichton, James, "The Admirable", 89.

Crockat, Gilbert, *The Scotch Presbyterian Eloquence*, 10, 130, 185, n.7, 193, 198, n.27..

Croll, Morris W., 7.

Cromwell, Oliver, 39, 40, 44, 118, 162.

Cross Petition, 80, 81–82, 83, 85–86.

Cunningham, William, 9th Earl of Glencairn, 119.

Dalhousie, see Ramsay, William.

Dalrymple, Sir James, Lord President of the Court of Session, 141.

Dalrymple, Sir John, 1st Earl of Stair, 133.

Dalyell, Sir Thomas, of Binns, 141.

Davenant, John, Bp. of Salisbury, 65.

Descartes, René, 15.

Dickson, David, minister of Irvine, 41, 65.

Divine right, 90, 142–43; episcopacy, 111; of king, 127–29; of presbytery 52, 93, 96, 111, 177, 191.

Donaldson, Gordon, *Scotland, James V to James VII*, ix, 15.

Douglas, Robert, nonconforming minister, 120–21.

Douglas, William, 3rd Duke of Hamilton, 118, 125, 135, 136, 139, 181.

Drayton, Michael, 79.

Drummond, William, of Hawthornden, 7, 8, 12; career, 79; *ΣΚΙΑΜΑΧΙΑ* , 64, 80–89.

Dryden, John, 140, 141, 193.

Dunbar, Earl of, see Home, George.

Durie, see Gibson, Alexander, of, senior and junior.

Edward VI, 85.

Egerton, Sir Thomas, Lord Chancellor of England, 26–27.

Eglinton, Earl of, see Montgomerie, Hugh.

Elizabeth 1, 85.

Engagers, 39, 52, 92–94, 123.

enthusiasm, 142ff., 160–61, see also Johnston of Wariston, Rutherford, Peden.

Epiphanius of Constantia, 165.

Episcopal system, 3, 17, 24, 31, 46–47, 52, 68, 83, 136, 185.

Episcopalian controversialists, 10, 13, 64, 177–78.

Erasmus, 4.

Erastianism, 4, 133, 134, 149, 178; also Melvill's *True Narration*, 19–31 passim.

Erskine, Sir George, Lord Innerteil, Lord Clerk Register, 33.
Erskine, John, 9th Earl of Mar, 61.
Essex, Earl of, see Capel, Arthur.
Evagrius Scholasticus, 66.
Fagel, Caspar, Grand Pensionary of Holland, 181.
Fénelon, François de Salignac de la Mothe, 3.
Fenwicke, John, Newcastle Parliamentarian, 45, 48–52.
Ferdinand II, Holy Roman Emperor, 74 and n.115.
Ferguson, William, *Scotland, 1689 to the Present*, 15.
Fleming, Bartholomew, 35.
Fleming, John, 2nd Earl of Wigtown, 61.
Fletcher, John, King's Advocate, 120.
Forbes, John, of Corse, 2, 189.
Fraser, James, of Brea, covenanting minister, 194.
Galba, Roman Emperor, 74.
Galloway, Patrick, minister of St. Giles, 33–36.
Gellius, Aulus, *Noctes Atticae*, 95.
General Assembly, of Dundee, 1596, 17, 19; of Aberdeen, 1605, 18, 19, 20, 21–23; of Linlithgow, 1606, 23; of St. Andrews, 1617, 32; of Perth, 1618, 32; of Glasgow, 1638, 38, 52, 56, 58, 65, 122, 131; of Edinburgh, 1639, 56; 1642, 80, 82, 84; 1690 and 1692, 177.
Gibson, Alexander, of Durie, senior, 57.
Gibson, Alexander, of Durie, junior, 61.
Gillespie, George, minister of Wemyss, *A Dispute against the English Popish Ceremonies*, 8, 58.
Glasgow, Act of Council at, 1662, 132, 186.
Gledstanes, George, Archb. of St. Andrews, 22.
Glencairn, Earl of, see Cunningham, William.

Gordon, George, 2nd Marquis of Huntly, 57, 59, 71, 91.
Gordon, John, Dean of Salisbury, 19, 21.
Graham, James, 6th Earl, 1st Marquis of Montrose, 39, 59, 61, 70–71, 78, 79, 91.
Graham, John, of Claverhouse, Viscount Dundee, 112, 177, 193, 194.
Gregory, David, mathematician, 149.
Gregory, James, mathematician, 149.
Grotius, Hugo, 57.
Halifax, Lord, see Savile, George.
Hamilton, Sir Alexander, 59.
Hamilton, Anne, Duchess of Hamilton, 118, 121.
Hamilton, James, 3rd Marquis, 1st Duke of Hamilton, 56, 57, 131.
Hamilton, 3rd Duke of, see Douglas William.
Hamilton, John, minister of Ratho, 43.
Hamilton, Sir John, of Orbiston, Lord Justice Clerk, 52.
Hamilton, Sir Thomas, King's Advocate, 23.
Hammond, Henry, 128.
Harvey, William, 193.
Hatton, Lord, see Maitland, Charles.
Hay, Alexander, Scottish Secretary, 21, 23, 25, 27, 30.
Hay, John, Lord Yester, 61.
Hay, John, 2nd, Earl of Tweeddale, 118–132, 136.
Henderson, Alexander, minister of Leuchars, 37; *Remonstrance*, 1639, 58; *Instructions for Defensive Arms*, 58, 65, n.77, 69, n.95.
Henry, Prince of Wales, 22, 23, 79.
Henry VII, Holy Roman Emperor, 88.
Henryson, Patrick, session clerk of St. Giles, 35.
Hill, Christopher, *Winstanley, The Law of Freedom*, 8.

Nairne, James, minister of Bolton, 113, 120, n.2, 127, 135, 149.

Naphtali, see Stewart, Sir James, and Stirling, James.

Nicholson, James, minister of Chapel Royal, Stirling, 22.

Nicolson, Sir Thomas, King's Advocate, 120.

Nisbit, Sir William, Provost of Edinburgh, 33.

Northampton, Earl of, see Howard, Henry.

Nottingham, Earl of, see Howard, Charles.

Orr, Robert, covenanter, 137.

Ovid, *Tristia*, 30.

Pape, Charles, minister of Cullicudden, 95.

Parliament, English, 24, 38; Long Parliament, 44, 80, 81, 84, 86.

Parliament, Scottish, 40, 46, 89, 111, 131, 140–41, 194; function under monarchy, 75.

passive obedience, 22, 28, 57–58, 65, 70, 74–75, 126ff., 149, 157–58, 168.

Paterson, Walter, "Bishops' evangelist", 135.

Peden, Alexander, 9, 130; career, 171; *The Lord's Trumpet*, 171–76.

Pentland Rising, 112, 171, 173, 174.

persecution, 111–12, 177; Hawthornden and, 83–84; Urquhart and, 89, 96; Kirkton and, 137ff.; Mackenzie and, 140–41, 143ff.; Leighton and, 149; Barclay and, 162–63, 166ff.; Peden and, 171ff.; Sage and, 178ff.

Perth, Five Articles of, 32.

Presbyterian: controversialists, 8–10, 13, 44, 52; historians, 4–6; hypocrisy, 64ff., 78, 87, 90, 94ff., 193ff.; ministers' general character, 124–25; ministers' *Humble Address* to James VII, 184–85; model church, 4–5, 18–19, 50, 131–32; right of resistance, 13, 125–26; system, 17, 37, 66–67, 83, 91, 92, 132ff. see also divine right of presbytery; unruliness, 65ff., 78,

82, 87–89, 91ff., 125–27, 142, 144, 155, 159, 180ff.

Presbyterianism and literary culture, 2–3.

Prayerbook, 37, 52.

Primrose, Sir Archibald, Lord Clerk Register, 119–20.

Protesters, 40, 44, 98, 111.

"Phineas fact", 13.

Pitcairne, Archibald, career, 193; *The Assembly*, 1–2, 194–200.

Polycarp, Bp. of Smyrna, 165.

Poor Man's Cup of Cold Water, see MacWard, Robert.

Quakers, 14, 162ff., 180.

Rabelais, François, *Gargantua and Pantagruel*, 89.

Ramsay, Andrew, minister of St. Giles, 2, 33.

Ramsay, William, 1st Earl of Dalhousie, 61.

Remonstrants, 40.

Renwick, James, field preacher, 172.

Resolutioners, 40, 52, 111.

Ridpath, George, Presbyterian pamphleteer, 10.

Right, Claim of, 177.

right reason, 166, 169, 191.

Rights, Bill of, 178.

Rivet, André, 57.

Roberts, Jane, mistress of Charles II, 113.

Robertson, William, 3.

Rochester, Earl of, see Wilmot, John.

Rollock, Henry, minister of Greyfriars, 62.

Rothes, Earls of, see Leslie.

Rule, Gilbert, Principal of Edinburgh University, 2, 10, 11, 194, 196, n.20.

Rullion Green, Battle of, 112.

Russell, William, Lord Russell, 113.

Rutherford, Samuel, 38, 98; career, 44; *A Free Disputation*, 150; *Letters*, 45–52, 171; *Lex Rex*, 10, 13, 44.

Sage, John, nonjuring bp., 80, 83, n.123; career, 178–79; controver-